"The volume at hand is a wel
professional study. In an or
the profound meaning of th
eloquently so, Dr Laos travels
civilizations…the author offer
confrontations, the spirituality
issues that humanity faces toda
– Dr Elias D. Kallioras, Former
Assembly of Black Sea Econor

"Nicolas Laos offers a rati
esotericism. Establishing connec
Kairos (the right or opportune n
an ecumenical esoteric system o
opens new possibilities of dialog
advanced sciences."
– Metropolitan Daniel (de Jesú
Latin America (Ukrainian Ortho

"Dr Nicolas Laos is an outstan
analytical mind assists the read
of the Greek word "esotericism'
of "Kairos" that focuses on the
reality of the world and the rea
book is a masterpiece for any poli
understand the complexities that
today. Excellent work!"
– Dr John M. Nomikos, Director, I
and American Studies (RIEAS)
Council for Intelligence Studies

The
Kairological Qabalah

REDISCOVERING WESTERN ESOTERICISM

WITHIN PHILOSOPHY, SCIENCE AND

THE REVOLUTIONARY SECRETS OF FREEMASONRY,

ROSICRUCIANISM AND THE ILLUMINATI

Dr Nicolas Laos

"Man is the architect and manager of his own fate."

WHITE CRANE
PUBLISHING

The
Kairological Qabalah

REDISCOVERING WESTERN ESOTERICISM WITHIN
PHILOSOPHY, SCIENCE AND THE REVOLUTIONARY SECRETS OF
FREEMASONRY, ROSICRUCIANISM AND THE ILLUMINATI

Dr Nicolas Laos

Produced, Designed, Illustrated and Edited by
White Crane Publishing Ltd
2 Red House Square,
Moulton Park,
Northampton,
Northamptonshire,
NN3 6WL. United Kingdom

www.whitecranepublishing.com

First Published 2012

British Library Catalogue-in-Publication Data:
A CIP record for this book is available from the
British Library.

ISBN: 978-1-907347-09-2 (Hardback)
First Edition.

The views of the author do
not necessarily reflect that
of the publisher.

To the memory of Adam Weishaupt (1748—1830) and to every servant of the ideal of anthropocentric cosmopolitanism.

CONTENTS

LIST OF ILLUSTRATIONS

LIST OF TABLES

INTRODUCTION

UNLIKE an animal, the human being does not relate to other beings and things in the world in a direct way, but indirectly, through such expressions of the intentionality of human consciousness as values, technology and institutions. Therefore, ultimately, man is the architect of the reality in which he lives and a morally responsible being. Furthermore, for the same reason, man continually encounters questions about meaning. These awarenesses have put an indelible imprint on my research and teaching activities in the fields of philosophy and mathematical modelling as well as on my work as a political and economic consultant. Additionally, the previous realizations have guided my investigation of several Western esoteric societies as well as my research interests in the philosophy of religion and Church history.

The human being lives and acts in a reality that it is composed of the reality of the world (i.e. of a reality that is external to human consciousness) and of the reality of human consciousness. 'Kairos' (an ancient Greek term that means the opportune moment) is a measure of one's potential and opportunities for action as well as a value. According to James Kinneavy, the classical term kairos can be defined as "the right time and due measure"*. It is an intentional creation of human consciousness, and simultaneously it respects the difference between the reality of the world and the reality of consciousness. However, it is based on the awareness that, even though the reality of the world and the reality of consciousness are not naturally one, they are united together, and this unity allows conscious beings to utilize and restructure the world.

---

* James Kinneavy, "Kairos: A Neglected Concept in Classical Rhetoric", in J.D. Moss (ed.), *Rhetoric and Praxis: The Contribution of Classical Rhetoric to Practical Reasoning*, Washington, D.C.: Catholic University Press, 1986.

The dynamic unity between the structure of the world (exoteric reality) and the structure of human consciousness (esoteric reality) led me to understand and study the reality of the world as a tank of opportunities and the reality of consciousness as a tank of intentions. Additionally, the previous awareness led me to a dialectical transcendence of philosophical realism and idealism through the concept of kairos. My ultimate goal is to show the submissiveness of reality to the intentionality of human consciousness, without lapsing into arbitrary idealistic arguments, thus developing a new humanism, which utilizes relevant theorems of cybernetics, quantum physics, quantum informatics and psychology.

Furthermore, through the concept of kairos, I have created a synthesis among philosophy, science and those, carefully selected, elements of Freemasonry, Rosicrucianism and the Order of the Illuminati which are useful for the building of a humanistic world along the lines of the arguments that I put forward in this book. Thus, I have created the concept of the Kairological Qabalah, which is studied in this book, and which is the keystone of the Kairological Society, which I have founded in order to operate as a philosophical and policy-oriented think-tank, as an exclusive private membership club and as a specialized and innovative consultancy organization focused on what I call 'reality creation consulting'.

THE MEANING OF WESTERN ESOTERICISM

Before we start our itinerary looking for general principles in the labyrinthine and sometimes even dark paths of esotericism, we need to examine some concepts whose prolonged use gives rise to a feeling of familiarity for them, but it leaves their meaning ambiguous.

Let us start by examining the very theme of this work. I deal with the ideas, currents and 'schools' that have shaped Western esotericism. But what do the terms 'Western' and 'esotericism' mean for a methodic and systematic student of the spiritual history of man? How can one define the East and the West? Which region is the West and why? Which region is the East and why? How 'near' is the Near East and to what is it 'near'? How 'far' is the Far East and from what is it 'far'? Which are the borders of the Middle East? Is Japan, i.e. the so-called "country of the rising sun", which lies to the West of San Francisco, an Eastern or a Western country; and, if it has become a Western country, when and why did it become Western?

Is Australia a Western country for its aboriginal people, too, or is it Western only for a portion of its overall population? Is the Republic of South Africa a Western country, or is it the edge of the South? The previous questions make it amply clear that, by referring to the cardinal points, we use some spatial frame of reference trying to understand history in terms of geocultural entities. Hence, in the context of the philosophy of history, the cardinal points inevitably include underlying cultural components.

The term 'esotericism' is controversial and is often confused with the colloquial adjectival sense of something that is obscure and technical or that pertains to the minutiae of a particular area of common knowledge. The term esotericism derives from the Greek root 'eso', which means inner. Plato, in his dialogue *Alcibiades*, uses the expression "ta eso", meaning the inner things, and, in his dialogue *Theaetetus*, he uses the expression "ta exo", meaning "the outside things". The Greek adjective 'esoterikos' (esoteric) was coined by the rhetorician and satirist Lucian of Samosata (2nd century A.D.) in his book *The Auction of Lives* (paragraph 26). The term 'esoteric' first appeared in English in Thomas Stanley's *History of Philosophy*, which was published in 1701. Thomas Stanley used the term esoteric in order to describe the mystery-school of Pythagoras, since the Pythagoreans were divided into the exoteric circle (under training) and the esoteric circle (admitted into the 'inner' circle). The corresponding noun 'esotericism' was coined by the French philosopher and historian Jacques Matter in his book *Histoire Critique Du Gnosticisme* (1828), and it was popularized by the 19th century French occult author and ceremonial magician Eliphas Lévi (born Alphonse Louis Constant).

One of the most influential attempts to explain what unites the various currents designated by 'esotericism' in the scholarly sense is due to the prominent French scholar Antoine Faivre, who held a chair in the École Pratique des Hautes Études at the Sorbonne. Faivre was a University Professor of Germanic Studies at the University of Haute-Normandie, and also he was the director of the *Cahiers de l'hermétisme* and of the *Bibliothèque de l'hermétisme*. Faivre's definition of esotericism is based on his argument that the following four essential characteristics are present in the esoteric currents*: (i)

---

* Antoine Faivre, *Access to Western Esotericism*, New York: State University of New York Press, 1994.

a theory of correspondences among all parts of the invisible and the visible cosmos, (ii) the conviction that nature is a living entity owing to a divine presence or life-force, (iii) the need for mediating elements (e.g. symbols, rituals, angels, visions) in order to access spiritual knowledge, and (iv) an experience of personal and spiritual transmutation when arriving at this inner knowledge. However, the previous definition of esotericism is mainly descriptive, since it refers to certain behaviors, but it says nothing about the final causes of the different esoteric behaviors. Thus, Faivre's definition is not as general as Faivre and his followers assert, and it tends to limit 'esotericism' to particular esoteric behaviors (i.e. to particular belief systems and spiritual practices), instead of offering a broad understanding of the motives that underpin the exhibition of esoteric behaviors. In this book, I follow a teleological approach to the concept of esotericism, in order to articulate a general definition of esotericism. My argument is that (if one wants to avoid the risks of lapsing into intellectual atavism and of fixating esotericists on particular stages of man's spiritual development) esotericism should be studied as a dynamic cultural phenomenon and particularly as an expression of man's attempt to know himself, to discern himself from the world and to impose his intentionality on the world.

One of my major arguments is that esotericism as such, i.e. the essence of esotericism (apart from the differences among particular esoteric 'schools' and currents), consists in giving witness to the reality of the human being and in particular to the autonomy of man, by focusing on the power of human consciousness's intentionality and on the outer reality's submissiveness to the intentionality of human consciousness. Additionally, the dynamic continuity between the structure of the world and the structure of human consciousness is the truth that serves as the foundation of the grand synthesis among philosophy, science and esotericism, which I propose in this book. Thus, following the previous adogmatic and teleological approach to esotericism, I understand esotericism as a program of personality creation and spiritual emancipation and as a Promethean erection of human consciousness, which can be expressed in many different ways, such as: ceremonial magic, art, science, philosophy, religion, etc.

According to my rationale, esotericism is based on the thesis that every object of consciousness exists not in itself but inextricably united with the meaning that is assigned to it by consciousness.

Therefore, every manipulation of the meanings that are assigned to things and make the world meaningful is equivalent to a manipulation of the reality of the world itself by consciousness. This is, according to my rationale, the ultimate 'secret' of esotericism's power and significance. Furthermore, inherent in my previous argument is a powerful political message, since the moral autonomy that is achieved through and underpinned by my interpretation of Western esotericism implies a high level of personal and social autonomy.

A REMARK ABOUT RELIGION, SPIRITUALITY AND SECULARISM

Given that I use many of the methodological and stylistic characteristics of 'philosophical anthropology' (as the latter has been formed and delineated by such philosophers as Max Scheler, Ernst Cassirer, Martin Heidegger, Hans-Georg Gadamer, Hans Jonas, Maurice Merleau-Ponty, Paul Ricoeur, etc.), I put emphasis on the study of the human being as a "symbolic animal", according to Ernst Cassirer's terminology[*], as well as on methodic studies in "symbolic anthropology" and the "imaginary", according to Gilbert Durand's terminology[†]. When I refer to the imaginary, I mean the set of values, institutions, laws and symbols common to a particular social group. Therefore, due to the fact that my work is focused on the creative and symbolic dimension of the social world, I dare to challenge and, in fact, cross borders among different 'camps' of cultures and mentalities.

My goal is to throw light on the ontological potential of the human being, on the autonomy of the human being and on the meaning of existence, and not to show reverence to the borders of any particular attitude toward religion and science. Therefore, my arguments and ideas challenge every religious/theistic/atheistic form of fundamentalism. After all, whenever I argue over matters of religion, I stress that, in my opinion, the most important issue is not *whether you believe in God or not*, but *how and why you believe or disbelieve in God*. And whenever I participate in debates about

---

[*] Ernst Cassirer, *The Philosophy of Symbolic Forms*, Volume One: Language, Volume Two: Mythical Thought, trans. R. Manheim, New Haven: Yale University Press, 1955.

[†] Gilbert Durand, *Les Structures Anthropologiques de l'Imaginaire: Introduction à l'Archétypologie Générale*, Paris: P.U.F., 1963.

religious fundamentalism, I argue that, in order to liberate humanity from religious fundamentalism, we must first of all disengage God Himself from religious fundamentalism, cultivate 'symbolic thought' and understand the 'Church' as a mystery.

The term secularism is derived from the Latin word 'saeculum', which means century. 'Saeculum' is the Latin translation of the Hebrew word 'olam', which means century and eternity. In the Biblical language, the term saeculum means world, too; e.g. one may refer to *Matthew* 13:22, *Luke* 16:8, *Romans* 1:25, etc. Furthermore, in the Middle Ages, 'seculares' were the lay members of the clergy, whereas 'regulares' were monks living in accordance with the rules ('regulae') of their monastic orders.

The phenomenon of the integration of the Church (as a community founded on 'mystery') into the historical world is called secularism. However, it should be stressed that the term world has two different meanings in the Bible and in the work of the Church Fathers: when the term world has a positive meaning, it is understood as the objectivation of God's creative will; when the term world has a negative meaning, it is understood as the negative passions and everything that characterizes the spirit of the flesh, i.e. as the deprivation of the Holy Spirit.

In the Western Church, secularism took the form of 'Papocaesarism', i.e. the Roman Church attempted to subordinate the State to its authority, and, given the power vacuum that was created in the Western Roman Empire as a consequence of barbarian invasions and of the transfer of the Empire's capital to Constantinople (by Emperor Constantine the Great in 330 A.D.), the Pope (Bishop of Rome) became a quasi emperor. On the other hand, in the Eastern Church, secularism took the form of 'Caesaropapism', since the new imperial capital, i.e. Constantinople (the "New Rome"), was simultaneously the seat of the Roman Emperor and of the Patriarch of Constantinople and the latter was submissive to the Emperor's attempts to subordinate the Church to the State in exchange for political and social prerogatives and imperial protection. Thus, in both the Western Roman Empire and the Eastern Roman Empire, Church authorities degraded Christianity, from a proposal of man's deification, to a method of moralization in accordance with secular expediences.

Many Greek Church Fathers have analyzed and emphasized the difference between the secularized form of religion and the unsecularized form of religion, and they have identified the true Church of Christ with the non-secularized form of religion, i.e. with 'mystery'. The secularized form of religion consists in a system of teachings and rituals whose purpose is to establish a link between man and an abstract God who inhabits the 'Heavens' and manages the world from up there, whereas man (at least his body) remains down here. In the context of the secularized form of religion, man has to conform to certain formalized practices and procedures in order to be connected with God. Therefore, in the context of the secularized form of religion, historical practices and historical institutions play the protagonistic role in man's attempt to be united with God.

On one hand, the understanding of the esoteric content of the Bible and the Greek Church Fathers' teachings implies that Church is the mystical Body of the Incarnate Logos of God (i.e. Christ), and in this way there exists a communion between man and God in the person of Christ. The secularized form of religion in general and secularized Churches in particular emphasize the observance of an objective order, beautiful ceremonial work, imposing temples and compliance with an established, usually highly formalized, moral and behavioral code. On the other hand, a non-secularized form of religion in general and non-secularized Churches in particular emphasize 'mystery', psychological cure, the endowment of human life with meaning, and the deification of man through his personal (and, therefore, 'mysterious') relationship with the Deity.

I deem it useful to make these remarks, because some of my readers may feel uncomfortable with my use of myth and symbology, and they may defend various forms of positivism/objectivism, irrespective of whether they endorse a form of scientism, anti-religious secularism or a particular religious system. I would like to clarify my point on this matter: my goal is to articulate a synthetic approach to the creativity and the itinerary of the human spirit through a creative re-interpretation of foundational elements of civilization.

I chose the sub-title 'Rediscovering Western Esotericism' in order to describe my attempt to throw new light on what happens in the inner ('eso') world of the Western man and of the Western society, i.e. in that spiritual locus from where religion, spirituality, art and science emerge, and to explain how the creativity of the human spirit is objectivated in historical becoming. Hence, the present book presupposes that its readers are familiar with 'symbolic thought', or at least they intend to employ symbolic thought, and that they are ready to cross borders among different mental/cultural 'camps'.

THE STRUCTURE OF THIS BOOK

I have divided this book into three parts. Part One is concerned with the methodic study of the emergence and development of Western esotericism. This part discusses the historical context of the phenomena of Western esotericism and why knowing this is important. If one asks some other people about their identity, a story soon appears. One's identity is inextricably connected with what has happened to him and with what he has done. Moreover, listening to people's biographical narratives is in many ways similar to the psychoanalytical process. Thus, this part is an attempt to use philosophical anthropology, psychoanalysis and history in order to investigate the identity (and the genealogy) of the Western world.

In particular, Part One is divided into the following three chapters:

1. *Esotericism as an Object of Historical Research:* esotericism and the study of history; and the relation among esotericism, culture and civilization.

2. *The Noachites and the Spiritual Horizon of Western Esotericism:* The term Noachite literally means child of Noah. In the mythological context of the book of *Genesis*, the sons of Noah were Shem, Japheth and Ham, and the nations of the Bible descended from them: Hebrews, Chaldeans, Assyrians, Persians and Syrians descended from Shem; the descendants of Japheth were the Greek tribes; Canaanites, Egyptians, Philistines, Hittites and Amorites descended from Ham. Hence, *Genesis* helps one define the geographical structure of the ecumene. Furthermore, in this chapter, I argue that the mythological narrative of *Genesis* urges one to interpret Noah's children as different archetypal cultural communities, and, therefore, it helps one to study what I call 'geoculture', i.e. the distribution of cultural characteristics in space. In

addition, I draw useful information for my geocultural studies from Plato's *Timaeus*, i.e. a philosophical text that belongs to the 'Japhethite' spiritual tradition, and from Ibn Khaldun's *Muqaddimah*, i.e. a historical text that is concerned with Ham's descendants. Thus, in this chapter, I set the conceptual framework of my research work, and I clarify the geographical and the spiritual substances of the 'ecumene'

3. *The Creation of the Japhethite Ecumene and the Foundations of Western Esotericism:* In this chapter, I study the rise of the 'Japhethite ecumene' and the communication among different ancient cultural communities. In particular, I pay special attention to the following issues: the creation of the ecumene by the Greek Emperor Alexander the Great; the Punic Wars; the communication between the Celts and the Greeks; the communication between the Romans and the Greeks; the communication between the Hebrews and the Greeks; the synthesis between the spirit of the East and the spirit of the West within the context of the Greek culture; the Orientalization of Greece and the Hellenization of the East; the Christianization of the Japhethite ecumene; the Greek conception of reason and the adventure of ratio in the Middle Ages; the controversy between Neoplatonism and Gnosticism; and Hesychasm, which is the most influential tradition of the Eastern Roman Empire's Christocentric mysticism.

Part Two is concerned with what I call the Kairological Qabalah. This Part is divided into the following four chapters:

1. *Kairos and Qabalah:* In this chapter, I study the Greek concept of kairos, and I redefine the Qabalah (arguably the most important symbol of Western esotericism), thus giving rise to a new way of thinking about the nature of reality (ontology), about the study of knowledge and justified belief (epistemology), about the submissiveness of reality to the intentionality of human consciousness, and about the philosophical correspondences of the well-known Qabalistic 'Tree of Life'. Thus, I define a new

Qabalah, which I call the 'Kairological Qabalah', and it is the epitome of the history of philosophy. In particular, I articulate an original synthesis between Kairos, the ancient Greek god/archetype of the opportune moment (signifying the imposition of the intentionality of human consciousness on reality), and the Qabalah of Western esotericism, as a structural theory of ontology and cognition.

2. *The Kairological Left Pillar:* the three left-pillar sephiroth (levels of reality) of the Kairological Qabalah, i.e. Binah, Geburah and Hod, interpreted according to my philosophical synthesis between Kairos and the Qabalah.

3. *The Kairological Right Pillar:* the three right-pillar sephiroth (levels of reality) of the Kairological Qabalah, i.e. Chokmah, Chesed and Netzach, interpreted according to my philosophical synthesis between Kairos and the Qabalah.

4. *The Kairological Middle Pillar:* the five middle-pillar sephiroth (levels of reality) of the Kairological Qabalah, i.e. Kether, Daat, Yesod, Tiphareth and Malkuth, interpreted according to my philosophical synthesis between Kairos and the Qabalah.

5. *Greek Humanism and the Mystery of God Incarnate:* from the Greek philosophical conception of theoretical life to the Incarnate Logos; Gematria and the secret of number thirty-three.

Part Three is concerned with the methodic study of Western esoteric fraternities, morality and politics from the perspective of the Kairological Qabalah. Furthermore, in this part, I try to answer the following question: which elements of the Freemasons', the Rosicrucians', the Illuminati's and other old Western esoteric fraternities' traditions and folklore are not only valuable for museums, but can be significant in the life of a mature person in an era marked by the accomplishments of cybernetics, genetics, psychoanalysis, philosophical anthropology, quantum physics, nanotechnology, globalization, modern democracy, international human rights law and massive political awakening? Part Three is divided into the following three chapters:

1. *The Rituals and Teachings of Esoteric Fraternities: the Masonic legacy:* Symbolic Masonry and the Holy Royal Arch; the Templars' legacy and the spiritual itinerary of the Knights Kadosh; the Rosicrucian legacy; the Illuminati's legacy; the legacy of Thelemic Magick.

2. *The Relation between Western Esotericism and Morality:* the nature of moral consciousness; the value of moral consciousness; the moral criterion.

3. *The Political Dimension of Western Esotericism and the Kairological Qabalah:* politicized Western esoteric fraternities; the interplay between politics and esotericism; civil society and human autonomy; the political ramifications of the Kairological Qabalah.

BASIC DEFINITIONS

Throughout this book, my approach to 'Western esotericism' is founded on the following definitions, through which I clarify what I mean by the terms 'esotericism' and 'Western':

Definition of Esotericism: Esotericism is a system of methods, practices and theories that are concerned with the reality of the human being and, more specifically, with the self-knowledge of the human being, the creation of personality and the imposition of man's intentionality on reality. Furthermore, my definition of esotericism is founded on the thesis that there is a dynamic continuity between the structure of the world and the structure of human consciousness.

Corollary: The different forms through which esotericism is manifested are ceremonial magic (the most archaic form), religion, science, art and philosophy.

Definition of 'Western' cultural structures: I call a cultural structure 'Western' if and only if it is founded on a synthesis of the following four principles: metaphysical depth, reason, tradition and technology (this thesis is clarified and defended in Part One).

Nicolas Laos
President and Founder,
Kairological Society — Reality Restructuring Resources Ltd
May 2012

ACKNOWLEDGEMENTS

I WISH to express my gratitude to the members of the steering committee of the "Kairological Society — Reality Restructuring Resources Ltd", a philosophy and policy oriented think-tank, private exclusive membership club and consultancy organization, which I have founded on the basis of the ideas and values expressed in this book.

Additionally, I wish to gratefully cite the persons who have played key role in my education by the institutions where I encountered them. This list is not exhaustive by any means, but it is representative. At the University of La Verne (California), where I studied Mathematics, Politics and Humanities, and from where I graduated in 1996 with departmental honors, Professor Themistocles M. Rassias (currently Professor at the National Technical University of Athens) introduced me in advanced mathematical analysis and helped me to complete my book *Topics in Mathematical Analysis and Differential Geometry* (New Jersey, London, Singapore, Hong Kong: World Scientific Publishing Co., 1998), Professor Vassilios Christides (founding President of the Institute for Graeco-Oriental and African Studies) and Professor Paul Angelides taught me important courses in history and humanities, and Professor Rehavia U. Yakovee opened to me the world of international politics. At the University of Rousse (Bulgaria), Professor Svetoslav Jordanov Bilchev, hosted me, co-operated with me in preparing and publishing research papers in algebraic geometry and differentiable dynamics, and he discussed with me interesting problems in geometry, number theory and cybernetics. At the University of Kent's London Centre of International Relations, Professor Hazel Smith and Professor Michael Nicholson played a key role in my international-political education, and they helped me to complete a research project entitled *Theory Construction and Empirical Relevance in International Relations* (published in 2000 by Ant. N. Sakkoulas Publishers). At the Royal Institute of International Affairs (Chatham House), Mr William Hopkinson, former Head of the Chatham House's International Security Program, opened to me the scholarly charity of this prestigious institution in 1999. At the Academy of Athens, the gifted philosopher Professor Evangelos Moutsopoulos' work broadened my thought in the fields of ontology, cognition and ethics, and Professor Moutsopoulos contributed some of his thoughts to my research project *International Relations as an Object of Science*. At the Metropolitan University of London, Professor Kelvin Knight, Director of the Centre for Contemporary Aristotelian Studies in Ethics and Politics, gave me the opportunity to become a member of this creative research institution. At the Saint Andrew's Theological Academy in Mexico, the Metropolitan Dr Daniel de Jesús Ruiz Flores of Mexico and All Latin America gave me significant opportunities to develop my research program in Philosophy, on the basis of which I ultimately earned my Doctoral Degree in Philosophy from that school. The Chairman of the Saint Elias Seminary and Graduate School (Virginia), the Rt. Rev. Dr William C. Baron, has been particularly encouraging and supportive toward my interdisciplinary research and teaching interests in Philosophy, Politics and Spirituality, and his institution has awarded me the honorary degree of Doctor of Divinity. At the Business Schools of European University (Montreux, Switzerland) and the Free European School of Economics (Brittnau, Switzerland), Dr Dirk Craen, President of the first, and Dr Friedrich Frei, Rector of the latter, have given me creative opportunities to accomplish my academic goals in Business Administration and Finance. At the Hellenic American University (Athens, Greece), Professor George Hagerty (currently the President of St. John International University, Turin) applauded my research work in Cultural Diplomacy and wrote a foreword for my book *Foundations of Cultural Diplomacy* (New York: Algora Publishing, 2011).

Fortunately, I have been given several opportunities to test my philosophical arguments and political visions against the critical judgment of scholars from different academic disciplines, and of creative researchers associated with the RAND Corporation and the Delft University of Technology, with whom we worked together in order to create a cutting edge workshop on policy analysis at the Hellenic American Union, Athens, Greece, in May 2012. In the context of the previous research project, my communication with Dr Warren E. Walker (Professor of Policy Analysis at the Delft University of Technology, and Operations Research scholar associated with the RAND Corporation), Dr Adnan Rahman (Principal and Director of the International Division of Cambridge Systematics and former Director of Business Development at RAND Europe), Mr Marc Leipoldt (Managing Director of Global Risk Advisory Services), Mr Dimitris Vayenas (IT expert with rich industrial experience), Dr John M. Nomikos (Director of the Research Institute for European and American Studies), and other people from industry, government, banking and academia has helped me to elucidate the critical yet elusive interdependence between philosophy and politics.

My publisher, David Campbell, and my editor (project manager), Alasdair Urquhart, not only improved the clarity of my case but were persuasive in pressing me to try to make a transition from academic writing to creative writing and to organize my material in an effective way. Moreover, I am intellectually indebted to several learned members of Freemasonic, Rosicrucian and Templar Orders from different countries as well as to such chivalric and charitable fraternities as the United Grand Priories of the Hospitaller Order of Saint Lazarus of Jerusalem (under the administration of Master-General John Baron Dudley von Sydow von Hoff and under the patronage of the distinguished British educationalist Sir Robert Balchin the Lord Lingfield) and the Grand Priory of the Mediterranean of the Hospitaller Order of Saint Lazarus of Jerusalem (under the administration of Chancellor Chev. Massimo J. Ellul), because all of them have contributed, in various ways, to the chiselling of my mind and have given me opportunities for reflection.

The
Kairological Qabalah

PART ONE

THE EMERGENCE AND DEVELOPMENT OF WESTERN ESOTERICISM

THIS part discusses the historical context of the phenomena of esotericism and explains why the study of Western esotericism in historical context is important. In general, this part sets the stage for the delineation of the Kairological Qabalah, which I have created as a new way of thinking about esotericism, and which is the main topic of Part Two.

1

ESOTERICISM AS AN OBJECT
OF HISTORICAL RESEARCH

PHILOSOPHY of history is concerned with the becoming of humanity, i.e. with the itinerary followed by humanity and with the temporal framework in which this itinerary is integrated. Every researcher of history encounters philosophical questions about the nature of historical evidence, the meaning of objectivity, the degree to which objectivity is possible, etc., and the kind of answers he gives to the previous questions determines his overall research work in the field of history. Furthermore, from the perspective of my thesis about the dynamic continuity between the structure of the world and the structure of consciousness, the principal preoccupation of historical research lies in shedding light on the fundamental significations, known also as values, and the ultimate motives of the historical subjects under investigation.

ESOTERICISM AND THE STUDY OF HISTORY

We often have the feeling that historical 'events' provide us with cognitive security and that, due to this feeling of cognitive security, we can depend on them, because they never change, in contrast with the continually changing interpretations of them by men. But how can one intellectually legitimize his decision to treat historical events as objective (or 'crude') evidence? Isn't one's decision to depend on 'objective evidence' simply a way of *interpreting* what an event is? How can one define an event? When does an event begin, and when does it end? How do the initial and the final conditions of an event determine its significance and evaluation?

Until recently, historians believed that an event exists objectively, i.e. independently of human consciousness, and that, if we are not careful enough, we may stumble over it, or that it can smash up our interpretation of it. This is the position of historical positivism. However, in the 20th century, many of the Enlightenment's certainties were destroyed; one of them was the belief in so-called cold, crude facts*. Thus, today, historians ask: What is an event? Historical events are not 'given', they are not material realities buried somewhere in time. We cannot bring them back to the historical surface, clean them up and then exhibit them to our contemporaries under strong spotlights. A piece of historical research has nothing in common with a museum's showcase. Thus, today, historians have rediscovered what philosophers had been saying about history and what esotericists had been experiencing even before the Enlightenment: events are not pieces of objective evidence, and, therefore, they do not exist in some 'exoteric' record accessible by our observational skills.

For instance, a student of the history of the Bavarian Illuminati must know that the founder of the Bavarian Illuminati was Adam Weishaupt and not Baron von Knigge and that the Order of the Bavarian Illuminati was founded in 1776. But a serious and spiritually demanding student of the history of the Bavarian Illuminati will search behind the previous facts in order to analyze the motives that guided Weishaupt's historical action, and he will seek to understand the existential purpose and the ethos of the Bavarian Illuminati. In general, the most spiritually fruitful approach to history is focused on the analysis of people's and societies' systems of fundamental significations, or values.

In the Bible, the above truth was stressed by Simeon when he prophesized that Jesus Christ would have a paradoxical effect on Israel and on people in general and that he would be "a sign which shall be spoken against" (*Luke* 2:34). Indeed, Christ being a person and a Mystery, and not an archaeological object, is open to several, different interpretations, according to each person's way of relating to the Christ Mystery and according to each person's ethos. After all,

---

* See: F. Braudel, "Histoire et sciences socials: la langue durée", *Annales*, Vol. 4, 1958, pp. 725-753; E.H. Carr, *What Is History?*, London: Penguin, 1961.

Jesus Christ himself said that men can know God the Father through God the Son and that the knowledge of God the Son presupposes a mystical participation and progress in God the Holy Spirit: "the Comforter [Paraclete] the Holy Ghost, whom the Father will send in my name, he shall teach you all things, and bring all things to your remembrance, whatsoever I have said unto you" (*John* 14:26). In other words, according to the Bible, orthodox Christology depends on a peculiar cultural attitude (participation in the Holy Spirit and psychological openness toward Christ's Gospel), and, therefore, the institution of the 'Church of Christ' is nothing more and nothing less than the community of people who participate in a common *experiential* knowledge of God through His Incarnate Logos, Jesus Christ.

Hence, in order to understand the Mystery of Christ, we must bear in mind Gabriel Marcel's distinction between 'problem' and 'mystery'. The distinction between 'problem' and 'mystery' hinges on the notion of participation. Marcel explains the distinction between problem and mystery as follows: a problem is something that one meets, and it is clearly differentiated from the intentionality of the observer's consciousness, whereas a mystery is something in which a person's intentionality is embedded*. A mystery is a peculiar problem that feeds back into its own structure. Thus, the initiates of the Christ Mystery understand Jesus Christ as the Archetype of the Divinized Man, whereas those who approach Jesus Christ as if he were merely an archaeological problem articulate a totally different Christology, e.g. they use fragmented and controversial archaeological information in order to challenge orthodox Christology by formulating intriguing speculations about Jesus' family and personal life, and sometimes they write 'masterpieces' of "pop pseudohistory", as Laura Miller characterized Michael Baigent's book *Holy Blood, Holy Grail* in a book review published in *The New York Times* on 22 February 2004. Furthermore, many Christian Church authorities, in their attempt to defend their doctrines against heretics and to impose their doctrines in an intellectually coercive manner, try to transform theological beliefs into coercive 'objective' truths, and, therefore, they repeat the heretics' errant Christological methodology, since they degrade Christology into an archaeological problem.

---

* Gabriel Marcel, *Being and Having*, trans. K. Farrer, Westminister: Dacre Press, 1949, p. 117.

ESOTERICISM, CULTURE AND CIVILIZATION

In order to place the study of esotericism within a philosophically and scientifically rigorous framework and in order to avoid charlatanism and spiritually sterile speculation, we must study esotericism as a cultural phenomenon. Hence, we must clarify two more concepts, namely: civilization and culture. From a broad perspective, the concept of civilization includes the concept of culture, but, from a narrower perspective, 'civilization' can be differentiated from 'culture' on the basis of the argument that 'civilization' is simultaneously the means and the result of the collective consciousness's attempt to achieve for itself better terms for its adaptation to the world, whereas 'culture' is the result of man's reflection on his life. Civilization is a structure that consists of technology and institutions. On the other hand, culture is a reflective attitude toward institutions and an attempt to transcend institutions through myth, whose complex structure reflects the structure of institutions. In fact, 'myth'* is the spiritual core of the elements of civilization, and, therefore, it should be clearly distinguished from the notion of 'tale'. The creation of tales is an unsuccessful attempt to satisfy humans' quest for an inspiring and spiritually life-giving myth. In other words, tales are unsuccessful substitutes for myth. Myth is the most important manifestation and the core of culture. Myth translates experienced reality into a symbolic language, and in this way it leads toward the experiential participation of the collective consciousness in the same experience of reality, since myth makes possible the partaking of all areas of the conscious and the unconscious mind into the same experience of reality.

The primary purpose of civilization is to exert control over untamed forces and hence to transform them into forces that are controlled by human consciousness in order, ultimately, to harmonize all controlled forces with each other and with human reason. Human reason, under its different manifestations (namely, technical, scientific, and moral ones), oversees the successive phases of civilization and evaluates them according to its own dispositions. The dispositions of human reason are subject to change according to

---

* See: C.G. Jung, "The Relations Between the Ego and the Unconscious", in J. Campbell (ed.), *The Portable Jung*, New York: Penguin Books, 1971; Claude Lévi-Strauss, *The Raw and the Cooked*, trans. John and Doreen Weightman, Chicago: The University of Chicago Press, 1969.

the manner in which each society understands its needs. In general, irrespective of whether a civilization gives priority to materialistic pursuits or to more spiritual pursuits, the essence of 'civilization' primarily consists in the objectivation of the intentionality of consciousness through the construction of technological systems (e.g. machines, tools, etc.) and through institutions, whereas the essence of 'culture' primarily consists in the objectivation of the intentionality of consciousness through artistic creation, philosophy and scientific theories and models. However, civilization and culture are neither contradictory nor incompatible to each other. Even though civilization corresponds to 'technical construction' and culture corresponds to 'spiritual creation', culture is embodied in civilization and underpins civilization, and, additionally, civilization underpins the integration of culture into history.

Hence, there is a dialectical relation between civilization and culture, both at the level of their essences and at the level of their manifestations. Civilization seems to be founded on a concrete set of knowledge[*], whereas culture seems to be founded on a concrete set of experiences. In terms of civilization, the progress of humanity consists in the technological and institutional progress of society. On the other hand, in terms of culture, the progress of humanity is evaluated according to the spiritual deepening of the human being. Thus, as Christopher Bamford has pointed out in his book *An Endless Trace: The Passionate Pursuit of Wisdom in the West*, two powerful motives weave beneath the surface of the West's spiritual history: the desire to understand and the desire to love[†].

Following the above conceptions of culture and civilization as well as the above philosophy of history, I treat the historical study of esotericism as the methodic and systematic study of the itinerary of the human spirit.

---

[*] 'Knowledge' is an intellectual function according to which one constantly considers that an object corresponds to reality. Knowledge presupposes a correspondence between thing and intellect. This argument has been put forward by Aristotle in his *Metaphysics* 1011b25 as follows: "To say of what is that it is not, or of what is not that it is, is false, while to say of what is that it is, and of what is not that it is not, is true", and virtually identical assertions can be found in Plato (*Cratylus* 385b2, *Sophist* 263b).

[†] Christopher Bamford, *An Endless Trace: The Passionate Pursuit of Wisdom in the West*, New York: Codhill Press, 2003. Moreover, see: Rudolf Steiner, *The Science of Knowing: Outline of an Epistemology, Implicit in the Ghoetean World View*, trans. W. Lindeman, New York: Mercury Press, 1988.

2

THE NOACHITES AND THE SPIRITUAL
HORIZON OF WESTERN ESOTERICISM

THE principal preoccupation of this chapter lies in establishing the cardinal points of the spiritual horizon of the so-called 'Western world' in general and of Western esotericism in particular. I do this by focusing on three characteristic historical sources: the first belongs to the sphere of myth, the book of *Genesis*, the first book of the Bible; the second belongs to the sphere of philosophy, Plato's *Timaeus*; and the third belongs to the sphere of historiography, Ibn Khaldun's *Muqaddimah* (*Prolegomena*).

I show that the Hebrews, the Egyptians, the Arabs and the Greeks represent four principles that can be understood as the four cardinal points of the so-called 'Japhethite man', i.e. of the 'Western' or European man. In particular, the Hebrews represent the principle of metaphysical depth, the Egyptians represent the principle of tradition, the Arabs represent the principle of the utilization of man's intellectual power as a means for the accumulation of material possessions (or technology), and the Greeks represent the principle of reason. In the history of the European civilization, i.e. of the 'Japhethite world', the previous four concepts always co-exist and interact with each other, and they are interwoven with each other. None of the previous four principles exists completely separated from the other three principles. *The synthesis of the previous four principles is the defining characteristic of Western esotericism and of the Western culture in general.*

Thus, for instance, exactly because a European mystic, such

as Symeon the New Theologian (949—1022 A.D.) in the Eastern Roman Empire and Meister Eckhart (ca. 1260 — ca. 1327 A.D.) in the Western Roman Empire, is spiritually embedded in a synthesis of the previous four principles, European mysticism can never be identified with any Oriental school of mystical belief, such as Tibetan mysticism, Sikhism, Jainism, etc., or with any African school of mysticism. It goes without saying that there are common elements among all these schools of mystical belief, and, therefore, these schools of mystical belief can communicate with each other. But, whenever these different schools of mystical belief communicate with each other, they are heavily dependent on a task of translation, since the previous schools of mystical belief represent different spiritual realities. Any attempt to arbitrarily unify different spiritual realities reduces to an attempt to eliminate the existential otherness of the different spiritual systems, and, ultimately, it throws all spiritual communities, or cultures, into a chaotic and impersonal melting pot, which, in the Bible, is described by the metaphor of the Tower of Babel.

THE GENEALOGY OF THE NOACHITES

We read in *Genesis* 9:20-27: "And Noah began to be a husbandman, and planted a vineyard: and he drank of the wine, and was drunken. And he was uncovered within his tent. And Ham, the father of Canaan, saw the nakedness of his father, and told his two brethren without. And Shem and Japheth took a garment, and laid it upon their shoulders, and went backward, and covered the nakedness of their father. And their faces were backward, and they saw not their father's nakedness. And Noah awoke from his wine, and knew what his younger son had done unto him. And he said, Cursed be Canaan; A servant of servants shall he be unto his brethren. And he said, Blessed be Yehovah, the God of Shem; And let Canaan be his servant. God enlarge Japheth, And let him dwell in the tents of Shem; And let Canaan be his servant. And Noah lived after the flood three hundred and fifty years. And all the days of Noah were nine hundred and fifty years: and he died".

Noah is an emblematic figure in several systems of Western esotericism. Freemasonry is a characteristic case in point. One of the earliest surviving documents of Freemasonry, the *Graham Manuscript*, apparently dated 24 October 1726, explicitly refers to the sons of Noah seeking the secret that their dead father had possessed in a manner similar to part of the Hiramic Legend of the Third Degree of Symbolic Masonry. Hence, this manuscript gives a Noah story, rather than a Hiramic one as the legend of the Third Degree of Symbolic Masonry (see Chapter 9). Additionally, if one looks at Anderson's 1738 Constitutions of Freemasonry, he realizes the key importance of Noah for early Freemasons: Freemasons see themselves as true Noachites, i.e. as children of Noah.

The three sons of Noah are three very well-known persons. Shem is the father of the Hebrews and a forebear of Abraham (1 *Chronicles* 1:17-27). Ham is the father of Canaan and Mizraim (*Genesis* 10:6, 1 *Chronicles* 1:8), and, according to Clement of Alexandria* (*Homily* IX, 3-7), the races of the Egyptians, the Babylonians and the Persians are descended from Mizraim. Japheth is the father of Javan, and the sons of Javan are Elishah, Tarshish, the Kittim and the Rodanim (*Genesis* 10:2-4). Thus, the Bible tells us that Japheth was the father of Ion (Javan) and, therefore, the father of the Greeks[†]. According to Greek mythology, Ion was the son of Apollo and Creusa, daughter of Erechtheus and wife of Xuthus, and, when his mother abandoned him, he was saved and raised by a priestess of the Delphic Oracle. His story is told in the tragedy *Ion* by Euripides. According to mythological accounts, Ion is the father of a primary Greek tribe, the Ionians.

Many philologists[‡] equate Iapetos (or Japetus), who, according to the ancient Greek mythology, was the Titan of mortal life, the son of Uranus and Gaia, with Japheth, who, according to the Bible, was one of Noah's sons, for the following reasons:

1. there is a linguistic connection between the names Iapetos and Japheth;

---

[*] Titus Flavius Clemens (died ca. 215 A.D.), known as Clement of Alexandria, was a very influential Christian theologian and the head of the noted Catechetical School of Alexandria. He is counted as one of the early Greek Church Fathers. The works of Clement of Alexandria were first edited by P. Victorius (Florence, 1550). The most complete edition is that of J. Potter, *Clementis Alexandrini opera quae extant omnia* (Oxford, 1715; Venice, 1757), reproduced in J.P. Migne, *Patrologia Gaeca*, Vol. VIII, IX.

[†] G.W. Bromiley (ed.), *The International Standard Bible Encyclopedia*, Vol. II, fully revised, Michigan: Wm. B. Eerdmans Publishing, 1994, pp. 971ff.

[‡] See: M.L. West, *Hesiod: Theogony*, edited with prolegomena and commentary, Oxford: Clarendon Press, 1966.

2. according to the Greek mythology, Cronus, a brother of Iapetos castrated their father, which echoes the sinful act of Ham, the brother of Japheth;

3. both Japheth and Iapetos are related to a deluge: the first through his father Noah, and the latter through his grand-son Deucalion;

4. Iapetos was the husband of Asia.

The Biblical story of Noah has great ontological significance. First of all, it is interesting that Noah cursed his son Ham, because the latter saw him naked. This attitude of Noah should not be interpreted as an expression of anger by a prudish old man. It has a much deeper meaning.

The name Noah means 'relief'. The father of Noah was Lamech, the sixth generation descendant of Cain (*Genesis* 4:18). Lamech named his son Noah, prophesizing that Noah "shall comfort us in our work and in the toil of our hands, which cometh because of the ground which Yehovah hath cursed" (*Genesis* 5:29). Noah relieved the humankind and, in general, every animate being from the curse of the Deluge. Thus, according to *Matthew* 24:36-39, Noah can be considered a type of Christ: "But of that day and hour knoweth no one, not even the angels of heaven, but my Father only. And as were the days of Noah, so shall be the coming of the Son of man. For as in those days which were before the flood they were eating and drinking, marrying and giving in marriage, until the day that Noah entered into the ark, and they knew not until the flood came, and took them all away; so shall be the coming of the Son of man".

In particular, we can identify the following correspondences between Noah and Jesus Christ:

Table 1: Correspondences Between Noah and Jesus Christ

Noah	Jesus Christ
Divine Judgement	Divine Judgement
Salvation	Salvation
Wooden Ark	Wooden Cross
Exit from the Ark	Resurrection
Blessing of Sons	Blessing of Apostles
Covenant	Covenant

However, we can also identify the following differences between Noah and Jesus Christ:

Table 2: Differences Between Noah and Jesus Christ

Noah	Jesus Christ
Deluge	Baptism
Inebriation	Holy Communion
Clothing	"Divided his garments by casting lots"

Furthermore, according to *Genesis* (9:20), Noah is the first farmer. He transformed (or one could even use the term 'transmuted') the 'cursed' land into a nourisher of the human being, and also he transformed labor into a source of reward. One day, as he had passed from labor to refreshment, Noah drank wine from his vineyard, he became inebriated, and he put off his clothes.

Nakedness is a kind of revelation, namely, it reveals one's body. In the context of Biblical anthropology, the human body is not merely a system of flesh and bones, but it is something much more than that. The human body discloses the whole human being. In other words, the human body is an integral expression of man's mental life and the mediator between the reality of consciousness and the reality of the external world. Thus, Merleau-Ponty argues that the permanence of our body leads to the conclusion that the body is not an object of the world, but it is our means of communication with the world*. In addition, the Apostle Paul wrote that the body is meant "for the Lord, and the Lord for the body" (1 *Corinthians* 6:13). Since the body substantiates the human person, the disclosure of the naked body cannot take place without certain presuppositions. The revelation of a person's body means the revelation of what that person really is, and, therefore, this act presupposes a deep awareness of the holiness of that moment, i.e. it presupposes a kind of initiation. 'Initiation' means the ability to see when your eyes are shut, i.e. it means the ability to see beyond sensual phenomena. The presence of any being of the sensual world in human consciousness is determined by the significance that human consciousness ascribes to it. Thus, the ability to see beyond sensual phenomena means that one is able to see the spiritual reality in which the objects of his consciousness are embedded. In the context of the previous analysis, showing one's body without initiation is an ontological degradation of the human being, since, in this way, men behave like animals.

If we are not 'initiated', the human body is clothed, which means that one's being is concealed. Thus, according to the book of *Genesis*, God covers the fallen man with clothes: "And Yehovah God made for Adam and for his wife coats of skins, and clothed them" (*Genesis* 3:21). Furthermore, on several occasions, the Bible stresses the social and cultural functions performed by clothing: "Life's prime needs are water, bread, and clothing, a house, too, for decent privacy" (*Sirach* 29:21). According to *Deuteronomy*, food and clothing are some of God's blessings (*Deuteronomy* 10:18), whereas, if man is abandoned by God's grace, he lives "in hunger and thirst, in nakedness and utter poverty" (*Deuteronomy* 28:48). Clothes protect us from adverse environmental conditions, and, therefore, according to *Exodus* 22:26, "if thou at all take thy neighbour's garment to pledge, thou shalt restore it unto him before the sun goeth down". Clothing helps us distinguish between male and female, and it can function as a symbol of their relations (*Deuteronomy* 22:5). Furthermore, clothing indicates social life, since giving one's clothes to someone else is a sign of brotherhood (1 *Samuel* 18:3-4), and, according to *Ezekiel* 18:7, justice requires that we should "clothe the naked". In the same spirit, Isaiah teaches that the act of "clothing the naked when you see them"

---

* M. Merleau-Ponty, *Phenomenology of Perception*, London: Routledge Classics, 2002 (originally published in 1945), p. 106.

is an act of spiritual rebirth (*Isaiah* 58:7). Moreover, Jesus Christ said: "And if any man would go to law with thee, and take away thy coat, let him have thy cloke also" (*Matthew* 5:40), meaning that we must make our own personhood available to the fellow human that seeks a true communion with us. Clothing, by being an objectivation of the intentionality of human consciousness, implies that our body can exist in many different ways that reflect our personhood, and not only in accordance with the impersonal and coercive logic of nature.

After the previous analysis, we are able to understand the meaning of Ham's act. Ham disgraced initiation, i.e. he disgraced the human personhood by treating the human being as if it were merely an object of the natural world. Shem and Japheth did the opposite: "Shem and Japheth took a garment, and laid it upon their shoulders, and went backward, and covered the nakedness of their father" (*Genesis* 9:23). In other words, Shem and Japheth safeguarded the personal (as opposed to impersonal-natural) mode of existence of the human being, and they showed respect to the existential otherness of Noah in particular and of every human being in general, instead of treating them like same units of the natural world. Thus, Noah cursed Ham and prophesized the following: "Blessed be Yehovah, the God of Shem; And let Canaan be his servant. God enlarge Japheth, And let him dwell in the tents of Shem; And let Canaan be his servant" (*Genesis* 9:26-27). Thus, Japheth, the founder of the Greek civilization, will worship the God of Shem, but Japheth will not reign only in the land of Shem. Japheth's dominion will expand worldwide.

In *Genesis* 9:26-27, behind the seemingly simple words of Noah, a cosmogenesis takes place. Noah divides the world in half: he exalts Shem to the sublime historical 'office' of the founder of the religion of the nations that descended from Shem, but he offers the entire earth to Japheth. Noah's prophecy is clear: on the one hand, "Blessed be Yehovah, the God of Shem" – namely, Shem is the custodian of the true religion, i.e. he is invested with the supreme religious authority – but, on the other hand, "God enlarge Japheth" – namely, Japheth is invested with the supreme secular and political authority. Hence, in *Genesis* 9:26-27, we read, in terms of a mythological language, the story of the division of the world between two different (but not mutually incompatible) spiritual forces: the spiritual force that is represented by Shem consists in religious faith and in the worship of the true God, and the spiritual force that is represented by Japheth consists in reason (logos) and historical action.

JAPHETH'S DESCENDANTS: ANCIENT GREEKS AND THE QUEST FOR KNOWLEDGE

Let us now turn our attention to the words of one of Japheth's descendants, namely Plato. In his book *Timaeus*, 21e-25b, Plato narrates a conversation between Egyptian priests and Solon. Solon, a great Athenian sage, told the Egyptians the most ancient Greek traditions, such as the legend about Deucalion and Pyrrha after the Flood and the genealogy of Deucalion's and Pyrrha's descendants (*Timaeus*, 22a). Then an old Egyptian priest said to Solon that "Greeks are always children", in the sense that "there is not such a thing as an old Greek" (ibid, 22b). And on hearing this, Solon asked him to clarify what he meant by that statement (ibid, 22b). And the Egyptian priest replied that Greeks are "young in soul" and that they do not possess ancient beliefs derived from old tradition, nor do they preserve old scientific propositions (ibid, 22b). In other words, the Egyptian priest observes that the Greeks do not have long traditions about anything; they do not preserve old forms of knowledge. For the Egyptians, Plato's Greece is a country without anything old. Plato agrees on that, and he points out that tradition is an important notion on the basis of which one can distinguish between different civilizations.

Solon was speaking to the Egyptian priests about the creation of man and a very ancient deluge. Both Solon and the Egyptian priests believed that Solon's teachings about the creation of man and the deluge were based on rational grounds. Then why did the Egyptian priest say that "Greeks are always children"? Because, according to this Egyptian priest, the Greeks do not possess belief systems that are ancient and derived from old tradition. The Greeks produce and disseminate new knowledge. The Greeks' arguments, opinions and interpretations about reality are 'ashlars' perfectly chiselled, but they are not old, in the sense that they are continually subject to re-examination, and the Greek mind is open and ready to chisel new 'ashlars' without any fear about the future status of the previous ones. On the other hand, in the context of the Egyptian culture, knowledge is like a pebble that has been smoothed by its prolonged exposure to the influence of the air and the water.

According to the Egyptian priest, the Greeks' dynamic relation with tradition is, first of all, due to the climate of Greece: in Egypt, the water does not pour down over the Egyptian fields from above, but it tends naturally to well up from below, and, therefore, what is preserved in Egypt is reckoned to be very old; on the other hand, according to the Egyptian priest, in Greece and generally in places where there is no excessive heat or cold, there always exists some human stock (ibid, 22e). Hence, the natural climate of Greece makes the Greeks feel secure about the preservation of their nation and of their stock of knowledge, and, therefore, they do not need to depend on rigid traditional structures for their survival. In particular, the Egyptian priest mentioned that, when, goddess Athina established the city of Athens, she chose the specific geographical spot because she perceived therein a climate that was duly blended and that would bring forth men of high intellectual qualities (ibid, 24c). Furthermore, the Egyptian priest said to Solon that the Greeks' dynamic relation with tradition is related to the use of written language: events that are noble or great or in any way conspicuous are recorded and preserved in Egyptian temples, whereas, according to the Egyptian priest, the Greeks and the others lack certain memories, because they started using written language later than the Egyptians.

The Egyptian priest, referring to goddess Athina, the founder of Athens, as "a lover of war and a lover of wisdom" (ibid, 24d), argues that the two fundamental attributes of what we might call the 'Western man' – since Solon is an ancient representative of the 'Western man' – are love for wisdom (or 'philosophy') and love for war. Many centuries later, in his book *History of Philosophy*, Georg Wilhelm Friedrich Hegel* pointed out that the Western world's philosophical, scientific and artistic endowment has taken its root in Greek life and has been created by the Greek spirit. Moreover, Hegel pointed out that, even though Greeks received the substantial beginnings of their religion, culture and social institutions, more or less from Asia, Syria and Egypt, they have so greatly assimilated them and they have so much adapted them to their own mentality and, hence, changed them, that their civilization and culture are essentially their own. Finally, in his *Lectures on the Philosophy of History*, Hegel argues that Greece is an archetype of "the cheerful

---

* G.W.F. Hegel, "Greek Philosophy – Introduction", *Lectures on the History of Philosophy*, trans. E.S. Haldane and F.H. Simson, London, 1892—1896 (originally published in 1825—1826).

aspect of youthful freshness" and that, in the Greek civilization and culture, Achilles is the ideal youth of poetry and Alexander the Great is the ideal youth of political reality*; these two Greek personifications of youth were in contest with Asia.

It is important to notice that it is Solon who traveled to Egypt. It is not an Egyptian priest or a Chaldean Magus who visited the 'Agora' of Athens. Thales, Pythagoras, Solon, Herodotus, Plato and so many other Greek scholars and explorers travel around the world seeking knowledge, whereas the Asian adepts are not engaged in risky knowledge adventures. Furthermore, in the context of the classical Greek philosophy, 'tradition' does not signify continuous conformity to and repetition of specific answers to specific questions, but it signifies commitment to a specific way of posing questions and of giving meaning to historical action. Thus, according to the Greek conception of tradition, the acquisition of new knowledge and societal changes in general do not contradict the continuity of tradition.

Solon traveled to Egypt in order to gather new knowledge. When the Egyptian priest comments that "Greeks are always children", Solon's response is to ask him to explain what he means by this statement. In other words, Solon's response to the Egyptian priest's argument is: prove it! Solon's response reveals the following spiritual principles of the Greek culture: rational accountability and rational autonomy. Moreover, the city of Athens from the 8th until the 5th century B.C. is the first society in the history of mankind that founded its operation on a continuous critical evaluation and re-evaluation of its own self. It is the first society in the history of mankind that demands from itself to be able to explain (to itself and to others) why it is what it is. Thus, whereas all societies institutionalize mechanisms for the coercive imposition of their 'logos' (values-norms) on their members, the Athenian democracy is the first society in the history of mankind that institutionalized mechanisms of rational self-control (i.e. reflective political attitude), too. In this context, as we read in Thucydides' *Peloponnesian War*†, Pericles (ca. 495—429 B.C.), one of the most prominent and influential statesmen and generals of

---

* G.W.F. Hegel, "Part II: The Greek World", *Lectures on the Philosophy of History*, trans. J. Sibree, New York: Dover, 1956 (originally published posthumously in 1837).

† Thucydides, *The Peloponnesian War*, trans. B. Jowett, Oxford: Clarendon Press, 1900 ("Funeral Oration of Pericles").

Athens, argued that, in the Athenian political system, the principles of freedom and respect for law are united and also the activities of the city are based on the voluntary co-operation and on the critical thought of the citizens.

HAM'S DESCENDANTS AND THE ARABO-ISLAMIC CIVILIZATION

Now, it is useful to listen to the voice of one of Ham's descendants, namely Ibn Khaldun (1332—1406 A.D.). In the Biblical view, the Arabs are descendants of Ham. Ibn Khaldun was an Arab historiographer and historian born in North Africa, in present-day Tunisia, and is often viewed as one of the forerunners of modern historiography, sociology and economics. In 1377, Ibn Khaldun wrote the book *Muqaddimah*, also known as Ibn Khaldun's *Prolegomena*, in which he records an early view of world history[*].

Some modern scholars argue that Ibn Khaldun's *Prolegomena* is one of the first works dealing with the philosophy of history. But Ibn Khaldun himself clearly denies that he is an *Arab* philosopher, and instead he argues that he is a student of the *Greek* intellectual heritage. In particular, in the "Preliminary Remarks" included in the first book of his *Prolegomena*, Ibn Khaldun writes that there are no such things as Persian, Chaldean, Syrian or Coptic sciences and that only the Greeks' sciences have come down to us.

Like the Egyptian priest who is quoted by Plato in *Timaeus*, Ibn Khaldun admits that the natural climate plays an important role in the development of civilization. In particular, in the "Second Prefaratory Discussion", in the first book of his *Prolegomena*, Ibn Khaldun divides the cultivated part of the earth into seven zones, and he observes that the level of civilization in each of them depends on the natural climate. However, Ibn Khaldun assigns great importance to the economic and sociological characteristics of civilization, too. In his chapter on "Bedouin Civilization, Savage Nations and Tribes and their Conditions [of Life] Including Several Basic and Explanatory Statements", Ibn Khaldun argues that the differences of condition among people are the result of economic factors, and he observes that "sedentary people" (i.e. the inhabitants of cities and countries, some of whom are craftsmen and others are merchants) earn more

---

[*] Ibn Khaldun, *The Muqaddimah*, Princeton, NJ: Princeton University Press, 1967 (originally published in 1377).

and live more comfortably than Bedouins, because they live above subsistence level. In addition, in his chapter "On the various aspects of making a living, such as profit and the crafts", Ibn Khaldun writes that the Arabs, of all people, are least familiar with crafts, because the centre of the Arabs' life is in the desert and the Arabs are more remote from sedentary civilization than anybody else, whereas the non-Arabs in the East and the Christian Mediterranean nations are very well versed in the crafts because they have developed sedentary civilizations.

Then how can one explain the flourishing of the Arab civilization during the Middle Ages? Ibn Khaldun deals with the previous question in his chapter on "The various kinds of sciences". First of all, Ibn Khaldun points out that his contemporaries' sciences were cultivated by the two greatest pre-Islamic civilizations, i.e. by the Persian civilization and the Greek civilization. According to Ibn Khaldun, when the Muslims conquered Persia, Sa'd ibn Abi Waqqas wrote to 'Umar ibn al-Khattab, asking him for permission to take the Persians' scientific books and distribute them as booty among the Muslims, and 'Umar ordered him to destroy them on the grounds that Islam was a self-sufficient system of knowledge. Thus, due to the Muslims, the sciences of the Persians were lost. Furthermore, Ibn Khaldun points out that the Greek scientific books continued to exist during the Roman Empire, and, when the Arabs deprived the Byzantines [Rum], as well as all other nations, of their realms, they came in touch with Greek scientific works. Ibn Khaldun writes that, at the beginning, the Arabs disregarded the crafts, but, eventually, they developed a sedentary civilization, they became versed in many different crafts and sciences, and, ultimately, they desired to study philosophy. Thus, Abu Ja'far al-Mansur, who is often considered the true founder of the Abbasid Dynasty, sent to the Byzantine Emperor and asked him to send him translations of Greek mathematical texts. The Byzantine Emperor sent him Euclid's book and some works on physics. Later on, al-Ma'mun, another learned Abbasid caliph, sent ambassadors to the Byzantine emperors, and those Arab ambassadors conducted deep and methodic studies in the Greek sciences and had them copied in the Arabic language. Thus, a good deal of scientific knowledge was amassed and preserved by the medieval Arabs.

Finally, Ibn Khaldun stressed the importance of the economic character of civilization, and, therefore, he devoted a large part of his *Prolegomena* to a methodic and systematic study of political economy*. Under the influence of Ibn Khaldun's idea that craftsmen and industrialists play a significant role in a country's growth, prosperity and power, the Ottoman Sultan Selim I, after having successfully extended his dominion over Egypt in 1517, took back with him from Cairo to Constantinople (Istanbul) the best artificers of his time. In modern terminology, Selim I applied a technology transfer policy.

THE CARDINAL POINTS OF THE SPIRITUAL HORIZON OF WESTERN ESOTERICISM

According to the book of *Genesis*, Noah distributed different spiritual characteristics among different people. His sons were equal to each other, in the sense that they all sprang from the same source, but each one of them was different from his brothers, in the sense that each of Noah's sons had his own distinctive spiritual identity. In order to understand Western esotericism, we must bear in mind what is meant by the term 'Western' (or European). As a conclusion of this chapter, the 'Western' (or European) man is a synthesis of the following spiritual characteristics, which, in the context of the book of *Genesis*, are symbolically represented by the Hebrews, the Egyptians, the Arabs and the Greeks: metaphysical depth (symbolically represented by the Hebrews), tradition (symbolically represented by the Egyptians), technology (symbolically represented by the Arabs), and reason (symbolically represented by the Greeks). In the next chapter, I study the historical context in which this synthesis took place, i.e. I study the creation and the development of the Western spiritual identity within the context of what I call the 'Japhethite ecumene'.

---

* See for instance: Abdol Soofi, "Economics of Ibn Khaldun Revisited", *History of Political Economy*, Vol. 27, 1995, pp. 387-404.

3

THE CREATION OF THE JAPHETHITE
ECUMENE AND THE FOUNDATIONS
OF WESTERN ESOTERICISM

THE historical context within which the synthesis among the
principles of 'metaphysical depth', 'tradition', 'technology' and
'reason' took place and gave rise to the Western spiritual identity,
according to the arguments that I put forward in Chapter 1, was the
'Japhethite ecumene', which was created by Alexander the Great.
Thus, the Japhethite ecumene is the 'womb' of the Western spirituality
and civilization in general and of Western esotericism in particular.

The term 'ecumene' is a Greek word that means 'inhabited
world'. However, it is not merely a geographical/geopolitical term.
In contrast with the term 'empire', which refers only (or at least
primarily) to a geopolitical phenomenon, the term 'ecumene' refers
primarily to a cultural phenomenon. In particular, 'ecumene' means
that a group of people participates not only in the same geographical/
geopolitical entity, but also in a common spiritual horizon.

THE GENESIS OF THE ECUMENE

In 334 B.C., Alexander the Great had already liberated the Greek
inhabitants of Ionia from the Persian yoke, and he went to Gordium,
the Phrygian capital, to spend the winter. In April 333 B.C.,
Alexander the Great solved the famous Gordian Knot, and, thus,
Gordium became the starting point of Alexander's operation for the
conquest of Asia.

Arguably, when Alexander the Great was still in Gordium, he had not already conceived the notion of ecumene, at least in its fullness. It would be superficial to assume that Alexander the Great invaded the cradles of so many, great and ancient civilizations without being influenced by them. However, irrespective of the extent to which and the manner in which Alexander the Great understood the notion of ecumene when he started his expedition to Asia, we know for sure that, in the last year of his life, Alexander the Great had a deep understanding of the notion of ecumene, and, in fact, he had created the ecumene. According to Arrian's *Anabasis* (Book VII, 11), Alexander the Great "prayed for other blessings, and especially that harmony and community of rule might exist between the Macedonians and the Persians". In fact, Alexander the Great did not simply found an empire; he founded the 'ecumene', i.e. he founded the first 'global' order in the history of mankind[*]. In other words, his work cannot be restricted to the narrow framework of a particular historical period or of a particular people. Thus, Hermann Bengtson[†] argues that neither the Roman Empire, nor the triumph of Christianity's march, nor the Byzantine Empire, nor the Arab civilization could have been created without Alexander the Great and his cosmogonic work.

Alexander's ecumene consisted of the Persian Empire and Greece. Alexander the Great wanted to expand his dominion over the vast Indian Peninsula, but his army refused to follow him, and, in particular, according to Arrian's *Anabasis* (Book V, 27), general Coenus said to Alexander the Great: "Do not lead us now against our will…Self-control in the midst of success is the noblest of all virtues, O king". This statement by Coenus determined the Eastern limits of the ecumene. In the ecumene of Alexander the Great and his Epigones, Greece was the 'Western world' and the area of the former Persian Empire was the 'Eastern world'.

The system of the fundamental significations, i.e. the value system, that spiritually underpinned the ecumene, which was founded by Alexander the Great, was 'Western', and particularly Greek, and not Asian. Classical Greek culture was based on reason. Thus, the

---

[*]   For more details, on this issue, see: Nicolas Laos, *Foundations of Cultural Diplomacy: Politics Among Cultures and the Moral Autonomy of Man*, New York: Algora Publishing, 2011.

[†]   Hermann Bengtson, *History of Greece: From the Beginnings to the Byzantine Era*, trans. E.F. Bloedow, Ottawa: University of Ottawa Press, 1997.

Athenian city-state was a society that founded its operation on the continuous critical evaluation and re-evaluation of itself. This is the essence of rational autonomy, which underpins the classical Greek education and political thought. The term 'autonomy' comes from the Greek word 'autonomos', which has two roots: 'autos', which means 'by itself', and 'nomos', which means 'law' and 'tradition'. The root 'autos' refers to individual freedom, and the root 'nomos' refers to a free and unbiased institution of a rational order (as opposed to chaos), which expresses the rational operation of consciousness. Thus, 'autonomy' is opposite to 'heteronomy', which consists in a situation where 'nomos' (legal order) is dictated by an authority that is beyond criticism and is not accountable to the citizens. Additionally, 'autonomy' is opposite to 'anomy', which consists in a situation that is characterized by absence of law. Autonomy means that men live by laws that express their intentionality and are subject to criticism, but they are not results of arbitrary idealistic action. The classical Athenians developed a system of continuous autonomy where the people (demos) voted constantly on matters of government and law and where the elected rulers (the archons) were asked to enforce them.

The great Greek poet Aeschylus, in his play *Persians*, verse 242, refers to the autonomous character of the Greek society by writing the following about the Greeks: "Slaves to no lord, they own no kingly power". On the other hand, Persia was a heteronomous society. Thus, Aeschylus, in his play *Persians*, 212—214, writes that, in the context of the Persian society, King Xerxes' rule was absolute and, therefore, it was the foundation and cause of the Persian society's heteronomous character. The antithesis between autonomy (Greek society) and heteronomy (Persian society) created an unbridgeable cultural chasm between West and East. Aeschylus, in his play *Persians*, 181—196, refers to this cultural chasm in terms of a prophetic dream that was seen by King Xerxes' mother; in that dream, two gorgeously vested women, one adorned in Persian robes and the other wearing the Doric garb, were fighting against each other.

However, Alexander the Great envisioned the Greek society and the Persian society (namely, the two sisters that Xerxes' mother saw in the above-mentioned dream) as the two horses of the chariot of his 'ecumene'. In his book *On the Fortune or the Virtue of Alexander*, I, 329a-d, Plutarch points out that Alexander the Great gave effect to

Zeno's cosmopolitan political ideal. Zeno, the founder of Stoicism, wrote in his *Republic* that we should consider all men to be of one community and one polity and that we should all have a common life and common order. Furthermore, Plutarch (ibid) points out that Alexander the Great did not follow Aristotle's advice to treat the Greeks as if he were their leader, and other peoples as if he were their master. Instead, according to Plutarch (ibid), Alexander the Great believed that he came as a heaven-sent governor to all and as a mediator for the whole world, and, therefore, those whom he could not persuade to unite with him, he conquered by force of arms, but he bade all his subjects consider as their fatherland the whole inhabited earth, as their polity his camp, as akin to them all virtuous men, and as foreigners only the wicked. Thus, Alexander the Great created a multicultural polity. With respect to Alexander the Great's attitude toward Asia, Plutarch (ibid, I, 330c-e) emphasizes that Alexander did not overrun Asia like a robber, but Alexander's goal was to render all upon earth subject to one law of reason and one form of government.

Instead of building up an empire merely by establishing regimes based on physical-spatial unity, Alexander the Great was founding new cities that were loci of the Greek 'paideia'*, and, at the apex of his imperial career, he declared the brotherhood of all men, thus uniting space with time. He was the first global leader that transcended national differences, and he anticipated the Apostle Paul's universalism by forging a spiritual unity between the Greeks and the barbarians[†]. Alexander the Great wanted to conquer the barbarians primarily by penetrating and conquering their minds, i.e. by applying 'soft power'.

---

* See: W.W. Jaeger, *Paideia: The Ideals of Greek Culture*, Oxford: Oxford University Press, 1945. In this famous research work, Jaeger explains that 'paideia' is a word we translate as education, but which, according to ancient Greeks, means not only the rearing and education of children ('pais' is the simple Greek for child), but also culture and civilization, and, generally, the spiritual accomplishments of an age or people. It was rendered in Latin as 'humanitas'. As Jaeger put it in the much quoted Introduction of his book *Paideia*, whereas other systems of paideia were centered on gods, kings and / or spirits, the Greek system of paideia was the first cultural proposal that was centered on man. Hence, according to Jaeger, men must see, in the traditional heroes Pindar glorified, an idealization of their selves.

† See: W.W. Tarn, "Alexander: The Conquest of the Far East", in *Cambridge Ancient History*, Vol. VI, Cambridge: Cambridge University Press, 1933.

THE PUNIC WARS

The Punic Wars were a series of three wars fought between Rome and Carthage from 264 B.C. to 146 B.C. They played a decisive role in the fate of the ecumene. They started in 264 B.C., when the Roman Republic decided to ally itself with a group of robbers and pirates, namely the Mamertines (which means 'sons of Mars'), who were living in Messina, which was besieged by Hieron II, King of Syracuse, and by the Carthaginians. In his *Histories*, I, 12:5, Polybius explains the historical significance of the First Punic War: it was "the first warlike expedition of the Romans beyond the shores of Italy", i.e. beyond their natural borders. In 264 B.C., the decision of the Roman Republic to plunge its armed forces in a war outside its natural borders signals the beginning of a series of wars between Rome and Carthage, which was the greatest power in the Western Mediterranean. The Punic Wars lasted for 82 years. In 146 B.C., the Romans eventually defeated the Carthaginians, and Carthage was destroyed by the Roman general Scipio Aemilianus.

As a consequence of the victory of Rome in the Punic Wars, the entire Western Mediterranean was placed under the rule of Rome. Thus, in his *Histories*, I, 3:3-6, Polybius argues that the Roman conquest of Carthage is the most important milestone of the history of the ecumene, because, after the Roman conquest of Carthage, "the affairs of Italy and Libya are involved with those of Asia and Greece, and the tendency of all is to unity".

In September 200 B.C., two Roman legions were deployed in Epirus. According to Polybius' *Histories*, XVIII, 47:2, after defeating the Macedonians, the Romans demanded from Antiochus III the Great, the 6th ruler of the Seleucid Empire, never to "cross over into Europe with an army". In reality, Antiochus III accepted the Roman dominion over Europe, since, in his reply to the Romans, he attempted to justify the invasion of Thrace (a part of Europe) by his army, and he demanded from the Romans to split the ecumene into East and West, i.e. into Asia and Europe. Thus, as we read in Polybius' *Histories*, XVIII, 51:2, Antiochus III claimed that the Romans "should refrain entirely from interfering in the affairs of Asia, seeing that he never in the least degree interposed in those of Italy". Rome did not compromise with Antiochus' proposal, and its legions eventually conquered Greece and, in 190

B.C., under the command of Lucius Cornelius Scipio, the Roman legions crossed the Hellespont and sought Antiochus in his own kingdom.

Under the Roman dominion, the ecumene underwent major changes: the geopolitical and the cultural significance of the East was dramatically reduced; the borders of the ecumene expanded northwards; and the Atlantic Ocean became the Western border of the ecumene. The cultural consequences of the previous changes in the ecumene were significant. The Roman Empire became, involuntarily, the geopolitical framework within which different nations assumed leading cultural roles. In the context of the Roman Empire, four nations assumed leading cultural roles: the Hebrews, the Greeks, the Romans and the Celts. However, before the Roman Empire, the Greeks had already created various networks of communication between Greece, on the one hand, and the Celts, the Romans and the Hebrews on the other.

THE COMMUNICATION BETWEEN THE CELTS AND THE GREEKS

The Celts and the Greeks had intimate contacts with each other since the prehistoric years. The megalithic architecture, the use of copper, the building of walls around cities, and the erection of ancient edifices are gifts of the Aegean civilizations to the rest of the European peoples[*]. By the 14th century B.C., trade relations between Mycenae[†] and the Celts had become very active, and, in the 6th century B.C., Greeks from Phocaea founded Marseille, which soon became a major centre for the dissemination of the Greek civilization among the Celts. In his *Geographica*, IV, 181, Strabo writes that Marseille was a training-school for the barbarians, it was schooling the Galatae to be fond enough of the Greeks to write even their contracts in Greek, and it had become one of the most important educational centres in the Roman Empire.

In his *De bello gallico*, I, 29:1, Gaius Julius Caesar writes that: "In the camp of the Helvetii, lists were found, drawn up in Greek characters". Moreover, in *De bello gallico*, VI, 14:4, Gaius Julius

---

[*]   See: C.F.C. Hawkes, *The Prehistoric Foundations of Europe to the Mycenaean Age*, London: Methuen and Co., 1940.

[†]   Its name was given to one of the greatest civilizations of Greek prehistory, the Mycenaean civilization. The construction of the palace and fortification wall currently visible began ca. 1350 B.C.

Caesar writes that, the Druids, namely the priests of the Celts, "in their public and private transactions, they use Greek characters".

THE COMMUNICATION BETWEEN THE ROMANS AND THE GREEKS

Like the communication between the Celts and the Greeks, the communication between the Romans and the Greeks is a very ancient phenomenon. In general, the civilization of prehistoric Europe was founded on the Mycenaean civilization. Rome, in particular, was created by the Etruscans and by the inhabitants of Kimi (current Cuma), the first Greek colony in Italy, and of the Greek cities of Sicily. The Roman (Latin) alphabet was derived from the Greek one, and the first known Roman author is the Greek dramatist and epic poet Livius Andronicus (3rd century B.C.). Moreover, the Greek gods were adopted by the Romans during the classical era, i.e. long before the Hellenistic era. For instance, the Temple of Demeter in Rome was built by Greek artificers in 493 B.C.

In the course of the 14th and 13th centuries B.C., the development of Mycenaean navigation and trade made a great contribution to the development of the Mycenaean economy. The Mycenaeans developed commercial relations with Syria and Palestine. Carl J. Richard* writes that the Mycenaeans had very active trade relations with Egypt, Palestine, Anatolia, Syria, Sicily, Southern Italy, Cyprus, Crete, and the Aegean islands. Thus, it was very easy for the Hebrews and the Greeks to communicate with each other, given that there were Hebrews in Palestine, Lebanon, Babylon, Egypt and elsewhere in the Middle East. However, before the Hellenistic years, the Greeks seem to be rather indifferent toward the Hebrews.

THE COMMUNICATION BETWEEN THE HEBREWS AND THE GREEKS

In his book *Antiquities of the Jews*, Titus Flavius Josephus (37 — ca. 100 A.D.), also called Joseph ben Matityahu, studied methodically the relations between the Greeks and the Hebrews. Josephus, "an ethnic Jew and priest of Jerusalem"†, had studied the Greek language and culture, and, in his book *Jewish War*, he introduces himself with the Hellenized version of his name: Iosepos.

---

* C.J. Richard, *Twelve Greeks and Romans Who Changed the World*, Oxford: Rowman & Littlefield Publishers, 2003, p. 8.

† Josephus, *Jewish War*, I, 3.

In his polemical work *Against Apion*, I, 12:60-68, Josephus wrote about the relations between the Hebrews and the Greeks, and he attempted, among other things, to explain why the Greeks seemed to be rather indifferent toward the Hebrews. In particular, Josephus argued that the Greeks had not made extensive references to the Hebrew people in their writings because the Hebrews did not inhabit a maritime country, they did not delight in merchandise, and they strongly avoided mixing with other cultures. In addition, in his *Against Apion*, I, 12:171, Josephus made the following comments on Herodotus' *History*, II, 104, and on the poetry of Cherilus, in order to show that the Greeks had in fact paid some attention to the Hebrews: Herodotus mentioned that "the Syrians that are in Palestine are circumcised", and this is, according to Josephus, an indirect reference to the Jews; Cherilus, a still more ancient writer, and a poet, in his enumeration of all the nations that came to the assistance of King Xerxes, in his expedition against Greece, wrote also the following sentences, which, according to Josephus, are a reference to the Hebrews: "At the last there passed over a people, wonderful to be beheld; for they were speaking the Phoenician tongue with their mouths; they were dwelling in the Solymean mountains, near a broad lake: their heads were sooty; they had round rasures on them; their heads and faces were like nasty horse-heads also, that had been hardened in the smoke".

But, as it has been pointed out by Kostas Friligos[*], the arguments through which Josephus tries to enhance the image of ancient Judaism and explain why, for so many centuries, the Greeks were indifferent toward the Hebrew civilization are not correct, because of the following reasons: (i) when Cherilus mentions the Solymean mountains, he does not refer to the Hebrews' land, but to a mountain mentioned in Homer's *Odyssey* (E 383): in contrast to Josephus' arguments, the Solymean mountains were in the area of Lycia and not in Syria, whereas Jerusalem was built near Mount Zion; (ii) when Cherilous and Herodotus refer to people with "round rasures", they do not refer to the Hebrews, but they refer to Arab nations, as it is clarified in Herodotus' *The Histories*, III, 8, and, furthermore, in contrast to Josephus' arguments, according to *Leviticus* 19:27, the Hebrews were not allowed to cut the hair at the sides of their head;

---

[*]   Kostas Friligos (trans. and intro.), *Josephus, Against Apion*, Athens: Daedalus – I. Zacharopoulos Publications (in Greek).

(iii) in contrast to Josephus' arguments, Herodotus (ibid, VII, 70) clarifies that, when the Greeks refer to people whose "heads and faces were like nasty horse-heads", they mean the Ethiopians of Asia and not the Hebrews.

Even though, among the Greeks, the references to the Hebrews are of marginal significance, the Old Testament pays great attention to the Greeks. In *Genesis* 10:4-5, we read: "And the sons of Javan; Elishah, and Tarshish, Kittim, and Rodanim. By these were the isles of the Gentiles divided in their lands; everyone after his tongue, after their families, in their nations". The names of the previous islands, which were inhabited by the Ionian Greeks, are often mentioned in the Bible when the latter refers to the Greeks. In *Isaiah* 66:18-19, we read the following impressive prophecy: "For I [know] their works and their thoughts: it shall come, that I will gather all nations and tongues; and they shall come, and see my glory. And I will set a sign among them, and I will send those that escape of them unto the nations, [to] Tarshish, Pul, and Lud, that draw the bow, [to] Tubal, and Javan, [to] the isles afar off, that have not heard my fame, neither have seen my glory; and they shall declare my glory among the Gentiles". In addition, in *Zechariah* 9:13-14, we read: "When I have bent Judah for me, filled the bow with Ephraim, and raised up thy sons, O Zion, against thy sons, O Greece, and made thee as the sword of a mighty man".

THE ORIENTALIZATION OF GREECE
AND THE HELLENIZATION OF THE EAST

The creation of the ecumene caused immigration to increase dramatically and intensified the communication among different peoples. Moreover, the Roman dominion over the Mediterranean led to the establishment of the 'Pax Romana', which encouraged the development of international trade and united all the coastal peoples of the Mediterranean into a single Mediterranean economy. However, behind these well-known and rather obvious observations, some intellectually challenging and thought-provoking questions emerge: Why was the ecumene culturally divided into two parts? In other words, why did the East choose to express itself in Greek and not in Latin? Why, apart from Matthew's Gospel, which was written in Aramaic, were all the other books of the New Testament written in Greek and not in Latin? Why did the Egyptian historian and priest Manetho (ca. 3rd century B.C.) write the history of his country in Greek? Why did so many people from the East with Hellenized names write and speak in Greek and ignore Latin? And conversely: Why did the Celts, in the West, eventually choose the Latin language, even though, in the early stages of their civilization, they were using the Greek language? The above questions can be reduced to the following 'critical question': how and why did the Adriatic Sea become the border between East and West, instead of Ionia? When Emperor Diocletian divided the Roman Empire into Eastern and Western halves (ca. 293 A.D.), the border between East and West was the Aegean Sea, but, when Emperor Theodosius the Great (346—395 A.D.) divided the Roman Empire between his two sons, Arcadius in the East and Honorius in the West, the Adriatic Sea became the new border between East and West. How and why did Greece become a part of the East, how and why did the Greeks accept to become an Eastern nation, whereas for many centuries they were considering themselves Westerners, and how and why did the Easterners accept the Greeks as a part of the East, whereas for many centuries the Easterners were believing that the Greeks were Westerners? The previous question becomes even more difficult when we bear in mind the deep relationship between Rome and the Greek spirit. In fact, Jacques Pirenne[*] argues that the Roman Empire was a "Hellenistic state", and F.E. Peters[†] uses the terms "Latin Hellenism" and "Greek Hellenism" in order to describe the extent of the cultural influence of Greece on Rome. The cultural dominion of Greece over Rome has been explained by H.I. Marrou[‡] as follows: there was never an autonomous Italian civilization, because Rome and Italy were embedded in the Greek civilization, and, therefore, Latin education is a peculiar variation of the Greek culture.

Then how and why did the Greeks and the Romans separate from each other, following different spiritual paths? The answer is that Alexander the Great's cosmo-conception established a strong relationship between East and West. In this context, Greece underwent a process of Orientalization, and the East (mainly, the

---

[*]   Jacques Pirenne, *The Tides of History*, Vol. I, trans. L. Edwards, New York: E.P. Dutton & Co., 1962.

[†]   F.E. Peters, *The Harvest of Hellenism: A History of the Near East from Alexander the Great to the Triumph of Christianity*, New York: Simon and Schuster, 1971.

[‡]   H.I. Marrou, *A History of Education in Antiquity*, trans. G. Lamb, Wisconsin: The University of Wisconsin Press, 1982.

Middle East, Persia and Northern Egypt) underwent a process of Hellenization. Thus, the 'Greek' became an archetypal Man of East and West, whereas the 'Roman' never managed to assimilate Alexander the Great's ecumenical ideal and ethos. Therefore, in order to study the genealogy of the Western culture, one must analyze the Orientalization of Greece and the Hellenization of the East.

First of all, the creation of the ecumene was intimately related to the levelling of different peoples, i.e. to the intermixture of the civilizations of different nations, and the development of religious syncretism*. The levelling of the different peoples of the ecumene was followed by the intensification of the individualization of man. The individual was not any more a member of a homogeneous cultural community or a citizen of a city-state. In the context of the vast ecumene, the individual was feeling that it was too small to make a significant impact on historical becoming, and, therefore, the individual started to live for its own sake. In other words, the individual's primary goal was the survival and the intensification of its individuality. Thus, naturally, the Greek psyche turns toward Eastern religious doctrines of salvation and toward Eastern ascetic traditions and tries to imitate them. In particular, as we read in Arrian's book *The Discourses of Epictetus*, III, 22, the philosopher Epictetus described himself as a man "without a city, without a house, without possessions, without a slave" and as a man who has "no wife, no children, no praetorium, but only the earth and heavens, and one poor cloak".

The levelling of the peoples of the ecumene was followed by the levelling of the different gods of the ecumene, namely by religious syncretism. The Greek philosopher and historian Dio Chrysostom (ca. 40 — ca. 120 A.D.), in his *Rhodian Oration*, 11, writes that many people combine all the gods and make of them "one single force and power, so that it makes no difference at all whether you are honoring this one or that one".

A characteristic example of the religious syncretism of the Hellenistic era is the Hermetic cult. Tobias Churton[†] writes about the history of the Hermetic cult that, a century after Alexander the Great conquered Egypt and founded his city, Alexandria, in 331

---

* 'Syncretism' is a Greek word that means fusion.

† Tobias Churton, *The Golden Builders: Alchemists, Rosicrucians, and the First Freemasons*, Boston: Red Weel/Weiser, 2005, pp. 3-4.

B.C., Greek settlers in Alexandria had begun to apply the epithet "megistos kai megistos theos megas" (greatest and greatest the great god) to Hermes and that this dignity derives from the epithet "two times great", which Egyptians had applied to Hermes' Egyptian equivalent, the god Thoth. The Graeco-Egyptian Thoth-Hermes was the spirit of inventiveness. Sometime between the first century B.C. and the end of the first century A.D., a new figure appeared: "Hermes Trismegistus" (Thrice Greatest Hermes), a name with which Greek settlers in Egypt unified the Greek god Hermes and the Egyptian god Thoth, since both were associated with magical knowledge, the dead and healing. According to the Hermeticists' legends, the *Hermetica* was a collection of forty-two books of Egyptian magical wisdom that were written by Hermes Trismegistus, who was believed to be an ancient patriarch of civilization.

On the other hand, it should be mentioned that the Orientalization of Greece did not eliminate the Greek spirit. Therefore, the Greeks eventually adopted Christianity as a metaphysical proposal that completes and perfects the classical Greek humanistic philosophy, and they rejected Eastern schools of mystical belief (especially Asian spiritualism), which were not only opposite to the classical Greek humanistic spirit but also they were aiming for the spiritual dominion of Asia over Europe. The Greeks were deeply fascinated by the idea of the Incarnation of the Divine Logos, because they wanted to transcend the antithesis between body and soul by arriving at a new synthesis between body and soul (or between matter and spirit), and not by negating the body (or the material world).

Even though the civilizations of Mesopotamia, Egypt and Persia were covering vast areas of the East, the Eastern civilization that eventually exerted the most significant influence on the Greek spirituality in particular and on the culture of the ecumene in general was that of the Hebrews, who were a small nation living in the humble land of Jordan River valley.

Before becoming able to exert a significant cultural influence on the Greeks, the Hebrews were to a large extent Hellenized. The very term 'Hellenism', which refers to the use of the Greek language and the adoption of the Greek culture, was originally connected with the policy of a Hellenized Jewish high priest named Jason, and it was originally used by the Maccabees in order to describe the erosion of the Jewish culture as a result of the communication between the Hebrews and the Greeks. In particular, as we read in the Bible, in 2

Maccabees 4:7-13, the Maccabees (who were a Jewish rebel army who took control of Judea) revolted against the Greeks and attempted to reduce the influence of Hellenism and Hellenized Judaism. Additionally, the term 'Judaism', which refers to the observance of the morals and customs of the Jewish tradition, appeared for the first time in 2 *Maccabees* 2:21: "…and of the heavenly manifestations accorded to the heroes who fought bravely for Judaism…"

The Hellenization of the Jews was first of all manifested in the field of language. The part of the Jews that was Hellenized most rapidly was the one that was living in Egypt. Many Jews of Egypt used to take Greek names, such as: Apollonius, Artemidoros, Diodotus, Demetrius, Dionysus, Diophantus, Heracleia, Heracledes, Hermeias, Theodotus, Theodorus, Dositheus, Jason, etc. Even among the Maccabees, one can find Greek names, e.g. two generals of the Maccabees' army had Greek names: Dositheus and Sosipatrus. Moreover, in the fourth book of *Maccabees*, the classical Greek term 'polity' is used by the Jews in order to refer collectively to the faithful to the Torah.

Not only were the Jews of Egypt taking Greek names but also they were proud of their Greek education and were adopting Greek habits. The Jews of Egypt developed a highly Hellenized literature: the historiographer Demetrius, a Jewish courtier of Ptolemy IV, wrote an exposition of the Jewish religion following a philosophical style, which indicates the Greek spiritual influence on the Jews of Egypt; Artapanus of Alexandria, another famous Hellenized Jew, wrote an allegorical novel in which Moses is presented as the founder of the Orphic Mysteries[*]; a Jew named Ezekiel composed a Greek tragedy on the theme of the Exodus; Philo the Elder wrote an epic *On Jerusalem* in Homeric hexameters; Theodotus wrote an epic *On Shechem* (Shechem is mentioned in the Hebrew Bible as an Israelite city of the tribe of Manasseh) connecting the name of Shechem with Sikimios, the son of the Greek god Hermes; the Jewish philosopher Aristobulus of Paneas coined the theory that Pythagoras and Plato knew the Bible.

---

[*] The Orphic cult was one of the most ancient Greek monotheistic religious systems. According to the initiates of the Orphic Mysteries, there is only one divine King-Lord, who is self-caused, everything that has been created has been created by Him (the One), and all the different gods of the ancient Greek pantheon are different manifestations of the omnipotent One. See for instance: W.K.C. Guthrie, *Orpheus and Greek Religion: A Study of the Orphic Movement*, revised edition, Princeton, N.J.: Princeton University Press, 1993.

Therefore, the relations between Hellenism and Judaism are characterized by a duplex movement: Hellenism makes a pilgrimage to the East, since, as we read in Josephus' *Antiquities of the Jews*, many Greeks turned their minds toward Jewish monotheism because it was radically and uncompromisingly distinct from any kind of idolatry; and Judaism makes its exodus from its narrow geographical and ethnic limits toward Hellenism. The consequences of the previous duplex movement became cosmogonic when Christianity was born and Rome fell.

THE GREEK CONCEPTION OF REASON AND THE ADVENTURE OF RATIO IN THE MIDDLE AGES: RUDIMENTS AND RAMIFICATIONS

The study of Aristotle's *Logic* was an arduous task even in the ancient era. In his *Topica*, I, 1, the Roman philosopher and statesman Cicero (106—143 B.C.) mentions that Aristotle "was not known to the rhetorician, inasmuch as he is not much known even to philosophers, except to a very few", because "the obscurity of the subject" deterred them from Aristotle's books. This "obscurity" created a need for the publication of explanatory comments on and introductory textbooks in Aristotle's philosophy. One such textbook was Cicero's *Topica* (Cicero wrote *Topica* for the benefit of his friend Gaius Trebatius Testa). Another such textbook was Porphyry's *Introduction to the Logical Categories of Aristotle* (known simply as the *Introduction*).

Porphyry (ca. 234 — ca. 305 A.D.) was a Syrian student of Plotinus. In 268, he experienced a major depressive episode, and he wanted to commit suicide. His teacher deterred him from committing suicide. As we read in Porphyry's book *On the Life of Plotinus*, 11, Plotinus told Porphyry that the tendency to commit suicide does not spring "from reason but from mere melancholy" and advised Porphyry "to leave Rome". Porphyry obeyed and left for Sicily, where, in 270, he learned about Plotinus' death. A few years after Plotinus' death, Porphyry returned to Rome and became the head of Plotinus' school there. During his stay in Sicily, Porphyry wrote his *Introduction*.

The publication of Porphyry's *Introduction* was an amazing success in both the West and the East. In the 6th century, the Roman philosopher Boethius translated Porphyry's *Introduction* in Latin, and, in the same century, the Syrian theologian Sergius of Resaina translated this famous book in the Syrian language. Moreover, in the 8th century, Porphyry's *Introduction* was translated in the Armenian language, and, in the 10th century, it was translated in Arabic. In both the Western Roman Empire and the Arab Empire, Porphyry's *Introduction* was the first systematic educational textbook in logic.

Even though the Western medieval scholars were claiming that their philosophical systems were founded on classical Greek philosophy, their direct access to the original classical Greek philosophical texts was limited, and they were at the mercy of inaccurate Latin translations of classical Greek philosophical texts and of introductory textbooks. Thus, the medieval West interpreted classical Greek philosophy in a manner that served the medieval West's own historical needs and goals.

In the years of Augustine of Hippo and Boethius and throughout the Middle Ages, the West was understanding and defining the Greek metaphysical term 'ousia' (essence) as a universal, i.e. as a general concept. Thus, in contrast with the Greek philosophical tradition, the West interpreted Plato's 'ideas' as logically self-subsistent entities. But, in the context of classical Greek philosophy, the 'intellect' is not indiscriminately identified with the 'mind', and, furthermore, knowledge is not limited within the boundaries of the intellect. In other words, classical Greek philosophy never attempted to isolate the power of knowing from the power of feeling and will, and it never subjected the latter to the first.

In the context of classical Greek philosophy, cognition does not produce knowledge by itself (whenever cognition produces knowledge by itself, that knowledge is considered imagination), but it is viewed as a process whereby the mind receives and processes sense-data. In particular, in Plato's *Timaeus*, 45d, the soul, like the body, is characterized by "that sensation which we now term 'seeing'"; and, in Aristotle's *On Sense and the Sensible*, 438b10, the soul operates as the centre of sensation. Hence, the classical Greek philosophy of vision is focused on an external light that allows one to see an image without the mediation of any subject's mental representations. Since, according to Plato's and Aristotle's theories of the vision of light, an image can be seen independently of (and prior to) the images formed in the mind, it follows that, in the context of classical Greek philosophy, knowledge is obtained by the transition of the mind from its own world to the external reality of an idea, and not by the transfer of an idea into the mind, where it would give rise to a representational theory of the entire object of vision through a combination of concepts. In other words, in the context of classical Greek philosophy, knowledge is obtained through pure experience, i.e. without the mediation of any mental representations, and, therefore, it is based on a vision that is prior to conceptual thinking.

In the context of Plato's philosophy, cognition is not based on bodily sensations, but this does not mean that it is based on representations created by a subjective mind; instead, according to Plato's philosophy, cognition is based on a peculiar mental *sensation*. Thus, according to Plato, the mind does not reproduce an external object through a visualization or conceptualization process, nor does it create mental models of an external object, but it *participates* in the transcendental idea of an external object, and, therefore, it knows an external object due to the experience of the light of the corresponding idea. It is this dependence of knowledge on the light of the idea that prevented Platonism from lapsing into the problems of the nominalists' individualistic subjectivism and from committing the mistakes of the medieval West's philosophical realism. Moreover, according to Plato's *Republic*, those artists who, through their art, transform truth into a mental representation have no place in Plato's ideal republic.

Thomas Aquinas and generally the medieval Western scholars ignored that, when Plato created the term idea, which is one of the most controversial philosophical terms, he simultaneously asserted that vision is the most representative sense of human mental life. Thus, the medieval West ignored that, in the context of Plato's philosophy, knowledge, i.e. consciousness's relation with truth, is primarily a spiritual *experience*, and, for this reason, it primarily consists in a psychological state and only secondarily in the discovery of causal relations. As Plato himself argues in his *Theaetetus*, 184d, the unity of the 'idea' as vision makes psychological unity possible: "it would be strange indeed, my boy, if there are many senses ensconced within us, as if we were so many wooden horses of Troy, and they do not all unite in one power, whether we should call it soul or something else, by which we perceive through these as instruments the objects of perception".

The medieval West's rationalism reduces the entire knowledge process to the formulation of causal relations, and additionally it attempts to know God through causal relations. Nevertheless, Plato's theory of ideas proposes a different way of knowing: an individual participates in the idea of human being due to psychological relationships among human individuals and not because one can logically conceive the notion of humanity. Thus, Plato's theory of ideas is founded on a simultaneously active and passive participation* of the spirit in social relations, and not on logical necessities.

Because, in the context of classical Greek philosophy, truth is not representational (i.e. it does not depend on mental images), the classical Greek philosophers do not identify the intellect with the mind. In particular, in his *Republic*, 511d-e, Plato argues as follows: "And I think you call the mental habit of geometers and their like mind or understanding and not reason because you regard understanding as something intermediate between opinion and reason...and arrange them in a proportion, considering that they participate in clearness and precision in the same degree as their objects partake of truth and reality".

Therefore, in contrast with Thomas Aquinas' philosophy, classical Greek philosophy does not subject action and will to the coercive logical authority of general concepts. Classical Greek philosophy does not subject action and will to the coercive logical authority of general concepts, because, according to classical Greek philosophy, the image of a thing exists as an energy of the given thing's essence, i.e. it is determined by (and it is an emanation from) the given thing's essence, and it is not created by the perceptive mind. Hence, according to classical Greek philosophy, the essence of the mind is not a self-regulating logical system.

On the other hand, medieval Western philosophy was dominated by the view that the essence of the mind is a self-regulating logical system, and, therefore, in the context of Latin theology, God is perceived as pure energy. Within God as pure energy, essence, energy, will, knowledge and power are identified with one another, and the archetypal reasons (logoi) of God coercively pervade the totality of the cosmos, so that, according to Latin theology, even the evil is perceived as one of God's reasons. The previous view is unacceptable by both classical Greek philosophy and the Greek Church Fathers, because, according to classical Greek philosophy and the Greek

---

* There are two general forms of 'participation': the one is passive, and the other is active. The passive form of participation refers primarily to those elements that beings have inherited from their common source and continue preserving them. Thus, this form of participation points to the dependence of beings on their source and/or on one another. The active form of participation refers primarily to the beings' attempt to create a situation that will allow them to transcend their current situation. Thus, this form of participation points to identification within the framework of common activities ('identification' is a process whereby a being assimilates an aspect, property, or attribute of another being and is transformed wholly or partially).

Church Fathers, God is absolutely good and absolutely free from any essential determination, and the source of evil is merely man's own freedom of choice.

According to the medieval West's philosophical realism in general and to Thomas Aquinas' philosophy in particular, God's creation of the universe is a temporal manifestation of the archetypal reasons (logoi) of God, and man knows the archetypal reasons (logoi) of God through the reasons of man's own intellect. Therefore, the medieval West's philosophical realism in general and Thomas Aquinas' philosophy in particular lead to the following conclusions: the same reason pervades both God and the whole of nature; both God's freedom and man's freedom obey the same, all-pervading reason; both God's will and man's will are subject to the same, all-pervading reason. According the previous philosophical path, necessity takes precedence over freedom, and, for this reason, in the medieval West, philosophical realism became an intellectual weapon whereby the Church of Rome (the Vatican) attempted to impose and consolidate its authority over its subjects, and, later, philosophical realism became an intellectual weapon whereby rationalist university professors attempted to become the new authoritarian priesthood of Western Europe. Things become radically different, and freedom takes precedence over necessity, if one accepts the Greek views about sensation and knowledge. In particular, in the context of the classical Greek philosophical tradition, reason is the resultant of logic and experience. Thus, Plotinus, the founder of Neoplatonism, in the seventh chapter of his book *On Eternity and Time*, maintains that, in order to know something, we must have an experiential relationship with it.

The Greek conception of reason, without undermining the significance of logical accountability, recognizes that logic is not a self-sufficient system and that the analytical method of knowledge is not the only method of knowledge. The Greek conception of reason is intimately related to empathy and communion, and, therefore, it endowed ancient Greeks with the capability of creating the 'ecumene', in the context of which the logic of the general system did not eliminate the virtue of discretion and, therefore, different cultural communities could co-exist as members of a global society ('ecumene'). Moreover, the Greek conception of reason implies that the knowledge of God is primarily founded on personal relationship (knowledge as communion) and not on syllogistic necessities.

Thus, as I have already mentioned, in the context of the Japhethite ecumene, the Greeks gave rise to a creative synthesis between logical accountability and Biblical transcendentalism.

In 20th century political thought, one of the most stunningly superficial approaches to Western rationality can be found in Samuel Huntington's book *The Clash of Civilizations and the Remaking of World Order** (1996), because Huntington has in mind only the Romans' and the medieval scholastics' approach to rationality (namely, rationality as logical accountability, logical consistency and syllogistic necessity), and he ignores both the significance of Plato's notion of spiritual vision (i.e. the experiential and, in a sense, mystical dimension of rationality) and the Greek synthesis between logical accountability and the East's transcendentalism, which took place in the context of Alexander the Great's ecumene and the Hellenistic Kingdoms. Therefore, at the political level, Huntington's paradigm of world-order construction is unable to lead to a complete understanding of the concept of ecumene, and it cannot address the substantial conceptual difference between Alexander the Great's 'ecumene' and George W. Bush's 'new world order'.

THE CONTROVERSY BETWEEN NEOPLATONISM AND GNOSTICISM

The three basic principles of Plotinus' metaphysics[†] are called by him 'the One' (or, equivalently, 'the Good'), Nous (Mind), and Soul. The One is the absolutely simple first principle of all. It is both 'self-caused' and the cause of being for everything else in the universe. Plotinus developed the idea of the One based on Plato's *Republic*, where Plotinus' One is named "the idea of good" (the 'Good'), and on Plato's *Parmenides*, where it is the subject of a series of deductions. Because of its absolute simplicity and transcendence, the One or the Good, is indescribable directly. Plotinus argues that we can only grasp it indirectly by deducing what it is not. This thesis is the essence of 'apophatic theology'. According to Plotinus, universe is an emanation from the One, an inevitable overflow of the One's infinite power or actuality. The first emanation from the One is Nous.

---

[*] S.P. Huntington, *The Clash of Civilizations and the Remaking of World Order*, New York: Touchstone, Rockefeller Center, 1996.

[†] See: L.P. Gerson (ed.), *The Cambridge Companion to Plotinus*, Cambridge: Cambridge University Press, 1996, and D. O'Meara, *Plotinus: An Introduction to the Enneads*, Oxford: Oxford University Press, 1993.

This emanation is a unified system of all the eternal and immutable entities that account for or explain the possibility of intelligible predication, i.e. the Platonic ideas. In other words, in the first stage of the divine emanation, the One contemplates the pure ideal cosmos. The second stage of the divine emanation is Soul, which is an image of Nous and less perfect than the original. In the highest life, namely, in the life of Nous, we find the highest form of desire, because that desire is eternally satisfied by contemplating the One through the entire array of ideas that are internal to it. Soul is a lower level of life, since it is the principle of desire for objects that are external to the agent of desire. One is paradigmatically what Nous is, and Nous is paradigmatically what Soul is. Thus, there are two phases of the Soul: in the first, it is turned toward Nous and therefore it acts as its archetype and contemplates ideas; in the second, it is turned toward the world of the senses and therefore it is impelled to bring order into matter. According to Plotinus, matter is to be identified with evil and privation of all form or intelligibility. However, for Plotinus, matter is evil *not in itself*, but matter is evil *only when it becomes an impediment to return to the One*. In other words, matter is evil when considered as a goal or end that is a polar opposite to the One.

Gnosticism (from Greek 'gnosis', which means knowledge) refers to a set of religious beliefs and spiritual practices based on the doctrine of salvation by a peculiar esoteric knowledge that promises to 'liberate' the soul from the material world. The roots of Gnosticism can be traced to non-Christian and pre-Christian Asian religious communities. In particular, Walter Bauer[*] and Christian Lassen[†] argue that Gnosticism is strongly related to the religions of India. According to Lassen, the Indian elements in the Gnostic 'schools' were derived from Buddhism, which exercised considerable influence on the intellectual life of Alexandria. R.A. Lipsius[‡] argues that the origins of Gnosticism are in Syria and Phoenicia. Adolf Hilgenfeld[§] argues that Gnosticism is strongly connected with later Mazdaism, i.e. with the worship of Ahura Mazda, who, in Zoroastrianism, is the source of all light and good.

---

[*]　Walter Bauer, *Orthodoxy and Heresy in Earliest Christianity*, trans. and ed. R. Kraft and G. Kroedel, Philadelphia: Fortress Press, 1971.

[†]　Christian Lassen, *Indische Alterthumskunde*, Bonn: H.B. König, 1847.

[‡]　R.A. Lipsius, *Der Gnosticismus*, Leipzig, 1860.

[§]　Adolf Hilgenfeld, *Die Ketzergeschichte des Urchristentums*, Leipzig, 1884.

Mainstream Gnosticism is marked by the following characteristics: notion of a supreme, monadic divinity, often called One, Source and Bythos (i.e. depth); the introduction by emanation of further divine beings, known as Aeons, which are aspects of the One, from which they proceeded; the introduction of a distinct creator god, called Demiurge, which is a later emanation from the One and an inferior or false god (often described as a lion-faced serpent). In *The Hypostasis of the Archons* or *The Reality of the Rulers* (Nag Hammadi Library, Codex II), which is a Gnostic exegesis of the book of *Genesis*, the Demiurge, the creator of the mankind and the material world, is described as a spiritually blind deity, because, due to his ignorance and arrogance, the Demiurge said, with his power, 'It is I who am God; there is none apart from me'. But, according to the previous Gnostic text, when the Demiurge said this, he sinned against the entirety, and a voice came forth from the One, saying, 'You are mistaken, Samael', which is 'god of the blind'*.

Neoplatonism provided several Gnostic schools with the idea of a continuum of degrees of being that lie between the extreme ontological poles of being and non-being. Thus, Gnostics developed various different hierarchies of ontological emanations, or divine beings, known as 'Aeons'. However, in contrast with Neoplatonism, the various Gnostic schools, adopted radically dualistic Asian religious traditions†, including the solipsism‡ of Hinduism, and they converged to the idea of the essential evil of this present existence. Gnostics developed various ritualistic systems through which they attempted to liberate their members from what they believed to be a corrupt sensuous world. On the other hand, Neoplatonism followed the Greek philosophical tradition, which was characterized by the joyful acknowledgment of and homage to the beautiful and the noble *in the sensuous world*. Thus, for instance, by the 3rd century

---

* For more details, see: Bentley Layton, "The Hypostasis of the Archons", *Harvard Theological Review*, Vol. 67, 1974, pp. 351-425.

† For instance, in Mazdaism, both Ahura Mazda, who is purely good, and his antithesis, the demon Ahriman, are absolute principles.

‡ The term 'solipsism' comes from Latin 'solus' (alone) and 'ipse' (self), and it is the view that the only reality is one's own consciousness. See: Ledger Wood, "Solipsism", in D.D. Runes (ed.), *Dictionary of Philosophy*, Totowa, NJ: Littlefield, Adams and Company, 1962. Moreover, solipsism plays a major role in many Eastern religious systems. In Hinduism, the *Isha Upanishad* asserts that, "for the enlightened, all that exists is nothing but the self" (sloka 6, 7). Similarly, Mahayana Buddhism challenged as illusion the idea that one can experience an 'objective' reality independent of individual perceiving intellects.

A.D., Neoplatonists, such as Plotinus, Porphyry and Amelius are all attacking the Sethian Gnostics.

If we travel in the corridors of the illustrated history of humanity, i.e. if we study history of art, we see that ancient agricultural civilizations (e.g. Egyptians, Babylonians, etc.) worshiped nature, and, thus, their gods usually had animal characteristics, and ancient nomadic civilizations (e.g. the Hebrews) worshiped the natural bond of blood, the power of the race. On the other hand, ancient Greek gods had human form. The human form of the ancient Greek gods was characterized by exceptional beauty, because it was expressing the human quest for perfection, and, according to ancient Greek mythology, the end of the human being's existence is man's participation in the Deity. Thus, through their mythology, Greeks gave priority to a personal approach to reality over the impersonal commands of nature and race, and, in this way, they created an anthropocentric civilization.

The humanism of the classical Greek aesthetics was transformed into a theological system by Christianity, since Christians identified the Greek value of beauty with Jesus Christ and, through Jesus Christ, Christianity stressed the personhood of God. According to Irenaeus of Lyons' book *Against Heresies*, 3, 19:1 (*Patrologia Graeca*, Vol. 7:1, 939), the central dogma of Christianity is that "the Word became man, and the Son of God became the Son of man: so that man, by entering into communion with the Word and thus receiving divine sonship, might become a son of God". Furthermore, Gregory of Nazianzus (also known as Gregory the Theologian) has stressed that the Christ Mystery signifies not only the Incarnation of the Divine Word but also the divinization of the human flesh (*Patrologia Graeca*, Vol. 36, 353B). Thus, ultimately, the Greeks adopted the Orthodox Christian Dogma of the Incarnation of the Divine Word, because they understood it as a metaphysical proposition that completed and perfected the classical Greek humanistic philosophy, and they rejected Gnosticism's extreme dualism, which was not only opposite to the classical Greek humanistic spirit but also it was aiming for the dominion of Asia's spirit over Europe.

Neoplatonism emphasized knowledge as participation or communion, expressing the Greek philosophical quest for man's participation in the Deity. However, Neoplatonism discerned itself from Gnosticism's negation of the material world. Thus, Neoplatonism implies that man can participate in the Deity without denouncing humanity for the sake of divinity. But the Neoplatonic teachings about man's participation in the Deity are based on a series of emanations from the One, and, therefore, Neoplatonism leaves the problem of man's freedom blurred. In particular, if the emanations from the One follow a mechanistic process, then man's participation in the Deity is not founded on man's free will, but it is a process that takes place independently of man's intentionality, like natural laws. Furthermore, if there is a bond of connaturality between God and the world, then the logic of the world is coercively imposed on man, and then man's freedom reduces to man's conformity to a necessary cosmic logos. The Orthodox Christian mysticism, which is called Hesychasm and emerged in the Eastern Roman Empire (the 'Greek East'), combined the Neoplatonists' quest for man's experiential knowledge of the Absolute (the transcendental One) with personal freedom and the ontology of particularity (personhood). Thus, the combination of the Greek conception of reason, which I explained in the previous section, with the Christian Gospel gave rise to the Greek East's Christian humanism.

HESYCHASM AND CHRISTIAN HUMANISM

The terms 'Hesychasm' and 'Hesychast' are derived from the Greek word for 'silence' or 'stillness', namely 'hesychia'. Thus, 'Hesychasm' ('hesychasmos') is the practice of silence, and the Hesychast ('ho hesychastes') one who follows this practice, striving thereby to achieve inner peace and freedom from passions and to be united with the Deity through the Jesus prayer. The "Jesus Prayer" exists in several forms: the most familiar formula is, "Lord Jesus Christ, Son of God, have mercy on me, a sinner", but it is sometimes shortened to "Lord Jesus Christ, have mercy on me", and Gregory Palamas, one of the most influential teachers and defenders of Hesychasm, was fond of a similar devotional entreaty, "Enlighten my darkness" (Photison mou to skotos).

Even though Hesychasm was a very old practice in the Greek East, the first analytical description of the Hesychasts' method of prayer in the Greek sources dates only from the late 13th century, in the work *On Vigilance and the Guarding of the Heart* by Nicephorus the Hesychast, a monk of Mount Athos. Moreover, there is a closely similar description in a work entitled *Method of Holy Prayer and Attentiveness*, which is attributed to Symeon the New Theologian

(949—1022 A.D.), a Byzantine Christian monk and poet, who is venerated as a saint in the Eastern Orthodox Church. In the previous texts, Nicephorus and Symeon the New Theologian describe the physical techniques that are used by Hesychasts as follows: (i) The aspirant is to sit with his head bowed, and, additionally, according to Symeon the New Theologian's *Method of Holy Prayer and Attentiveness*, the aspirant should rest his chin on his chest and direct his bodily eyes together with the mind toward the middle of his belly, that is toward his navel[*]. Other texts suggest that the aspirant's gaze should be fixed on the place of the heart. The Hesychast acknowledges in humility the Christ within; the all encompassing Love. In his inner silence, bows respectfully to his Archetype of the Perfected Man, the Lord of the Uncreated Light. (ii) The aspirant's breathing rhythm is to be slowed down. In particular, Symeon the New Theologian's *Method of Holy Prayer and Attentiveness* gives the following advice: "Restrain the inhalation of your breath through the nose, so as not to breathe in and out at your ease"[†]. (iii) As he controls his breathing, the Hesychast is at the same time to search inwardly for the place of the heart. In particular, Nicephorus the Hesychast writes that the Hesychast is to imagine his breath entering through the nostrils and then passing down within the lungs until it reaches the heart, and, in this way, he is to make his mind remain with the breath within the body, so that mind and heart are united[‡].

According to Hesychasm, the logoi[§] of Nature, which the Neoplatonists regarded as emanations from the One, are not emanations from God's essence, but they are God's wills. Therefore, God is neither determined by nor identified with any natural necessity, and the natural cosmos, of which the human species is a member, is not the realm of necessity. In his *Ambigua*, 7 (*Patrologia Graeca*, Vol. 91, 1080A), Maximus the Confessor[¶], who belongs to the

---

[*]   Symeon the New Theologian, *Method of Holy Prayer and Attentiveness*, Greek text and French trans. I. Hausherr, "La méthode d'oraison hésychaste", *Orientalia Christiana*, Vol. IX, 2, No.36, Rome, 1927, p. 164

[†]   Ibid, p. 164.

[‡]   Nicephorus of Mount Athos, *On Vigilance and the Guarding of the Heart*, in *Patrologia Graeca*, Vol. 147. Moreover, see: E. Kadloubovsky and G.E.H. Palmer (trans. and eds), *Writings from the Philokalia on Prayer of the Heart*, London: Faber, 1951, pp. 22-34.

[§]   The term 'logoi' is the plural form of the Greek word 'logos' (word/reason).

[¶]   Maximus the Confessor (ca. 580—662) was a Christian monk, theologian and scholar. He methodically and systematically supported the Council of Chalcedon's position that Jesus Christ

tradition of Hesychasm, argues that the logos (reason) of a being is not a substance, but the reason of that being's substance, and, therefore, it does not subsist in itself, but it only exists *potentially* in the Deity, as a yet unmanifested possibility. Following Dionysius the Areopagite, Maximus the Confessor names the logoi divine "wills"* (*thelemata*†). According to Maximus the Confessor's theology and according to Hesychasm in general, God is not related to the nature (essence) of the beings and things in the world, since the nature of the beings and things in the world is created whereas God's nature is uncreated, but God knows the beings and things in the world as realizations of His will, and, for this reason, His knowledge is equivalent to love. Hence, within the context of Hesychasm, free will and love take primacy over logical necessity.

Using Aristotle's concepts of being potentially and being actually, Maximus the Confessor explains that, within the Logos of God, all the logoi of the beings and things in the world exist potentially, and, through their actuality, they reveal the same work and presence of the Logos. In other words, in each creature, through its logoi, the Logos of God is made present and manifested. Thus, Maximus the Confessor compares our contemplation of the sensuous world with the meeting between Elizabeth and Mary the Mother of God, which is mentioned in *Luke* 1:39-56. In particular, according to Maximus the Confessor‡, in its material and bodily form, each and every human being represents John the Baptist in the womb of his mother Elizabeth, while the Logos of God is hidden in creatures as if in another womb (the womb of Mary the Mother of God).

Contrary to Origen§ and the Gnostics, who saw a decline in corporality and materiality, Maximus the Confessor writes that the creation of the world itself is a revelation of God's will, and the essence of this revelation is the presence of the Logos of God in the logoi of the creatures. This is considered by Maximus the Confessor to be an Embodiment of the Logos of God. In fact, Maximus the

---

had both a human and a divine will, fighting a heresy called Monotheletism (for Greek meaning 'one will'). Following the Asian legacy of transcendentalism, Monotheletism was an attempt to 'reduce' the human aspect of Christ by arguing that Christ had only one will, namely the divine one. Maximus the Confessor is a saint in both Eastern and Western Christianity.

* Maximus the Confessor, *Ambigua*, 7 (*Patrologia Graeca*, Vol. 91, 1085A).

† 'Thelemata' is the plural form of 'thelema', which is Greek for will.

‡ Maximus the Confessor, *Ambigua*, 6 (*Patrologia Graeca*, Vol. 91, 1068AB).

§ Origen was an influential early Alexandrian Christian scholar and theologian.

Confessor speaks about a triple Embodiment of the Logos[*]: in nature, in the Bible, and in the historic person of Christ.

In the 14th century A.D., Gregory Palamas (1296—1359), who is venerated as a saint in the Eastern Orthodox Church, exposed and defended Hesychasm in his book *In Defence of the Sacred Hesychasts* (*Hyper ton Hieros Hesychazonton*). In contrast to the Gnostics' mind-body dualism, Gregory Palamas, in the first triad of his sermons *In Defence of the Sacred Hesychasts*, stresses that Hesychasm regards it as evil for the mind to become a servant of the flesh, and not wrong for the mind to be in the body, because the body is not evil. Moreover, Gregory Palamas explains that the Hesychasts fight against the law of sin in order to banish it from the body and establish there the mind as an overseer. In particular, the Hesychasts lay down laws for every power of the soul and for every member of the body as is appropriate for it: to the senses they prescribe what they have to receive and in what measure, and this practice of spiritual law is called self-mastery; they bring the desiring part of the soul to that excellent state whose name is love; and they improve the intellectual part by banishing all that prevents the mind from soaring to God, and this part of the spiritual law is called 'nepsis', which is a state of watchfulness or sobriety. Thus, according to Gregory Palamas, *both the mind and the body* are partakers of the Deity.

According to the tradition of the Greek Church Fathers in general and the teachings of Gregory Palamas in particular, God's 'energy' is different from God's 'essence', in the sense that God's energy is the life-force of God's essence, but the fullness of God is present in God's energy according to God's own will. The Hesychasts maintain that man can participate in God's energies, which are known as wisdom, love, providence, creativity, etc., and man's ontological perfection, or deification, consists in man's participation in God's energies. However, the Hesychasts add, since God's energies are distinct from God's essence (even though God's energies are equally divine as God's essence), man's participation in God's energies implies that man participates in God, but simultaneously God's essence and hypostases (i.e. the three persons of the Trinity) remain totally transcendental, and, therefore, the relationship between God

---

[*]   Maximus the Confessor, *Questions to Thalassius*, 15 (*Patrologia Graeca*, Vol. 90, 297B-300A). See also: H.U. von Balthasar, *Cosmic Liturgy: The Universe According to Maximus the Confessor*, San Francisco: St Ignatius Press, 2003, p. 292.

and man is founded on free will and not on connaturality. In other words, God and man relate to each other through their wills without mixing their essences together. In the light of Hesychasm, the Will is our spiritual engine.

Man's participation in God's energies should not be understood as a relation between the most general concept ('Divine Being') and a less general one ('human being'), but as a free personal relationship between God and man. If man's participation in God's energies were reducible to a relation between concepts, then man's freedom would be dramatically reduced, because, in that case, man's reasons (logoi) would be logically determined and coercively subject to God's reasons. On the contrary, in the context of Hesychasm, the most genuine kind of theology consists in man's participation in God's energies, and man's participation in God's energies takes place if and to the extent that man is properly prepared psychologically. Thus, God's being is not a coercive universal. The relationship between God and man is based on free will and not on logical necessity. It is the medieval West's rationalism that, by reducing the relationship between God and man to a relation between a higher more general concept and a lower less general concept, mixes theology with logical necessity and coercion. For the Hesychasts, the most genuine kind of theology is the personal experience of one's participation in God's energies, and the tradition of the Church Fathers is nothing else than a record of such experiences and of their spiritual outcomes. In contrast with the Western rationalist schools of philosophy and theology, the Hesychasts follow the Greek conception of reason, and, therefore, they keep in mind Plato's thesis that humans can attain a personal experience of the absolute good, but they cannot logically deduce the absolute good from a deterministic chain of syllogisms.

Thus, Hesychasm is simultaneously opposite to Scholasticism (i.e. to the philosophical foundation of the medieval Roman Catholic Church) and to Gnosticism: Scholasticism identifies God's essence with God's energy, and, therefore, in order to protect the monotheistic doctrine of the distinction between God's uncreated essence and the natural world's created essence, it separates radically God from man, and it teaches that man can understand God as the most general concept, but, according to Scholasticism, man literally cannot participate in the Deity; Gnosticism teaches that man literally can participate in the Deity, but, since the Gnostics did not subscribe to the Hesychasts' doctrine of the distinction between God's essence and God's energy, Gnosticism endorses emanationism, and, therefore, in the context of Gnosticism, the human being is a member of a suffocating, logically determined and, therefore, coercive cosmic hierarchy. On the other hand, by stressing the essence-energies distinction, Hesychasm teaches that man literally can participate in the Deity, and, more specifically, in God's *uncreated energies*, but, since there is no *essential* bond between God and man, the relationship between God and man is based on freedom (free will) and not on any kind of logical necessity.

At this point, it is useful to add that the absence of any essential relationship between God and the natural world implies that there is no contradiction between the existence of God and any cosmological theory of the natural sciences. Physics is concerned with questions about the functions of the natural world. For instance, physics is concerned with questions of the following type[*]: What happened at or before the Big Bang? Was there really an initial singularity? What is the topology of space? Why is there an arrow of time; that is, why is the future so much different from the past? Are there non-local phenomena in quantum physics? Do the phenomena attributed to dark matter point not to some form of matter but actually to an extension of gravity? On other hand, the debate about the existence of God rises from a question whose nature is philosophical and not scientific, namely: *Why* does the natural world exist? Thus, if we understand God as the ultimate source of the significance, or purpose, of the beings and things in the world, then God's existence means that the natural world is meaningful, and His existence does not contradict any theorem of the natural sciences. Therefore, from the perspective of Hesychasm, no theorem of the natural sciences can prove or disprove the existence of God. According to the Bible, God created the world only by His own free will, without any pre-existent 'raw materials', and therefore He is the transcendental positive void that generates the significance of all the beings and things in the world. The Hesychasts strictly refuse to call God the 'Supreme Being', and, in general, they believe that the term being should not be used when one refers to God, since they insist on the total transcendentality and uknowability of God's essence. For

---

[*] See for instance: H. Price, *Time's Arrow and Archimedes' Point – New Directions for a Physics of Time*, Oxford: Oxford University Press, 1996, and S. Hawking and L. Mlodinow, *A Brief History of Time*, New York: Bantam, 2005.

instance, some Hesychasts were referring to God's essence by using the expression "the inconceivable nothing", thus stressing that the most genuine kind of theology is the mystery of man's participation in God's uncreated energies.

Given that God did not use any pre-existent 'raw materials' in order to create the world, i.e. given that God's essence is totally unrelated to the natural world, we cannot transform any theorems about the natural world into theological arguments. The creation of the world is a result of God's will (thelema) and not a result of God's essence, and, therefore, it is an expression of God's freedom. Furthermore, since the world is an objectivation of God's will and not an emanation from God's essence, the secret ultimate foundations of the universe are love and freedom and not logical necessity. Therefore, according to Hesychasm, the discoveries of science reveal results of God's *will*, but not God's *essence*.

The earliest Church Fathers and generally the Hesychasts never felt that their faith in God could be threatened by any theorem of the natural sciences, because they understood God as the totally transcendental source of the significance of all the beings and things in the world. From this perspective, every discovery of the natural sciences is a discovery of a particular result of God's *will*, but it reveals nothing about God's *essence*. However, in the Middle Ages, a conflict between religion and science was ignited because several scholastic theologians, who were speculating about God's essence, used arguments of philosophical realism in order to defend their faith and, in this way, they attempted to show that it was possible to syllogistically ascend from nature to God. Those scholastic theologians founded their theology upon the confirmation of certain cosmological hypothetico-deductive systems, which were convenient for their theological arguments; in this way, they reduced God to a concept whose validity was vulnerable to the disproof of certain cosmological theorems and to the proof of new cosmological theorems. Hence, for many Scholastics, faith in God became compatible only with certain scientific theorems and incompatible with others. For instance, the Roman Catholic Church felt obliged to oppose heliocentrism from 1616 to 1757. In other words, the naturalistic theology of several representatives of the medieval Roman Catholic Church, by deviating from the original Christian principle of the absolute transcendence of God's essence, gave rise to a kind of Christianity that prohibits and inhibits free scientific inquiry and progress. Thus, many Renaissance natural scientists reacted against the spiritual despotism of many Church authorities by indiscriminately discarding the Christian Dogma and espousing other approaches to religion that appeared to be friendlier to scientific research. On the other hand, Hesychasm leads to an understanding of God as the perfect archetype of the free person.

For the Hesychasts, man's mind is not a part ('spark') of God's essence, but it is the field in which the mystical meeting and union between God and man can take place freely and voluntarily. According to Hesychasm, the heart is the essence of the mind, and the mind is a power of the heart. Hence, the Hesychasts understand man's deification as a process in which man's mind is filled with God's energies. With regard to man's mind, Hesychasm has creatively assimilated the mystical tradition of the Jewish Patriarchs and Prophets. Thus, even though one should avoid speculation about parallel development, it can be argued that there are significant similarities between the Hesychastic notion of mind and the Qabalistic doctrine of the 'Neshamah', as it is presented in the *Sefer Ha-Zohar* (or *Book of Splendor*), an important text of Jewish mysticism, which first appeared in Spain in the 13th century A.D. and was published by a Jewish writer and rabbi named Moses de León* (ca. 1250—1305 A.D.). According to the *Zohar*, the Neshamah stands above all the parts of the soul, it is the supernal power by which man knows the Holy One and obeys His precepts, and also it is conceived as our spiritual umbilical cord that connects us to God and to each other. Similarly, in the context of Hesychasm, the mind is the vessel of God's grace in man, and, according to the Hesychasts, God's grace is the uncreated energy of God.

It is important to emphasize the difference between the Hesychastic idea of meditation, which is known as 'nepsis', and the Oriental idea of meditation, which is known as 'yoga'. The Oriental schools of meditation understand inner silence as a state in which the intellect is detached from the world of the senses. On the contrary, the Hesychasts maintain that the 'mind' (*nous*) should be differentiated from the 'intellect' (*dianoia*) and that it is the mind and not the intellect that must be detached from the world of the

---

* For an overview of the *Zohar* and the Jewish mysticism in general, see: D.C. Matt, *The Essential Kabbalah: The Heart of Jewish Mysticism*, San Francisco: Harper San Francisco, 1995.

senses. The Hesychasts maintain that the natural function of the intellect is to be concerned with the world of the senses in order to endow the world of the senses with a rational order that expresses the intentionality of the mind, but the mind is characterized by an enlightened intuition that transcends the intellect, and it is understood as the power of enlightened discretion, convincing the soul to direct its attention to certain elements-stimuli and to ward off others. In particular, according to Hesychasm, the natural function of the mind is to be directed to the Deity, the Transcendental One, and receive God's uncreated energy, and, therefore, it is the mind, and not the intellect, that must be detached from the world of the senses in order to function as a pure vessel of God's grace. Oriental meditation aims to detach the intellect from the world of the senses, and, therefore, it leads to yogic sleep (since the intellect cannot function without being actively involved in the world of the senses), whereas Hesychastic meditation leads to an experience of participation in God's uncreated energies without any experience of sleep and without the negation of the sensuous world.

The Hesychasts emphasize that man's deification is founded on freedom, and, therefore, they argue that man's participation in God's energies is primarily founded on man's psychological preparation and not on syllogistic necessities. As I mentioned above, the Hesychasts lay down laws for every power of the soul and for every member of the body as is appropriate for it, and they follow the Greek conception of reason. The Hesychasts argue that, when man's reason is subject to the sensibles and passions, it tends to subjugate the mind and it darkens the mind. Thus, the Hesychasts, by following their psychosomatic and praying practices, attempt to bring the mind back to its normal position, which is the heart, in order to be able, in a state of mental cleanness, to receive the light of God's truth, which leads to the deification of man. The Hesychasts do not pursue to project the mind outside the body, since they do not treat the body as a mortal prison of an immortal psychical substance, but they pursue to keep the mind inside the body, since the purpose of the mind is to oversee the entire psychosomatic substance of man and to eliminate all those logical and all those passionate elements of the soul that could impede the experience of divine illumination. Thus, according to the Hesychasts, the essence of psychotherapy is the safeguarding of the divine grace, which was given to man as mind, or freedom of the soul. By the term 'soul', the

Hesychasts understand the personal way in which the human being expresses life.

In the context of Hesychasm, man's soul is an energy of social life and the essence of personhood. On the other hand, in the context of the medieval West, rationalism attempted to transform the soul from an energy of social life into an organ of rational thought, and, therefore, it caused an enormous repression of the world of impulses, and this enormous repression of the world of impulses, in turn, caused a reaction that was expressed as an indiscriminate, occasionally nihilistic, attempt to legitimize individual impulses*. Thus, due to rationalism (and as a response to rationalism), man developed a second, underground soul, which is in continuous conflict with the socially recognized and legitimate soul. In other words, due to the Western conception of rationalism, man suffered a spiritual fragmentation into conscious and unconscious psychic worlds.

Given that, during the Middle Ages, many Western Europeans experienced rationalism in a psychologically traumatic way and as the philosophical underpinning of authoritarianism, Renaissance freethinkers and mystics (such as the Rosicrucians) rebelled against Scholasticism and against the scholastics' version of Christianity. During the Florentine Renaissance, Cosimo de' Medici took a personal interest in the new Platonic Academy that he determined to re-establish in 1439, under the influence of the Byzantine philosopher Gemistos Plethon, who taught Neoplatonism in Florence. Thus, serious ontological debates were ignited among Renaissance scholars, and the ancient Parmenidean question about being and non-being, which I study in Part Two, re-emerged. Moreover, in the 11th century Byzantium (Eastern Roman Empire), Michael Psellus, the leading intellectual of his time, monk, statesman, philosopher, historian, essayist and author of an imperially commissioned work on religious and other questions, managed to articulate a creative synthesis between philosophy and Orthodox Christian mysticism, and he argued that the study of philosophy helps man's intellectual development, and it does not necessarily (in fact, it should not) contradict the Orthodox Christian Dogma.

---

* Marquis de Sade's novel *Philosophy in the Bedroom* (1795) expressed this situation in a dramatic and eloquent manner (see: Marquis de Sade, *Justine, Philosophy in the Bedroom and Other Writings*, London: Arrow Books, 1965).

Many Renaissance mystics, such as Giovanni Pico della Mirandola (1463—1494), his nephew Francis, and Johann Reuchlin (1455—1522), a German humanist and teacher of Greek and Hebrew, were enthusiastic students of the Jewish Qabalah, which is a kind of Neoplatonism adapted to the Jewish religious traditions. But, due to the fact that many Renaissance mystics did not have sufficient knowledge of the history of philosophy and they were passionate for new and liberating spiritual experiences (after the West's exodus from the spiritually oppressive medieval regime of the Roman Catholic Church), confused Neoplatonism with Gnosticism, and, therefore, during their studies in the Jewish Qabalah and ancient Alexandrian mysticism (Hermeticism), they were fascinated by old (sometimes defunct) Asian spiritual traditions, whose adoption and revival by Renaissance mystics created new problems in the Western European psyche, since they gave rise to rigid dualistic philosophies and new prejudices and superstitions. This confusion between Gnosticism and Neoplatonism has been inherited by various Freemasonic Orders and by many modern esoteric fraternities that are strongly influenced by Gnosticism, such as the Theosophical Society, the Swedenborg Rite, the Hermetic Order of the Golden Dawn, the Ordo Templi Orientis, the Martinist Order, etc. Moreover, within many modern Freemasonic organizations (even within those Masonic Grand Lodges which officially abstain from religious debates), supporters of Gnosticism promote Gnostic religious doctrines by calling them 'philosophical' teachings (in order, under the cloak of philosophy, to bypass Grand Lodge regulations about religious affairs and to become more appealing to those Freemasons who are philosophically naïve and have a superficial knowledge of the history of philosophy and religion).

The Nicene Creed (4th century A.D.), which is the most widely accepted and used epitome of the Christian Faith and has been rejected by the Gnostics, stresses that the Incarnation of the Divine Word implies that our relationship with God is a deeply *human* affair and has nothing to do with the acquisition of a secret knowledge that is alien to what *we* really are. The mystery of God Incarnate does not mean that a mysterious being (e.g. Aeon/Angel) from another world took human form; this is a rather superficial attempt to interpret Christ. The mystery of God Incarnate means that the channel of God's love became a human being, thus making humans potentially partakers of God's way of life, which is love. Hence, the more deeply we understand and affirm our *humanity* (i.e. our soul-body complex) and the more deeply *humane* we become the more we know God. In other words, in contrast to the Gnostics' teachings, the purpose of Jesus Christ's Gospel was not to break man's soul-body complex and 'liberate' man from his body, but to reconcile us to ourselves, and, through this inner reconciliation, to lead us to deification.

The human being is characterized by particularity, whereas God is characterized by universality. However, the human being can participate in God's universality, through love and due to God's love, without sacrificing its ego, or personhood. Love is a *personal* affair, and, therefore, salvation through love implies that salvation is founded on a personal relationship between man and God, and not on any impersonal laws or mechanistic procedures. The incarnate manifestation of God's love is the incarnation of His Son-Logos. Thus, the Christ Mystery can be understood as an ontology of particularity, and, therefore, as the ultimate metaphysical foundation of humanism. Moreover, the Christ Mystery should be clearly distinguished from the bureaucratized religious systems of Christianity, which have been fabricated by authoritarian priesthoods in both Eastern and Western Europe (often in collaboration with authoritarian political elites).

THE CORRUPTION OF ORTHODOX CHRISTIANITY IN THE WESTERN ROMAN EMPIRE

The transfer of the Roman Empire's capital from Rome to Constantinople* (the so-called New Rome) had significant spiritual consequences. Constantinople became the Christian capital of the Roman Empire. The change of capital from Rome to Constantinople enhanced the impact of the Greek philosophical tradition on the development of Christian theology. In this way, the Eastern (Greek) Church assimilated the experience and the best organizational practices of the Western (Roman) Church and simultaneously it utilized the Greek philosophical heritage. The Eastern Church managed to develop under the direct protection of the Byzantine political system, since the Bishop of Constantinople had privileged access to and intimate cooperation with the Roman Emperor, whose

---

* Constantinople was founded in 330 A.D. at ancient Byzantium as the new capital of the Roman Empire by Constantine I, after whom it was named.

seat was in Constantinople. Additionally, the Eastern Church took control of the Byzantine educational system. On the other hand, as a result of the change of capital, the Church of Rome had to struggle for its growth without having any major centre of political authority next to it, and additionally it had to Christianize many hordes of barbarians and to integrate them into the Roman political and legal order. The Bishop of Constantinople was close to the Emperor, but the Bishop of Rome had been left alone. In a sense, the Bishop of Rome had to cover the political vacuum that was created in the Western Roman Empire after the change of capital, and he did so.

The Eastern Church chose to develop a theology that is focused on the interpretation of Christianity as the perfect road to the mystical deification of man. The Western Church decided to pursue a pragmatic attitude toward the very harsh geopolitical and geocultural reality that was formed in the Western Roman Empire after the transfer of the Roman Empire's capital from Rome to Constantinople. In fact, the Western Church decided to pursue a pragmatic attitude, even if that meant compromising the authentic humanistic ethos of Christ's Gospel. Hence, the Western Church chose to develop a theology that is focused on the moral and intellectual training of barbarians and on the creation of effective systems of social organization. In fact, in the Middle Ages, the Western Church was spiritually nourishing Western Europeans with its rationalist theological systems (scholasticism).

Contrary to popular arguments, in the Middle Ages, the Western Church was not the societal force that led supposedly illustrious Pagan civilizations down the path of superstition, prejudice and phobia. For instance, no one can seriously argue that the Goths, the Huns and the Saxons were living inside the light of reason, or *ratio*, before Christianity was imposed on them. Furthermore, Christianity was not the first religious community that talked about witches, mermaids, vampires, ghouls, magic brooms, sexual intercourse with the Devil, etc.; all these are concepts that have originally been developed by Pagans. However, following a pragmatic policy of expansion, Christianity purposely adopted many superstitions, and, in its attempt to speak in the language of the proselytes (converts from Paganism to Christianity) and to maximize its psychological influence on them, Christianity accepted to play in a cultural power game whose terms were to a large extent set by the Pagans' beliefs.

As a result of the above circumstances, the Western Church developed an authoritarian religious system founded on moral rationalism (I study this notion in Chapter 10), on philosophical realism (scholastic ontological arguments) and on psychologically terrorizing Pagan-inspired superstitions and prejudices. Thus, from the Renaissance onwards, many frustrated Western Europeans have been seeking an imaginary way out of the Vatican's spiritual despotism by romanticizing their Pagan past and by fabricating various tales and conspiracy theories about the roots of Christianity*.

The authoritarian ethos of the Roman Church was explicitly formulated by Pope Gelasius I (he was Bishop of Rome from 492 until his death in 496). Gelasius I affirmed the primacy of Rome over the entire Church, and, in his letter *Duo sunt*, written to Emperor Anastasius I in 494, he set forth a systematic theory of the relationship between institutional Church and State. According to Gelasius I, "this world" is governed by two sovereignties, the sacred authority of the priests ("auctoritas sacrata pontificum") and the royal power of kings and emperors ("regalis potestas"), but the emperor, being a child and not a father of the Church, was required to bow in submission to the priests, and especially to the Bishop of Rome, who was supposedly the highest among them, in all ecclesiastical matters. Hence, Gelasius I argued that the Bishop of Rome alone has "auctoritas" (ultimate authority), whereas the emperor has only "regia potestas" (royal power) for the conduct of temporal affairs (all these terms are taken from Roman law, and not from Christ's teachings of course).

In the Byzantine court, Gelasius' theory of the relationship between Church and State was incomprehensible, and, in fact, Emperor Anastasius I did not even deign to reply to Gelasius' letter. According to the Byzantines, Gelasius' ecclesiology was merely the result of his arrogance. On the other hand, in the Latin West, Gelasius' theory of the relationship between Church and State led, in later centuries, to the assertion of wide Papal claims to temporal power.

---

* Such romanticizations of Paganism and conspiracy theories about the Christian Church have recently gained much attention because of the popularity of such fictional works as *The Da Vinci Code* by Dan Brown, or *The Holy Blood and the Holy Grail*, a fictional work touted as a "historical work", by Michael Baigent (a well-known conspiracy theorist and editor of the magazine *Freemasonry Today*), Richard Leigh (a comparative literature scholar) and Henry Lincoln (an actor and screenwriter).

THE CORRUPTION OF ORTHODOX CHRISTIANITY
IN THE EASTERN ROMAN EMPIRE

In 586 A.D., Emperor Maurice gave the Bishop of the Imperial City (Constantinople) the title "Ecumenical Patriarch", which means universal bishop. In those days, Constantinople was the 'ecumenical' city, in the sense that it was the political, spiritual, economic and legislative centre of the ecumene, i.e. of the Roman Empire. Moreover, the Byzantines loved prestigious and impressive titles. Thus, even the chief librarian of the Imperial City was called "Ecumenical Librarian". In 586, the Bishop of Constantinople was John the Faster, and, even though he did not ask for the new title, "Ecumenical Patriarch", he accepted it. The title Ecumenical Patriarch was translated into Latin as "Universal Patriarch". Thus, alarmed at the thought that one bishop was claiming to himself authority over all the other bishops, the Pope of Rome Gregory I wrote to the Patriarch of Constantinople:

"I prey you, therefore, reflect that by your bold presumption the peace of the whole Church is troubled, and that you are at enmity with that grace which was given to all in common...Therefore, dearly beloved brother, love humility with all your heart. It is that which ensures peace among the brethren, and which preserves unity in the Holy Catholic Church...What will you say to Christ, who is the Head of the universal Church – what will you say to him at the moment of judgment – you who, by your title universal, would bring all his members into subjection to yourself? Whom, I prey you tell me, whom do you imitate by this perverse title if not [Lucifer] who, despising the legion of angels, his companions, endeavoured to mount to the highest?"

The above letter shows that Pope Gregory I directly rejected any claim about the Church of Constantinople's supremacy over the entire Church and also indirectly rejected the Latin Church's theory of the primacy of the Church of Rome over the entire Church. However, the Bishops of Constantinople, conforming to the Byzantine Emperors' politics of prestige, continued using their new title, Ecumenical Patriarch, and, in the 20th and the 21st centuries, the Patriarch of Constantinople is often called the "leader of the World orthodoxy". Furthermore, after the end of the Cold War and the collapse of the atheistic systems of the Soviet Bloc, in Eastern Europe, especially in Russia and Ukraine, and in the Balkans, especially in Greece,

Bulgaria and Serbia, the national Christian Orthodox Churches (known also as Eastern Orthodox Churches) often operate as state organizations, mingle Christianity and nationalism and subordinate Christ's universal and mystical Gospel to various folkloric elements, popular superstitions and political expediencies.

However, as I have already argued, great Greek Church Fathers and especially the mystical theologians of Byzantium were openly against both Papocaesarism (subjection of State to Church) and Caesaropapism (subjection of Church to State). Maximus the Confessor is a characteristic case in point. Gregory the son of Photinus, a representative of the Byzantine Emperor, asked Maximus the Confessor: "What, then, is not every Christian Emperor also a priest?" Maximus the Confessor answered: "He is not, for neither does he stand at the altar nor after the consecration of the bread does he elevate it saying 'Holy things for the Holy'. Nor does he baptize or anoint, or lay on hands and make bishops and priests and deacons; nor does he anoint churches, or wear the symbols of the priesthood". Moreover, as I have already argued, the Hesychasts (Orthodox Christian mystics) have emphasized an esoteric understanding of Christianity focused on the psychological cure and the deification of the human being.

PART TWO

THE KAIROLOGICAL QABALAH: THE SECRET MYSTERIES OF NATURE AND SCIENCE AND THE MASTERING OF REALITY

PART Two defines and explains the Kairological Qabalah and contrasts it against:

1. The Jewish Qabalah (sometimes also spelled Kabbalah), which is a system of Jewish mysticism inspired by Pythagoreanism and Neoplatonism,

2. The Hermetic Qabalah, which is a mystical school based on the philosophical religion of Hermes Trismegistus and Gnosticism, and

3. The traditional medieval Christian Qabalah (sometimes also spelled Cabala(h)), which is a system of Christian mysticism strongly influenced by Neoplatonism and Stoicism.

The Kairological Qabalah is a philosophy, an attitude and a way of life that are focused on the utilization and restructuring of reality by the intentionality of consciousness, on the ontology of particularity (personhood) and on the principle of personal and social autonomy. From the perspective of the Kairological Qabalah, man is the architect and the manager of his fate, and the ideal of divinization is intimately related to a deep affirmation of humanity as a soul-body nexus.

4

KAIROS AND QABALAH

NOW it is time to define and study the concepts of Kairos and Qabalah and to show the manner in which they can be fused into the concept of Kairological Qabalah, thus opening a new way of thinking about Western esotericism and giving rise to a new symbolic system for the understanding and practice of Western esotericism.

THE CONCEPT OF KAIROS

The concept of kairos refers to an opening or passageway, through which someone or something must travel at the proper moment and with effective force to achieve a goal. Hunter W. Stephenson[*] has drawn an analogy between kairos and archery by arguing that kairos represents the moment in which one may fire an arrow with sufficient force to penetrate the target. Whereas Stephenson uses phrases such as 'may be' and 'could be' in order to describe the kairic moment, Eric Charles White's interpretation of kairos emphasizes the element of urgency, referring to the tunnel-like aperture through which the arrow must pass and the critical time when action must take place[†].

In the context of ancient Greek mythology, the concept of kairos was personified as the Greek god of opportunity, and god Kairos

---

[*]   H.W. Stephenson, *Forecasting Opportunity: Kairos, Production and Writing*, Lanham, Maryland: University Press of America, 2005.

[†]   E.C. White, *Kaironomia: On the Will-to-Invent*, Ithaca, New York: Cornell University Press, 1987.

was a son of Zeus. For instance, Aesop (*Fables* 536; Plato, *Phaedrus* 5:8) writes that Kairos runs swiftly, balancing on the razor's edge, he is bald, but there is a lock of hair on his forehead, and he wears no clothes. According to Aesop, if one grasps Kairos from the front, he might be able to hold him, but, once Kairos has moved on, no one can pull him back. Thus, Kairos is a symbol of the 'opportune moment', i.e. of the brief moment in which things are possible. The famous Greek travelogue Pausanias, in his *Description of Greece*, 5.14.9, writes that, quite close to the entrance to the stadium at Olympia, there were two altars: one they called the altar of Hermes of the Games, the other the altar of Kairos (Opportunity). Ion of Khios, a 5th century B.C. poet, composed a hymn to Kairos; in Ion's hymn, Kairos is made out to be the youngest child of Zeus. Moreover, Callistratus, a Greek rhetorician who flourished in the 3rd/4th century A.D., in his *Descriptions* 6, wrote that Lysippos (a 4th century B.C. sculptor) wrought and set up a beautiful bronze statue of Kairos for the Sikyonians to look upon. Kairos was portrayed by Lysippos as follows: he had youthful beauty, suggesting that beauty is always opportune and that Kairos (Opportunity) is the only artificer of beauty; he had wings on his feet, suggesting his swiftness, and that, borne by the seasons, he goes rolling on through all eternity; there was a lock of hair on his forehead indicating that, while he is easy to catch as he approaches, yet, when he has passed by, the moment of action has likewise expired (see Figure 1).

Figure 1: The Image of the Ancient Greek God Kairos.

The relief is from a cloister at the monastery of St. John of Trogir, with an artist impression of the rest of the design.

Evangelos Moutsopoulos, a prominent modern Greek philosopher and academician, has pointed out that, in Aristotle's works on the sciences of nature, the notion of 'kairos' (i.e. 'opportune moment') is combined with the notion of 'metron' (i.e. 'right measure'), and it appears under the form of the temporal categories of 'not yet' or 'too early', and 'never again' or 'too late'*. In psychoanalysis, the concept of kairos plays a very important role, too. Daniel N. Stern, a prominent psychiatrist and psychoanalytic theorist, has stressed the importance of our "need for intersubjectivity", and, hence, our ability to share our mental states with other persons[†], and, he has focused on the so-called "now moments"[‡], during which the patient, most often unconsciously, needs the therapist to actively and directly intervene in the process of psychotherapy ("the moment of kairos"), thus transcending the normal role that the psychoanalyst plays in the context of psychotherapy. Harold Kelman, a leading scholar in psychoanalysis, describes kairos as the right and unique moment for the psychoanalyst to be "totally present" and to "actively intervene" in a longer psychological process within the patient, and he mentions that this opportunity is "unique and will not reappear"[§].

Kairology is founded on the notion of being 'kairic'. An element is said to be kairic if and only if it determines both the presence of reality in consciousness and the intervention of consciousness in reality. A 'kairic element' is not necessarily innate in objective reality, but it may be attributed to it by the consciousness that intends to gather knowledge about objective reality in order, through this knowledge, to utilize objective reality. Thus, throughout this book, I use the terms 'kairology', 'kairological' and 'kairic' as follows:

- 'kairology' is the methodic study of kairicity;

- 'kairological' is an adjective referring to something that is related to kairology or to someone who studies a problem by using kairology; and

---

[*]   Evangelos Moutsopoulos, "Kairos ou minimum critique dans les sciences de la nature selon Aristotle", *Revue Philosophique*, Vol. 24, 1999, pp. 481-491.

[†]   Lennart Ramberg, "In Dialogue with Daniel Stern: A Review and Discussion of the Present Moment in Psychotherapy and Everyday Life", *International Forum of Psychoanalysis*, Vol. 15, 2006, pp. 19-33.

[‡]   D.N. Stern, *The Present Moment in Psychotherapy and Everyday Life*, New York: Norton, 2004.

[§]   Harold Kelman, "Kairos: the Auspicious Moment", *The American Journal of Psychoanalysis*, Vol. XXIX, 1968; Harold Kelman, *Helping People*, New York: Science House, 1971.

- 'kairic' means that something or someone is characterized by kairicity.

THE CONCEPT OF QABALAH

'Qabalah' stands for an ecumenical esoteric system of correspondences and symbols, and it is a structural approach to the itinerary of the spirit. The word Qabalah is derived from Hebrew QBL, which means to receive, and in Rabbinic Hebrew it means tradition. It came to be used to name a specific Jewish mystical philosophy that emerged in France and Spain in the 13th century A.D.

The origins of the Qabalah can be traced back to the 4th century B.C., when, in the syncretistic context of Alexander the Great's Empire, Pythagoras' philosophy of numbers was introduced in the Middle East*. Thus, Pythagoreanism and Neoplatonism mingled with Jewish mysticism. The first known work in Hebrew Qabalah is the *Sefer Yezirah* (Book of Formation), which appeared in the 3rd century A.D., and it is an adaptation of Pythagorean numerology and Neoplatonism to Judaism. Moreover, according to Barry's *The Greek Qabalah*, one can find elements of Greek Qabalah outside of mainland Greece well before the 3rd century A.D. in Egyptian amulets, Roman graffiti, Gnostic traditions and early Christian writings.

The Qabalah uses notions and symbols of Jewish mysticism in order to give rise to a new, anthropocentric and esoteric system of man's progress, which plays a protagonistic role in the Western esoteric tradition. However, the Qabalah is not part of the Jewish or any other religion. Thus, in the English language, the spelling Qabalah is used in order to refer to the use of Qabalah in the context of Western esotericism, whereas the spelling Kabbalah is used in order to refer to the esoteric interpretation of Orthodox Rabbinic Judaism, and the spelling Cabala(h) is used in order to refer to the adaptation of Qabalah to Christianity.

THE QABALISTIC TREE OF LIFE

The Qabalistic symbol that is called the "Tree of Life" is frequently mentioned in the Old Testament. This tree contains ten fruits called

---

* Kieren Barry, *The Greek Qabalah: Alphabetic Mysticism and Numerology in the Ancient World*, York Beach, ME: Samuel Weiser, 1999.

the 'sephiroth' (emanations; singular form: 'sephirah'), and they are connected together by 22 paths corresponding to the Hebrew letters, alchemical and astrological principles (see Figure 2). The sephiroth have been referred to as "the ten faces of God", and, since, according to the Bible, humans were created in the image of God, the Tree of Life is a metaphor for the human being.

The Tree of Life is an attempt to describe the creation of the universe, and simultaneously it is an attempt to describe certain traits of the Divine. The ten sephiroth of the Tree of Life are here listed in order from the beginning to the end:

1. Kether: Crown.

2. Chokmah: Wisdom.

3. Binah: Understanding.

4. Chesed: Mercy.

5. Geburah: Judgment/Power.

6. Tiphareth: Beauty.

7. Netzach: Victory.

8. Hod: Splendor.

9. Yesod: Foundation.

10. Malkuth: Kingdom.

In addition, as shown in Figure 2, Daat (i.e. the 'hidden sephirah' of knowledge) is the conceptual location (mystical state) where all ten sephiroth in the Tree of Life exist in their perfected state of mutual sharing.

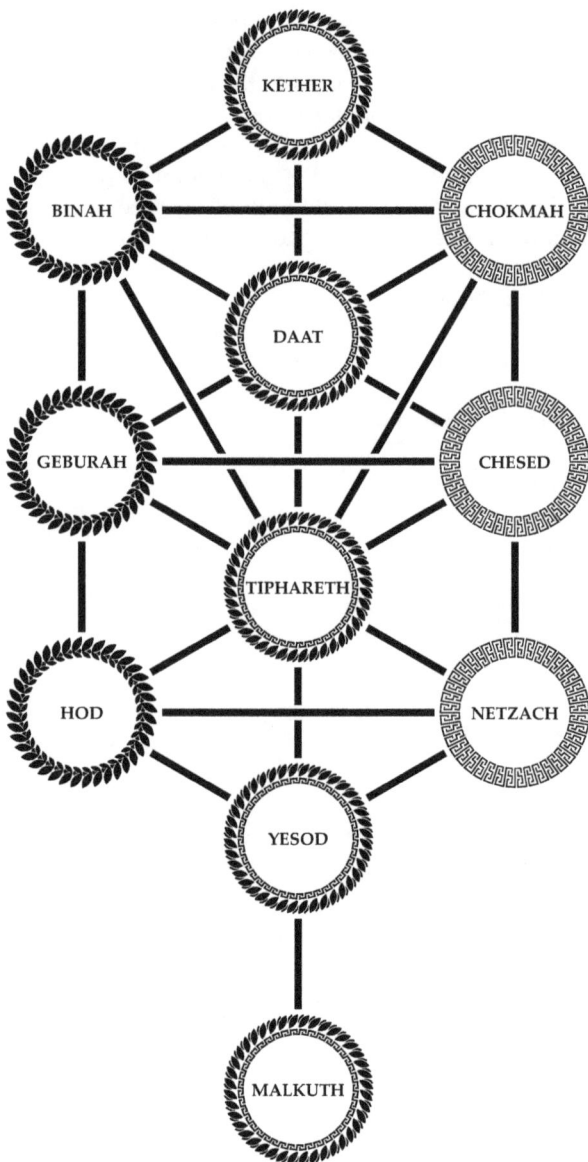

Figure 2: Tree of Life

The Jews' Qabalistic Tree of Life is a special version of the Pythagoreans' Tetractys. The Tetractys is a triangle consisting of ten points arranged in four rows (one, two, three and four points on each row) as follows:

Figure 3: The Tetractys.

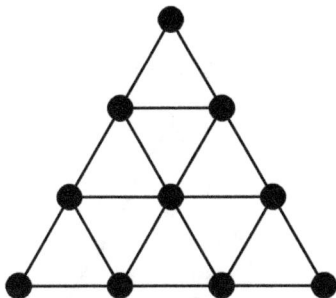

For Pythagoras and his followers, each row of the Tetractys holds these meanings:

- *First row:* the first row consists of a single point. This point symbolizes the First Cause, and it is associated with the virtue of wisdom.

- *Second row:* the second row consists of two points. The second row symbolizes "neikos", or strife. In the context of Pythagoreanism, strife is the power of division, and it is associated with the virtues of movement and impulse; movement and impulse, in turn, give birth to courage and strength.

- *Third row:* the third row consists of three points. The third row symbolizes "philotes", which means friendship and harmony. Philotes is the synthesis of physical beauty and mental balance.

- *Fourth row:* the fourth row consists of four points. The fourth row symbolizes the four elements of ancient Greek cosmology: earth, air, fire and water.

Like the Pythagoreans, the Jewish Qabalists believe that the Tetractys is an image of the structure of the universe, and they have paralleled the Tetractys with the Tree of Life. According to the Jewish Qabalists, the ten points of the Tetractys correspond to the ten sephiroth of the Tree of Life. Furthermore, the Jewish Qabalists have created a Tetractys of the letters of the Tetragrammaton (YHWH), which adds up to seventy two by the Jewish mystical numerology, as shown below:

Figure 4: The Tetragrammaton.

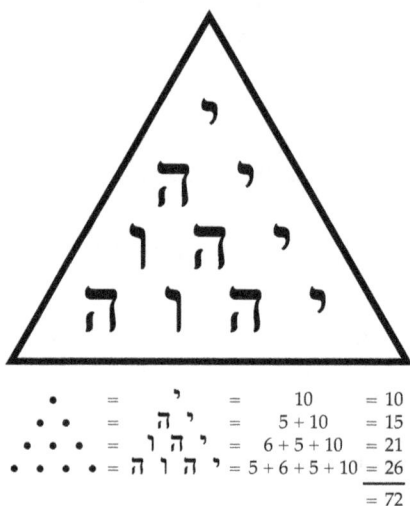

$$
\begin{array}{lllll}
\bullet & = & \text{י} & = & 10 & = 10 \\
\bullet\ \bullet & = & \text{י ה} & = & 5 + 10 & = 15 \\
\bullet\ \bullet\ \bullet & = & \text{י ה ו} & = & 6 + 5 + 10 & = 21 \\
\bullet\ \bullet\ \bullet\ \bullet & = & \text{י ה ו ה} & = & 5 + 6 + 5 + 10 & = 26 \\
& & & & & = 72
\end{array}
$$

The number 72 is considered holy for the Jewish Qabalists, because it signifies the 72 names of God[*].

THE SEPHIROTH OF THE TREE OF LIFE
ACCORDING TO THE CLASSICAL QABALISTIC THEORIES

In terms of the classical Qabalistic theories[†], the sephiroth of the Tree

---

[*] The 72 names of God are derived from the Book of Exodus, Chapter 14, verses 19-21: each of the verses contains 72 letters, and when combined they form 72 names, known collectively as the Shemhamphorasch, which is a corruption of the Hebrew term *Shem ha-Mephorash* (an old form of the Tetragrammaton).

[†] By the term 'classical Qabalistic theories', I refer to such classical Jewish Qabalistic texts as the

of Life can be interpreted as follows:

1. Kether: It refers to things that are above the mind's abilities of comprehension. In Jewish mysticism, the name of God associated with Kether is Ehyeh Asher Ehyeh, the name through which He revealed Himself to Moses from the burning bush, according to *Exodus* 3:1-15.

2. Chokmah: It refers to the primary ('beginning') force in the creative process. The first phrase in the Torah (in *Genesis*) is "in the beginning" (God created), which is translated "with Chokmah" (God created). In Jewish mysticism, the name of God associated with Chokmah is the Holy Tetragrammaton, Yod-He-Vau-He. In the context of non-Jewish traditional Western esoteric schools, Chokmah symbolizes the giver of life, and Kether symbolizes the precise moment of being and non-being, i.e. Chaos. In psychological terms, Chokmah symbolizes intuition.

3. Binah: According to the Jewish mystical text *Sefer Ha Bahir* (*Book of the Brightness*), Binah is described as "quarry of the Torah, treasury of wisdom, quarry of God's spirit, hewn out by the spirit of God". In Jewish mysticism, the name of God associated with Binah is Elohim. In the context of non-Jewish traditional Western esoteric schools, Kether is understood as energy, Chokmah as the conduit for the passing energy, and Binah as a reservoir that stores and catalyzes energy. In psychological terms, Binah symbolizes faith.

4. Chesed: According to the *Sefer Yezirah*, "Chesed contains all the holy powers, and from it emanate all spiritual

books *Sefer Yezirah* and *Sefer Ha Bahir* as well as to the Qabalistic teachings of such traditional Western esoteric schools as the Hermetic Order of the Golden Dawn, the Ordo Templi Orientis and several Rosicrucian Societies. See for instance: Papus (Gérard Encausse), *The Qabalah: Secret Tradition of the West*, York Beach, ME: Samuel Wesier, 2000 (originally published in 1903); Israel Regardie, *A Garden of Pomegranates: Skrying on the Tree of Life*, St Paul, Minnesota: Llewellyn Publications, 2002 (originally published in 1932); Dion Fortune, *Mystical Qabalah*, San Francisco: Red Wheel/Weiser, 2000 (originally published in 1935).

virtues". In the context of non-Jewish traditional Western esoteric schools, Chesed represents the formulation of divine ideas into concrete terms, and, therefore, it is associated with the Hierophant Taro card. In psychological terms, Chesed symbolizes control and obedience.

5. Geburah: Jewish mystics refer to Geburah as 'midat din', which means the attribute of judgment, since, in Jewish mysticism, Geburah is understood as God's mode of punishing the wicked and judging humanity in general. In the context of non-Jewish traditional Western esoteric schools, Geburah is the house of the will, it represents the Kundalini (absolute vitality), and it teaches the Magus that he must remove unnecessary things and that one thing is sacrificed for another. In psychological terms, Geburah symbolizes the ego and radical intelligence.

6. Tiphareth: It is the point of balance of the Tree of Life. In Jewish mysticism, in particular, it is the sephirah that integrates Chesed (compassion) and Geburah (judgment).

7. Netzach: In both Jewish and non-Jewish traditional esoteric teachings, Netzach is the sephirah of emotions, and it represents the virtues of endurance, fortitude and patience.

8. Hod: In both Jewish and non-Jewish traditional esoteric teachings, Hod is the house of perfected intellect, and it symbolizes logical rigor, the creation of forms and the elimination of illusions.

9. Yesod: According to Jewish mystics, Yesod translates concepts into actions that unite us with God. In the context of non-Jewish traditional Western esoteric schools, Yesod represents the individual unconscious and the collective unconscious as well as the sexual drive.

10. Malkuth: According to Jewish mystics, this sephirah does not emanate from God directly, but it emanates from God's creation, being the objectivation of the intentions of God's creative action. In the context of non-Jewish traditional Western esoteric schools, Malkuth is the physical representation of the Magus in his physical form, and, therefore, it is a symbol of the body and the sphere of the elements of the material world.

KAIROLOGICAL QABALAH: A NEW QABALAH AND ITS SIGNIFICANCE

I see all traditional Jewish and non-Jewish interpretations of the Qabalistic Tree of Life as expressions and results of advanced minds' intentions to ascend to higher levels of consciousness and to improve their existential conditions. Therefore, all traditional interpretations of the Qabalistic Tree of Life are significant and have some value for the spiritual progress of man. Furthermore, I see the Qabalistic Tree of Life as a powerful and effective tool whereby one can create a map of the spiritual itinerary of mankind and a philosophical compass.

On the other hand, the classical (Jewish and non-Jewish) Qabalistic theories have the following defects:

1. they are formulated in a language that impedes the creation of effective bridges between spirituality and science;

2. they are fixated in the ontological arguments of Hellenistic philosophical schools primarily of Gnostic character, and, therefore, not only are they unable to overcome the defects of Gnosticism, which I analyzed in Chapter 3, but also they ignore significant developments in the history of philosophy and in the history of science;

3. their Qabalah cannot operate as a continuously updated map of the spiritual itinerary of mankind.

In other words, the classical Qabalistic theories reflect very limited understanding of the different ways in which the creativity of the human spirit has been historically expressed (e.g. through philosophy, science, technology, religion, institutions, etc.), and they

71

tend to cause the fixation of the esotericist in particular segments of the West's cultural history.

Through the fusion of Kairos and Qabalah, I have created a new Qabalah, which I call the Kairological Qabalah. The Kairological Qabalah is an explosive liberating and illuminating experience, because it leads to a new humanistic synthesis between religion and science, between academic philosophy and esotericism, between spirit and matter, and generally between the reality of consciousness (which is, among other things, the realm of esoteric knowledge) and the reality of the world (which is, among other things, the realm of exoteric knowledge).

The Jewish Qabalah (also sometimes spelled Kabbalah) is a system of Jewish mysticism inspired by Pythagoreanism and Neoplatonism. The Hermetic Qabalah is a mystical school based on the philosophical religion of Hermes Trismegistus and Gnosticism. The traditional medieval Christian Qabalah (also sometimes spelled Cabala(h)) is a system of Christian mysticism strongly influenced by Neoplatonism and Stoicism. In contrast to the Jewish Qabalah, to the Hermetic Qabalah and to the traditional medieval Christian Qabalah, the Kairological Qabalah is a philosophy, an attitude and a way of life that are focused on the utilization and restructuring of reality by the intentionality of consciousness, on the ontology of particularity and on the principle of personal and social autonomy.

In the context of the Kairological Qabalah, Kether represents the reality of being in general, the Left-hand Pillar of the Tree of Life represents the reality of the world, the Right-hand Pillar represents the reality of consciousness, and the Middle Pillar represents the dynamic continuity and unity between the reality of consciousness and the reality of the world. In particular, according to my concept of Kairological Qabalah, the sephiroth of the Qabalistic Tree of Life must be interpreted in terms of the following correspondences:

1. Kether: The Reality of Being.

2. Chokmah: The Reality of Consciousness.

3. Binah: The Reality of the World.

4. Chesed: Historical Time.

5. Geburah: Natural Time.

6. Tiphareth: Kairicity.

7. Netzach: Space As a Creation of Consciousness.

8. Hod: Natural Space.

9. Yesod: Consciousness.

10. Malkuth: Brain.

5

THE KAIROLOGICAL LEFT-HAND PILLAR

THE Kairological Left-hand Pillar consists of the sephiroth of the Kairological Qabalah's Tree of Life that correspond to the reality that is external to human consciousness. The sephiroth of the Kairological Left-hand Pillar are Binah (the reality of the world), Geburah (natural time) and Hod (natural space).

BINAH: THE REALITY OF THE WORLD

Since experience provides us with images (irrespective of whether they are related or unrelated to each other) of a reality that seems to be external to our minds, it naturally follows that this reality is the cause of perception. Therefore, on the basis of the principle of causality, a mind-independent reality exists necessarily. The cosmological position that is founded on the previous syllogism is called (philosophical) realism.

Furthermore, realistic cosmological theories can be divided into two main groups: monism and dualism. According to monism, there is only one substance or principle that governs reality. If this principle is material, then the theories that follow are materialist, whereas, if this principle is spiritual, then the theories that follow are spiritualist. The materialist cosmologies are the oldest theories in the history of philosophy, and, in a sense, they reflect a naïve approach to reality. For instance, the reasoning that underpins the materialist cosmological models of the Ionian physicists (the most prominent of whom were Thales, Anaximander and Anaximenes) is the following:

observation shows that substances are changed into other substances (e.g. water becomes vapor) and, by similar process, the primal stuff must have been transmuted into the different substances found in our present world of experience. Monistic theories of the spiritualist type appeared later in the history of philosophy, and they were extreme positions of dualist theories.

Two of the most important examples of dualist realism are Platonism and Aristotelianism. It should be emphasized that it is a big mistake to characterize Platonism as an idealist philosophy only because it is idea-centred. On the contrary, Platonism is a realist philosophy because Plato argues that ideas are not mind-dependent abstractions, but they are the original, eternal transcendental archetypes of things, existing prior to things and apart from them and thus uninfluenced by the becoming of the manifest world. For Plato, ideas are apprehended by reason, not by sense; though sense can provide us with an indirect apprehension of ideas through the phenomena, which are shadows mimicking the idea of good. At this point, Plato's thought is influenced by the thought of Parmenides, according to whom, beings and non-beings cannot approach each other (or mingle with each other) because beings exist whereas non-beings do not exist.

However, during the last phase of his life, Plato, influenced by the critique of his philosophy by Aristotle, abandoned his thesis about the irreducibility of ideas (beings) and phenomena (non-beings) and accepted that reality consists of both beings (ideas) and non-beings (phenomena) as well as of almost-beings and almost-non-beings*. In other words, in his last dialogues, Plato identified a series of different ontological levels, and this series inspired Neoplatonism†, which, through the philosophical works of Plotinus, Proclus and Dionysius the Areopagite, developed the perception that there is a series of substances that communicate with each other, either through 'emanation' or through 'return to the origin', and that fill the space between the true being (the 'One') and the true non-being (matter). Plotinus, the founder of Neoplatonism, transformed Platonic dualism into a spiritualist theory, since, in Plotinian philosophy, the One (which is the absolutely simple first principle

---

* See especially Plato's dialogues *Timaeus* and *Sophist*.

† See: Dillon and Gerson (eds), *Neoplatonic Philosophy*; R.T. Wallis and J. Bregman (eds), *Neoplatonism and Gnosticism*, New York: State University of New York Press, 1992.

of all and of which the universe is an emanation) and the material world do not have the same ontological weight: the One is the true being whereas matter is to be identified with privation of all form. On the other hand, Proclus argued that matter has a degree of being. For Proclus, all things, including matter (which has in itself, apart from the forms existing in it, no 'being'), participate in the One and, therefore, in true being.

Aristotelianism is a dualistic realism, since it is based on the equality between two elements that are related to each other: matter and form. All objects are composed of a certain material arranged in a certain way. The material they are composed of is their matter, and the way it is arranged is their form. According to Aristotle*, all objects have matter, i.e. a material of which they are composed, and form, i.e. they are characterized by a certain way in which matter is arranged. The form of a thing makes a thing what it is. For instance, form allows us to distinguish between a vase and a sculpture. Whereas Plato asserts the separation of the form from the thing, Aristotle argues that every form is, like the Platonic 'idea', eternal, but, instead of being outside of matter, it is in matter; they coexist. In particular, 'form' is the manner in which 'matter' exists. Moreover, Aristotle identifies actuality with form, and hence substance, while identifying matter with potentiality. Potentiality is that state of being in which a being's program of existence has not been accomplished yet, but it is already firmly oriented toward a concrete purpose. Actuality is that state of being in which a being's program of existence has been accomplished, and the accomplishment of this program determines both the given being itself and the given being's behavior. For instance, as long as a pot remains stored in a cabinet, it exists potentially, but, when it is used in accordance with the purpose for which it has been constructed, it exists actually.

For Plato, reality has a transcendental existence, in the sense that it mainly lies beyond consciousness (irrespective of the fact that, as Plato writes in *Meno*, reality remains latent in consciousness and it can be perceived through the process of memory). On the other hand, for Aristotle, reality itself is formed in the world of the senses by matter and by the manifestation of a spiritual factor, namely, form

---

* See: Jonathan Barnes, *The Cambridge Companion to Aristotle*, Cambridge: Cambridge University Press, 1995; Georgios Anagnostopoulos, *The Blackwell Guide to Aristotle*, Oxford: Blackwell, 2007; Christopher Shields, *The Oxford Handbook on Aristotle*, Oxford: Oxford University Press, 2008.

(or species). This difference between Platonism and Aristotelianism inspired, throughout the Middle Ages, the controversy between realists and nominalists*. In medieval scholastic philosophy, realists (such as Johannes Scotus Eriugena and Anselm of Canterbury) argued that universals (species), e.g. 'humanity', 'nation', 'animal', 'beauty', 'circle', etc., are the ultimate realities (i.e. have essential or substantive reality), whereas nominalists (such as Roscellinus) argued that universals are merely linguistic signifiers ('names', hence the term nominalism) and that only individual objects have real existence.

In the Late Middle Ages, the prevailing philosophy was that of Thomas Aquinas (1225—1274), known also as Thomism. Thomism is a form of Aristotelianism[†] adapted to the spirit of Christianity[‡] in the manner that I explained in Chapter 3, and it became the official philosophy of the Roman Catholic Church. However, Platonism and Neoplatonism continued playing a major role in the course of philosophic thought, and they exerted important influence on the thought of George Berkeley and Hegel.

In modern philosophy, which originated in Western Europe in the 17th century, Descartes' dualism prevailed. Descartes distinguished two important concepts: extension (the property of taking up space) and thinking. He argued that the existence of the self can be known for certain because, at the very moment one doubts the proposition 'I exist', one is at the same time thinking and, therefore, existing. From this argument, known as 'the cogito', Descartes concluded that the essence of mind is thought. Additionally, in the *Second Meditation*, Descartes argues that he is a "thing that doubts, understands, affirms, denies, is willing, is unwilling, and also imagines and has sensory perceptions".

Descartes[§] distinguishes the notions of mind and body by arguing

---

* See: M.H. Carré, *Realists and Nominalists*, London: Oxford University Press, 1946; H.B. Veatch, *Realism and Nominalism Revisited*, Milwaukee: Marquette University Press, 1970.

† According to Thomas Aquinas' *De Principiis Naturae*, 1, "existence is twofold: one is essential existence or the substantial existence of a thing, for example man exists, and this is existence *simpliciter*. The other is accidental existence, for example man is white, and this is existence *secundum quid*". In Thomism, the definition of a being is "that which is", which is composed of two parts: "which" refers to its *quiddity* (literally 'whatness'), and 'is' refers to its *esse* (the Latin infinitive verb 'to be').

‡ See: C.F.J. Martin, *Thomas Aquinas: God and Explanations*, Edinburgh: Edinburgh University Press, 1997.

§ René Descartes, *The Philosophical Writings of Descartes*, trans. J. Cottingham, R. Stoothoff, D.

that, as regards body, we have only the notion of extension (which entails the notions of shape and motion), and, as regards the soul on its own, we have only the notion of thought (which includes perception and will). Furthermore, Descartes discusses the notion of mind-body union by arguing that, with respect to the soul and the body together, we have only the notion of mind-body union, from which derives our notion of the soul's power to move the body and the body's power to act on the soul and cause its sensations and passions*. In light of the previous arguments, Descartes concludes that voluntary bodily movements and sensations are not modes of the body alone, or the mind alone, but rather are modes of "the soul and the body together".

Modern philosophy is characterized by the notion that truth is not something to be handed down by authority or decreed by Papal Bulls, but something to be achieved by free and impartial inquiry. Descartes has been recognized as the founder of modern philosophy primarily because he founded his dualism, which leans toward spiritualism, on the perception that reason is self-reliant and that truth is interwoven with the 'cogito' principle ('I think').

The major representatives of Descartes' school are Nicolas Malebranche, Baruch de Spinoza and G.W. Leibniz. According to Malebranche, there is only one supreme Reason embracing the ideas of all possible things, and the material world is *terra incognita* (i.e. we do not know whether it exists or not). It is the idea of matter, not matter itself, which is the real immediate object of consciousness. Thus, for Malebranche, thought is the imposition of spirit (i.e. the substance in which the Absolute consists) on reality whenever consciousness perceives extended phenomena. For Spinoza, thought, which is the essential attribute of the mind, and extension, which is the essential attribute of the body, do not stand in mutual opposition, but they are interconnected due to a process of transition from the one to the other. Spinoza, inspired by Neoplatonism, unites God with nature, and thus he formulates a deterministic and pantheistic model of the universe. Whereas monotheism emphasizes the ontology of particularity and that the relationship between God and man is based on personal and, hence, free choice, pantheism, by fusing God and nature, transforms God into an impersonal coercive force, like

---

Murdoch and A. Kenny, Cambridge: Cambridge University Press, 1984—1991, p. 218.

*   Ibid, p. 218.

gravity, and, hence, pantheism eliminates personal freedom. Thus, in the suffocating atmosphere of life in Spinoza's pantheistic cosmos, man can experience and demonstrate his freedom only through madness (understood as a negation of the all-pervading, coercive cosmic logic) or through murder/suicide (understood as a negation of a life founded on necessity). On the contrary, Leibniz's version of Cartesianism attempted to protect the freedom of the individual through Leibniz's monadology.

For Leibniz, the notion of motion is more important than that of extension. According to Leibniz, the product of mass times velocity squared, which he called *vis viva* (the living force), is the real measure of force, as opposed to Descartes' force of motion (equivalent to the product of mass times velocity). Leibniz identified vis viva as the fundamental quantity of motion, as some active principle that was conserved and kept the universe from 'running down'. Leibniz's *Monadology* (1714) is a kind of spiritualist individualism, according to which a monad is a simple substance that cannot be divided into parts, the universe consists of an infinite number of monads, and each monad has its own perceptions: a simple or bare monad has unconscious perception, but does not have memory; a simple or ordinary soul has distinct perceptions, conscious awareness and memory; a rational soul or spirit is an even more highly developed monad, and it has self-consciousness and reason.

Another kind of monistic realism is materialism. According to Descartes, the entire reality is organized in a mechanistic manner, but the human being is an exception to this rule, because it has soul. However, Descartes' philosophy cannot offer convincing arguments on the basis of which one could accept that the human being is an exceptional entity in the mechanistic universe of Cartesianism. Thus, many post-Cartesian mechanistic philosophers, such as Ernst Haeckel, Julien Offray de La Mettrie and Karl Vogt, used the model of the mechanistic Cartesian universe in order to defend the argument that the human being is a machine-animal and that mind is merely an excretion of the brain. The epistemic problems of this 18th century materialistic monism are, first, that it is based on a completely objective view of the world, thus ignoring every subjective aspect of the inner states of consciousness*, and, second, that modern science (especially quantum mechanics) has refuted

---

* See: John Searle, *The Rediscovery of the Mind*, Cambridge, Mass.: MIT Press, 1992, pp. 50-54.

the mechanistic Cartesian world-conception and has shown that the description of nature is essentially probabilistic. Furthermore, the mechanistic analysis of life (which reduces the phenomenon of life to the difference between inorganic matter and alive matter and maintains that there is a continuity between these two forms of matter since they obey the same natural laws) contradicts the second law of thermodynamics, according to which the energy of matter tends to be reduced because certain forms of life produce large amounts of energy[*].

In contrast with the 18th century simplistic forms of materialism, Marx formulated scientific materialism (dialectical materialism and historical materialism), which was one of the many possible versions of Hegelianism. Marx borrowed from Hegel the notions of antithesis and its overcoming (synthesis), and he applied the Hegelian dialectical model to economics through the use of the concept of surplus value[†]. In Marxist economics, surplus value is the amount by which the value of the worker's product exceeds the wage the worker is paid. When the surplus value, created by the worker, is appropriated by the owner of capital, a 'dialectic' is created between the labor class and the capitalist class. The exploitation of the proletariat by the capitalist class leads to a class struggle. The competition among the capitalists functions according to the law of capital accumulation or the concentration of wealth in a few hands. The capitalist impulse is toward monopolistic structures, and, thus, finally, capital becomes more and more concentrated in the hands of the few, and unemployment grows as production becomes more technologically efficient. The result is overproduction and a crisis. The crisis of overproduction is resolved by opening new markets.

In addition, like Hegel before him, Marx attempted to apply the Hegelian dialectical model to cosmology, wishing to formulate a philosophy of nature, but he did not accomplish this project. Hegel himself was also unsuccessful in his own attempt to formulate a philosophy of nature on the basis of his dialectical model. However,

---

[*]   The thermodynamic degeneration that accompanies a sweeping or irreversible process cannot be repaired without compensation; see: W.S. Franklin, "The Second Law of Thermodynamics: Its Basis in Intuition and Common Sense", *The Popular Science Monthly*, March 1910, p. 239. The second law of thermodynamics is closely related to the concept of entropy, i.e. the disorder created during a thermodynamic process (in any closed system, the entropy of the system will either remain constant or increase).

[†]   Karl Marx, *Theories of Surplus Value*, New York: Prometheus Books, 2000.

it should be mentioned that Marx's dialectical materialism indicates that Marx was more careful than Hegel and also Marx's historical materialism indicates that Marx was more careful than Marquis de Condorcet and Auguste Comte: in contrast with Hegel, Condorcet and Comte, Marx did not specify exactly the moment of the beginning of the final stage of human society development. Thus, Marx's dialectical model is more versatile than the dialectical models of Hegel, Condorcet and Comte, but, exactly for this reason, it is susceptible to tautologies[*], i.e. to statements that are by definition true, since all possible states of the world can be consistent with them.

GEBURAH: NATURAL TIME

In man's spiritual life, 'time' occupies a conspicuous position. Time is associated with action and change but also with physical corruption and death. Thus, in the context of esotericism and art, time is often represented by a human skull or skeleton.

According to the traditional realist approach to the notion of time, time is part of the fundamental structure of the universe, a dimension in which events occur in sequence. Sir Isaac Newton subscribed to this realist thesis, and, therefore, it is sometimes referred to as Newtonian time. On the other hand, according to an alternative view, which has been endorsed by Immanuel Kant, 'time' does not refer to any kind of 'container' that events and objects 'move through', nor to any entity that 'flows', but it is part of a fundamental intellectual structure (together with space and number) within which consciousness sequences and compares events. This argument leads us to Chesed, which represents historical time and belongs to the Kairological Right-hand Pillar.

HOD: NATURAL SPACE

Like time, space is a mode of being, and it is complementary to time[†]. In the 19th century, the famous mathematician Hermann

---

[*] See: K.R. Popper, *Conjectures and Refutations: The Growth of Scientific Knowledge*, New York: Harper & Collins, 1968; Michael Nicholson, *Causes and Consequences in International Relations: A Conceptual Study*, London: Pinter, 1996, pp. 90-91.

[†] For further details, see: Nicolas Laos, *Topics in Mathematical Analysis and Differential Geometry*, London: World Scientific Publishing Co., 1998.

Minkowski, who has solved several difficult and important problems in mathematical physics and relativity theory, used the term "World point" in order to refer to a point of space at a point of time. However, like the temporal mode of being, the spatial mode of being is enriched through the experience and the application of a kairic mode of being. Thus, we move on to Netzach, which represents space as something created by consciousness and belongs to the Kairological Right-hand Pillar.

6

THE KAIROLOGICAL RIGHT-HAND PILLAR

THE Kairological Right-hand Pillar consists of the sephiroth
of the Kairological Qabalah's Tree of Life that correspond
to the reality that is determined by the intentionality of human
consciousness. The sephiroth of the Kairological Right-hand Pillar
are Chokmah (the reality of consciousness), Chesed (historical time)
and Netzach (space as a creation of consciousness).

CHOKMAH: THE REALITY OF CONSCIOUSNESS

According to the second general cosmological model to which one
can reduce the relations between external reality and consciousness,
the natures of these two factors are neither totally different from
each other nor opposite of each other. Whereas the representatives
of realism emphasize the principle of causality, the representatives
of idealism emphasize the principle of identity. In fact, in modern
philosophy, the basic argument of idealism is the following: if the
nature of reality were different from the nature of consciousness,
then it would be impossible for humans to know reality (i.e. not
only would we be unable to gather knowledge about the nature
of reality through analysis but also we would be unable to know
the substance and the meaning of reality). In fact, according to the
way in which modern philosophy understands idealism, idealism
presents the world not as something reflected in consciousness, but
as an extension and a projection of consciousness out of itself and
also as consciousness itself.

Idealism in its modern sense was first developed in the 18th century. Descartes was an involuntary precursor of modern idealism, because, starting from a 'methodical doubt', whose purpose is to use doubt as a route to certain knowledge by finding those things which are doubtless, he rejects every element of knowledge that can be doubted, and, therefore, for Descartes, consciousness is the ultimate foundation of reality and assurance. Another involuntary precursor of idealism was the empiricist philosopher John Locke[*]. In his *Essay Concerning Human Understanding*, Locke is concerned with the discovery of the source from which our knowledge springs, and he argues that, if it is true (as Descartes and others have argued) that we have an innate knowledge of principles, it cannot be explained why we question its validity. According to Locke, the mind does not possess any innate ideas, and the two sources of all our ideas are sensation (which supplies the mind with sensible qualities) and reflection (which supplies the mind with ideas of its own operation, e.g. perception, believing, doubting, willing, etc.).

The development of modern idealism took different forms in the 18th, the 19th and the 20th centuries. The most radical form of idealism is solipsism, according to which the only reality is one's own consciousness, and, therefore, knowledge of anything outside of one's own consciousness is unjustified. According to a moderate form of idealism, the sensible world is a degraded sensible appearance of an experienced conscious state that is the only reality. According to 'immaterialism', which is a form of idealism founded by George Berkeley[†] (Bishop of Cloyne) under the influence of Neoplatonism, there are not any mind-independent material objects at all. Berkeley argues that to exist means to be perceived, i.e. to be in the mind, and, therefore, bodies exist only when there is a mind that perceives or knows them. However, all the things we perceive (ideas) are inactive, and thus they cannot be the cause of sensations. Berkeley argues that the cause of the sensations is an immaterial, active substance called spirit. By the term 'spirit', Berkeley means a unified, active being, which, in so far as it perceives ideas, is called 'understanding', and, in so far as it creates (i.e. operates upon ideas), is called 'will'. Since all ideas are passive and inert and since the spirit is active and creative, there can be no idea formed of spirit,

---

[*] See: Jonathan Bennett, *Locke, Berkeley, Hume: Central Themes*, Oxford: Oxford University Press, 1971

[†] Ibid.

and thus we can perceive only the effects produced by the spirit but not the spirit itself.

David Hume* agrees with Descartes and Locke in requiring that genuine knowledge must be self-evident, but he argues that he has not found such knowledge anywhere except in mathematics, which merely analyzes its own concepts. According to Hume, the constitutive and fundamental elements of knowledge are impressions and ideas. By the term 'impression', Hume means a lively perception, which brings with it conviction or positive belief in the existence of a corresponding objective reality. All our sensations, passions and emotions as they make their first appearance in the mind are characteristic examples of impressions. By the term 'idea', Hume means a copy of a corresponding impression, left behind by the given impression, and hence ideas are less lively than perceptions. Ideas are faint perceptions of which we are conscious when we reflect on impressions, and they are copied by the memory and the imagination. According to Hume's law of association of ideas, impressions and ideas are linked together by an inclination to recall one another.

Hume's idealism is a form of skepticism. Hume discusses skepticism in his *Treatise of Human Nature*, Book I, Part IV, and in his *Inquiry Concerning Human Understanding*, Section XII, in order to deconstruct ordinary claims to knowledge. However, skepticism is neither a new phenomenon in the history of philosophy (since the father of skepticism is the ancient Greek philosopher Pyrrho) nor an unavoidable conclusion of the investigation of the problem of knowledge.

The different skeptical arguments can be divided into four groups:

1. The first form of skepticism emphasizes that we can know only very few of the qualities of any object of our consciousness, and thus the substance of every object of our consciousness remains unknown. However, in opposition to this argument, one can contend that limited knowledge does not mean invalid knowledge and that the knowledge of concrete, significant qualities of an object of our consciousness is a valid, significant form of knowledge of the given object.

---

*   Ibid.

2. The second form of skepticism emphasizes that the senses and reason can provide us with false impressions. Indeed, our senses are imperfect, i.e. fallible, and, under different circumstances, they can present the same sensible objects in different ways and with the same level of plausibility every time. Similarly, our intellect can confuse dreams with reality. However, in opposition to this argument, one can contend that the fallibility of sensible knowledge as well as dreams can be controlled by reason and that there are, at least within certain conceptual communities, evident truths and principles, such as the principle of contradiction* (i.e. contradictory statements cannot both at the same time be true).

3. The third form of skepticism contends that morality and legislation are different from one society to another, and, therefore, knowledge in the areas of morality and legislation is uncertain. However, one may counter-argue that these differences are due to different partial circumstances.

4. The fourth form of skepticism consists in the argument that our reason operates based on tautologies, i.e. logical statements in which the conclusion is equivalent to the premise. However, this skeptical argument can be opposed in two ways. First, one can counter-argue that the sin of being committed to a tautology is smaller than the sin of completely refusing to give any value to reason, since the latter is an obvious contradiction. Second, following Michael Nicholson, one can contend that the development of tautologies is only one, preliminary stage in the process of trying to develop a theory of some phenomenon; "a useful stage nevertheless"[†].

---

*   However, according to Lucien Lévy-Bruhl, the primitive mind does not address contradictions, since, according to Lévy-Bruhl's "law of participation", in the mind of primitive people, the same thing or phenomenon may at the same time be several entirely different forms of being. See: Lucien Lévy-Bruhl, *Primitive Mentality*, New York: AMS Press, 1978 (originally published in 1922).

†   Nicholson, *Causes and Consequences in International Relations*, pp. 96-97.

Kant said that he had been "awakened from his dogmatic slumbers" by studying Hume. However, Kant's philosophy undulates between realism and idealism, and Kant called his philosophy "critical". For Kant, there is a real world, independent of our minds, and he calls it the "noumenal world". Additionally, for Kant, the phenomenon is the image of the noumenon. Kant argues that consciousness cannot comprehend the essence of the noumenal world, but his refusal to accept the comprehension of the essence of the noumenal world by the conscious mind is a cognitive argument and not an ontological one (i.e. the noumenal world exists even though we cannot comprehend its essence). In his *Prolegomena to Any Future Metaphysics*, Kant accepts that the transcendental reality is doubtless. In fact, Kant asks if there are any propositions that seem to compel us on the basis of pure reason alone, and his answer is that there are such propositions, or ideas, and that they have been, historically, the very impulses that have inspired metaphysical speculations (i.e. psychological, cosmological, and theological ideas).

The most prominent representatives of the so-called romantic idealism were Johann Gottlieb Fichte and Friedrich Wilhelm Joseph Schelling. Fichte* argues that the only reality is the "ego" (i.e. consciousness) and that the "ego" alone creates the objects of its perception and becomes aware of itself by contrasting itself with everything that is alien to it. In Fichte's philosophy, all transcendental reality is contained in the "ego", and, therefore, Fichte eliminates the concept of the noumenon, since the noumenon is created by the "ego". Schelling†, following a path similar to Fichte's path, argues that the ego and all the things that are alien to the ego are functional forms of a unique reality that he called the "Absolute". The teachings of Fichte and Schelling about the dialectical antithesis between the ego and the things that are alien to the ego were systematized into a philosophy of transcendental idealism by Hegel.

Hegel argues that all life and movement are founded on contradiction, which rules the entire world. Everything tends to change and pass over into its opposite. But, according to Hegel, the opposites are opposites only with respect to one another, and not with respect to the unity or whole of which they form parts. In

---

* See: Robert Solomon, and Kathleen Higgins (eds), *Routledge History of Philosophy*, vol. VI: The Age of German Idealism, London: Routledge, 1993.

† Ibid.

Hegel's philosophy, God is the potential universe, the Idea, to which everything is reducible. With his transcendental idealism, Hegel attempted to avoid Kant's unknowable noumenal world, since he argued that Kant's doctrine of the unknowable is self-contradictory. However, Hegel fails to address the difference between 'knowing' and 'thinking'. The unknowable, i.e. Kant's noumenal world, can be thought and yet remain unknown, since it is not given in sensibility. Moreover, something may be an object of 'faith' without being an object of 'rational knowledge'. In other words, for Kant, the unknowable may have emotive, persuasive or imperative meaning. Thus, Kant's doctrine of the unknowable is not as self-contradictory as Hegel contends.

Hegel transcended the subject (i.e. the individual "ego") of the early German idealism (Fichte and Schelling) in order to ascend to a quantitavely higher (bigger), and, therefore, spiritually 'safer', subject, namely, the historical subject (i.e. the nation), which he called the "objective spirit". In Hegelianism, reason (*Logos*) is the self-consciousness of the "objective spirit", and thus it consists in the knowledge of a truth that is determined by historical becoming. Thus, Arthur Schopenhauer has argued that Hegelianism paralyzes mental power and stifles real thinking, and Karl Popper has argued that Hegelianism provides justifications for the absolute rule of Frederick William III and generally for statism.

According to Hegel, even though the world is historically created by the human being, the world has achieved its autonomy (from human consciousness). Furthermore, Hegelianism influenced the 19th century spiritualism, especially A. Rosmini and V. Gioberti in Italy, the neo-critical philosophers C. Remouvier and O. Hamelin, and the epistemologist L. Brunschvicg.

CHESED: HISTORICAL TIME

In the beginning of the *Transcendental Aesthetic*, Kant poses the following question: "what are space and time? Are they actual entities?" Later, in the *Transcendental Aesthetic*, Kant refers to the followers of Newton's position as the "mathematical investigators" of nature, who contend that space and time "subsist" on their own, and to the followers of Leibniz's position as the "metaphysicians of nature", who think that space and time "inhere" in objects and their relations. At the ontological level, Kant's position is that space and time do not exist independently of human experience but are "forms of intuition" (i.e. conditions of perception imposed by our own consciousness). In this way, he reconciles Newton and Leibniz: he agrees with Newton that space is an irrefutable reality for objects in experience (i.e. for the elements of the phenomenal world, which are the objects of scientific inquiry), but also he agrees with Leibniz that space is not an irrefutable reality in terms of things in themselves. At the epistemological level, unlike David Hume, Kant argues that the axioms of geometry are not self-evident or true in any logically necessary way. For Kant, the axioms of geometry are logically synthetic, i.e. they may be denied without contradiction, and, therefore, consistent non-Euclidean geometries are possible (as János Bolyai, Nikolai Ivanovich Lobachevsky and Bertrand Riemann actually accomplished). However, Kant argues that the axioms of geometry are known 'a priori' only because the axioms of Euclidean geometry, in particular, depend on our "pure intuition" of space, i.e. space as we can imaginatively visualize it.

Being goes through different states. The succession of these states is understood as 'time'. For this reason, time appears to be directly related to being itself, and, according to Aristotle, time is one of the modes of being. However, Jean Piaget, a pioneering Swiss epistemologist and psychologist, has shown that the development of the concept of time in consciousness takes place in parallel with the development of consciousness itself: initially, there is not one single time, but there is a collection of partial times, unrelated to each other, and each of them plays a different role in consciousness[*]. Consciousness refers to these partial times only when it intends to place a given experience in one of them. Only in a later stage, as consciousness extends its experiences, the previous unrelated partial times are gradually unified.

Piaget's research work on the concept of time extends Bergson's concept of time. According to Henri Bergson, duration is the only irrefutable reality and it constitutes the depth of the reality of the world and of consciousness, too. Duration, for Bergson, is a continuous flow that can be conceived through neither logic nor experience but only through intuition (i.e. through that operation of consciousness which Bergson called "sympathy"). In this way,

---

[*]   Jean Piaget, *The Child's Conception of Time*, trans. A.J. Pomerans, London: Routledge and Kegan Paul, 1969.

consciousness knows that its own self is duration, that it refers to the duration of its objects' existence, and also that, since it is duration, it is part of reality. Moreover, according to Bergsonism, time is a concept that is always conceived 'a posteriori' as a result of the interweaving between the divisible concept of time and the consciousness of the indivisible duration. In other words, time does not correspond to an ontological reality, but it is created by consciousness, since consciousness wishes to transcend the difficulties it encounters by analyzing them in a Cartesian way and thus making them measurable.

The movement of time is not uniform, since the velocity of time is subject to change, e.g. it may be rapid, imperceptible, etc. For this reason, time is subject to dilation* and condensation. These phenomena can be interpreted in two ways: first, there are different versions of time (astronomical time, biological time, psychological time, historical time); second, the elasticity of time allows the deformation of time by consciousness.

Furthermore, even though, in the "natural attitude", we think in terms of the dual temporal horizons of the past and the future, consciousness creates a third temporal horizon, which is called 'now', or 'present'. This 'now' does not belong only to time, but it belongs to consciousness, too. Consciousness tries to capture this 'now' in order to place itself within this 'now', and it experiences this 'now' as a kind of eternity that does not transcend consciousness but, instead, it is created by consciousness itself. According to Edmund Husserl, phenomenological time is essentially a 'form' that imposes itself upon mental processes, but this form is generated (constituted) by an activity of protention and retention that stems from the very core of consciousness. By means of this activity, consciousness draws its past into its present, and extends its present into its future. This activity is possible due to the intentionality of consciousness, i.e. due to the fact that consciousness is consciousness of its contents and, therefore, the contents of consciousness become conscious experiences. Hence, consciousness intervenes in the flow of reality.

Consciousness creates time in order to facilitate its activity. Far from becoming enslaved to its creations, consciousness forms kairic systems by means of which it reconstructs temporality, it affirms its

---

* See for instance: Steve Adams, *Relativity: An Introduction to Space-Time Physics*, London: Taylor & Francis, 2000.

freedom, and it subjugates the world. Thus, by utilizing kairos (i.e. the opportune moment), consciousness, ultimately, utilizes reality itself, and it perceives reality in a more creative and more ingenious way by taking a kairological stand.

The kairicity of consciousness signifies that consciousness is dynamically open to the world in order to intervene in the world and utilize it, and additionally it signifies a way according to which consciousness transcends the ordinary, natural mode of being in order to ascend to a better mode of being, i.e. to improve its existential conditions. Thus, due to kairicity, consciousness measures time not in deterministic and coercive units of natural time (e.g. seconds), but in possibilities and perceives reality as a tank of opportunities.

NETZACH: SPACE AS A CREATION OF CONSCIOUSNESS

Within the framework of a kairic mode of being, space and time are not any more natural-cosmic conditions of being, but they are creations of consciousness. Thus, to the extent that space and time are intentionally created by consciousness, and, therefore, they can be transcended by consciousness, space and time are not only modes of being, but they are also modes of well-being (i.e. modes of improving the existential conditions of being).

7

THE KAIROLOGICAL MIDDLE PILLAR

ONE of the major goals of philosophy is to identify the relations between consciousness and external reality. The various relations between consciousness and external reality are reducible to two general philosophical models ('schools'): realism and idealism. The Kairological Middle Pillar indicates that the reality of being is not one, but it is unified, in the sense that there is a dynamic continuity between the reality of the world and the reality of consciousness. The sephiroth of the Kairological Middle Pillar are Kether, Daat (the secret or 'shadow' sephirah), Tiphareth, Yesod and Malkuth.

KETHER: THE REALITY OF BEING

The primary problem of every philosophical endeavor consists in the identification of the reality of each and every object of the given philosophical endeavor, and particularly of that reality that can be conceived as the essential reality, namely, the reality of being. In the history of philosophy, the term 'being' refers to a self-sufficient reality, which endures either by being closed in its own self or by tending to transcend its nature and expanding itself beyond its normal limits. In the first case, being is static, whereas, in the latter, being is dynamic.

According to Parmenides[*], being is a totality, i.e. a unique set

---

[*]   See: Jonathan Barnes, *The Presocratic Philosophers*, 2nd edn, London: Routledge & Kegan Paul, 1982; P.K. Curd, *The Legacy of Parmenides: Eleatic Monism and Later Presocratic Thought*, Princeton: Princeton University Press, 1998

that imposes itself by being and is contrasted to everything that is not. In other words, according to Parmenides, being and non-being can never be reduced to each other. This dualistic argument is the intellectual root of Plato's classical conception of ideas as true beings, i.e. as existing in and for themselves, as having the character of substantiality. However, in his dialogue *Sophist*, Plato argues that being and non-being are the extreme terms of an ontological series whose intermediate terms are the non-being of being and the being of non-being. It is exactly by means of these intermediate terms that Plato[*] and the Neoplatonists[†] (e.g. Plotinus, Proclus and Dionysius the Areopagite) purport to explain the presence of the sensible world. In particular, Plotinus identifies four substances (One, Intellect, Soul and Matter), which are multiplied in Dionysius the Areopagite's work in order to become infinitesimal degrees of transition from the absolute being (which is called the 'idea of good' by Plato in his dialogues *Republic* and *Parmenides*, and the 'One' by Plotinus in his *Enneads*) to matter, which, for Dionysius the Areopagite, is not identified with absolute non-being. Proclus, by applying his views about the place of matter in the metaphysical hierarchy and carrying long-held views, like those of *Timaeus*, through to their conclusion, argues that matter is not the absolute non-being, but it has a degree of being. In modern philosophy, the Neoplatonic conception of a continuum of degrees of being can be found in the monistic philosophy of Spinoza.

Aristotle's ontology, which is systematically presented in his book *Metaphysics*, provides an integral, solid philosophical base for the interpretation of reality. Aristotle[‡] distinguishes between

---

[*]   See: Gail Fine (ed.), *Plato 1: Metaphysics and Epistemology*, Oxford: Oxford University Press, 1999; C.L. Griswold (ed.), *Platonic Writings, Platonic Readings*, London: Routledge, 1988; Laos, *Foundations of Cultural Diplomacy*; M.M. McCabe, *Plato's Individuals*, Princeton: Princeton University Press, 1994.

[†]   See: J.M. Dillon and L.P. Gerson (eds), *Neoplatonic Philosophy*, Indianapolis: Hackett, 2004; John Gregory (ed.), *The Neoplatonists: A Reader*, 2nd edition, London: Routledge, 1999; A.C. Lloyd, *The Anatomy of Neoplatonism*, Oxford: Oxford University Press, Reprint edition, 2005

[‡]   See: Laird Addis, "Aristotle and the Independence of Substances", *Philosophy and Phenomenological Research*, Vol. 54, 1972, pp. 699-708; Irving Block, "Substance in Aristotle", in G.C. Simmons (ed.), *Paideia: Special Aristotle Issue*, Brockport, NY: State University College at Buffalo and State University College at Brockport, 1978, pp. 59-64; David Charles, *Aristotle on Meaning and Essence*, Oxford: Clarendon Press, 2002; M.J. Cresswell, "Essence and Existence in Plato and Aristotle", *Theoria*, Vol. 37, 1971, pp. 91-113; Laos, *Foundations of Cultural Diplomacy*; C.D.C. Reeve, *Substantial Knowledge: Aristotle's Metaphysics*, Indianapolis: Hackett, 2000.

being 'potentially' and being 'actually'. This distinction is very important, because it presupposes a becoming according to which being is increasingly actualized and imposes itself in accordance with an innate archetypal form that is called entelechy by Aristotle and it is the program of the actualization of being, a program that remains unchanged irrespective of the partial changes that being undergoes. According to Aristotle, being is the simplest mental presence, but it is not absolutely simple. Aristotle conceived being as a resultant whose components are categories that constitute a system. These categories are substance, form, the relation between substance and form, time, and space, and they are qualities that can be identified with and attributed to being. Thus, Aristotle transcends Parmenides' absolute dichotomy between being and non-being and proposes a more dynamic ontology. In fact, the entire medieval[*] ontological thought was oscillating between Plato's and Aristotle's solutions to the problem of the antithesis between being and non-being, which was first posed by Parmenides and which has been playing a protagonistic role in philosophical research ever since.

Descartes[†] tried to reverse the scholastic ontology, which was primarily founded on Aristotelianism. In his *Metaphysical Meditations*, Descartes argued that being is present itself, i.e. it exists independently of consciousness, but simultaneously it is present in consciousness, which is consciousness of being and it underpins being. In Descartes' philosophy, existence is directly derived from the clear and distinct idea of a supremely perfect being. Moreover, according to Descartes' method of 'demonstration', whatever one clearly and distinctly perceives to be contained in the idea of something is true of that thing. Thus, in Descartes' philosophy, the reality of the world is interwoven with the mind that thinks about the world. With this argument, Descartes and his school (Nicolas Malebranche, Baruch de Spinoza and Gottfried Leibniz) founded modern ontology.

---

[*] See: J.J.E. Gracia and T.B. Noone, *A Companion to Philosophy in the Middle Ages*, Blackwell Companions to Philosophy, Oxford: Blackwell Publications, 2003; A.S. McGrade (ed.), *The Cambridge Companion to Medieval Philosophy*, Cambridge: Cambridge University Press, 2003.

[†] See: John Cottingham (ed.), *Descartes*, Oxford: Oxford University Press, 1998; E.M. Curley, "Analysis in the *Meditations*: The Quest for Clear and Distinct Ideas", in A.O. Rorty (ed.), *Essays on Descartes' Meditations*, Berkeley: University of California Press, 1986; M.D. Wilson, *Descartes*, London: Routledge & Kegan Paul, 1978.

Reacting against the extreme determinism and optimism of the rationalistic systems of Leibniz and especially of Wolff, Immanuel Kant[*], in his *Critique of Pure Reason*, admitted the existence of things-in-themselves (i.e. objects that exist independently of consciousness), but he argued that the thing-in-itself is rationally unknowable, and he simply accepted the transcendentality of the thing-in-itself. According to Kant's *Critique of Pure Reason*, Bxxvi-xxvii, we cannot *know* things-in-themselves, but we can at least *think* them as things in themselves, since otherwise we would be obliged to accept the absurd conclusion that there can be appearance without anything that appears.

In general, Kant argued that there are two different worlds. The first world is called the noumenal world[†], and it is the world of things outside of us, i.e. the things that exist independently of our minds. However, Kant argues that our consciousness cannot comprehend the essence of this world and that we can only perceive an altered version (a faint image) of this world, which Kant called the phenomenal world. The phenomenal world is the world that we perceive, i.e. the view we have of the world that is inside our minds. As I mentioned in Chapter 6, Kant's refusal to accept the comprehension of the essence of the noumenal world by the conscious mind is a cognitive argument and not an ontological one (i.e. Kant's thesis is that the noumenal world exists even though we cannot comprehend its essence).

On the other hand, Georg W.F. Hegel[‡], the father of German idealism, proposed a different solution to the old Parmenidean ontological problem. According to Hegel's *Phenomenology of Spirit*, the thing-in-itself (i.e. being) is the idea that moves far away from itself, i.e. gives rise to a contradiction, in order finally to return to its own self enriched by its voyage. In addition, by the term spirit or mind (*Geist*), Hegel refers to the idea realized. Therefore, according to Hegel, spirit is the subject that, after its exodus from its inner world and its adventure in the external world, returned to its own self. At the historical level, the Hegelian subject exists as the

---

[*]   See: Paul Guyer (ed.), *The Cambridge Companion to Kant's Critique of Pure Reason*, Cambridge: Cambridge University Press, 2010; Alan Wood, *Kant*, Oxford: Blackwell, 2005.

[†]   The elements of the noumenal world are called noumena (singular: noumenon).

[‡]   See: K.R. Westphal, "Hegel's Phenomenological Method and Analysis of Consciousness", in K.R. Westphal (ed.), *The Blackwell Guide to Hegel's Phenomenology of Spirit*, Oxford: Blackwell, 2009.

"nation" (*Volk*) and its spirit as "the spirit of the nation" (*Volkgeist*). Hegel's philosophy combines the concept of being with the concept of becoming, and, from this viewpoint it seems to follow Aristotle's philosophy. However, there is a difference between Aristotle's dynamic ontology and Hegel's dynamic ontology. According to Aristotle, the transition from potentiality to actuality indicates a becoming that is the realization of an ontological program, i.e. being realizes its existential purpose. On the other hand, according to Hegel, dialectic indicates a becoming that is a process of alienation.

Hegel[*] distinguishes between 'being-in-itself' (potentiality) and 'being-for-itself' (actuality). Hegel's dialectic is the teleological self-movement of reason in which that which is posited ('thesis') engenders its necessary limitation and negation ('antithesis') which is overcome through the development of a new thesis ('synthesis') which overcomes while preserving the prior moments. Intimately related to Hegel's dialectic is a process of 'alienation', which has been defined by Hegel as the condition in which there is a contradiction between the Spirit's (i.e. the historical subject's) existence and essence[†]. Moreover, Hegel argues that the previous alienation of being takes place in a rationally organized manner. For Hegel, time appears as the destiny and necessity of spirit that is not yet complete within itself, and, therefore, Hegel maintains, time appears as spirit's necessity to enrich the share that self-consciousness has in consciousness, i.e. to set in motion the immediacy of the "in-itself"[‡].

In modern philosophy, the philosophy of existence, known also as 'existentialism'[§], emphasized the distinction between the essence of being and the presence of being. The philosophy of existence has its roots in the works of Augustine of Hippo and Blaise Pascal, but its pioneer was S.A. Kierkegaard and its most important representative is Martin Heidegger. Whereas Aristotle's philosophy assigns primary significance to the essence of things (namely, to the attribute or set of attributes that makes an object what it fundamentally is, and which an object has by necessity, and without which it loses its identity), the philosophers of existence argue that what is ontologically significant

---

[*]   G.W.F. Hegel, *Lectures on the History of Philosophy*, 20-21.

[†]   G.W.F. Hegel, *The Philosophy of History*, 17ff.

[‡]   G.W.F. Hegel, *Phenomenology of Spirit*, paragraph 801.

[§]   See: Steven Earnshaw, *Existentialism: A Guide for the Perplexed*, London: Continuum, 2006; Thomas Flynn, *Existentialism: A Very Short Introduction*, Oxford: Oxford University Press, 2006; Robert Solomon (ed.), *Existentialism*, New York: Random House, 1974.

is not the essence of being but the presence of being, i.e. its existence. In other words, according to the existentialists, the only thing that is ontologically significant is the very fact that a being exists and is present, in one way or another, in front of me, or independently of me, or the manner in which it is identified with me. Thus, the only thing that has ontological significance is the fact that I am conscious of that which exists outside of me and the fact that I am conscious of my own existence. In particular, J.P. Sartre[*], an existentialist in whose thought the impact of Hegel's philosophy is very clear, emphasized that the objects of my consciousness exist not only 'in themselves' but also they exist 'for myself', and the same holds for my own existence, too.

The argument that the concepts 'essence' and 'presence' should not be identified with each other follows logically from the fact that essence can be conceived independently of its reality. For instance, I accept that Chimera is a mental creature that is not real in the external animal kingdom, but I can define Chimera by specifying its qualities (i.e. its essence): a monstrous fire-breathing female creature born by Typhon and Echidna, and composed of the parts of multiple animals: upon the body of a lioness with a tail that ended in a snake's head, the head of a goat arose on her back at the center of her spine. By defining Chimera, I specify its essence, but I do not argue for its existence. At the level of human consciousness, 'essence' and 'presence' are not identical to each other.

From the previous analysis of the philosophy of existence, it follows that, at the level of consciousness[†], existence is prior to essence, not so much in terms of chronological order as in terms of significance. In other words, consciousness assigns primary significance to the emergence of existence from non-existence, and thus ontology reduces to a 'genealogy' of existence. From this perspective, the first priority of the philosopher of existence is to explain how human existence and human knowledge progress from one level of being and one level of knowledge to another, and how consciousness gradually evolves, through confrontation with its own antinomies, from an immediate and unformed state toward a

---

[*]   See: Thomas Busch, *The Power of Consciousness and the Force of Circumstances in Sartre's Philosophy*, Bloomington: Indiana University Press, 1990.

[†]   According to the Bible, though, at the level of God (Divine Existence), essence is identified with presence, and, thus, we read: "I am that I am" (Exodus, 3:14).

condition of unity and integral self-experience. In particular, Karl Jaspers*, ascribed central status to 'limit situations' (*Grenzsituationen*), which are moments, usually accompanied by experiences of dread, guilt or acute anxiety, in which the human mind confronts the restrictions and pathological narrowness of its existing forms, and it allows itself to abandon the security of its limitedness and so to enter a new realm of self-consciousness. Additionally, Jaspers developed a theory of the 'unconditioned' (*das Unbedingte*), arguing that human limitations are neither absolute nor fixed, and, in general, human life is basically about growing and outgrowing our old, immature and less perfect ways.

DAAT: THE QUEST FOR KNOWLEDGE

Within the framework of the so-called archaic mentality, the knowledge of being is based on an experiential relation that is called 'participation' and emphasizes an assumed continuity between beings, ontological states and mental states. In other words, the objects that are experienced by consciousness form an ontological continuum, in the sense that consciousness moves toward these objects, it embraces them, and ultimately it completely assimilates them within itself. This process becomes clearer as philosophy becomes more rational and deeper. According to the archaic philosophizing consciousness, consciousness partakes of the reality of the world due to a series of transcendental and mysterious first causes, i.e. supernatural forces, which act according to a complex system of preferences known only by few initiated minds of 'magi', and thus these initiated minds can intervene in the operation of the world by activating or de-activating the previous forces according to their will, i.e. by subjugating the previous forces to their intentionality†. This archaic, or mystical, mentality is characterized by kairicity, in the sense that it leads to an intervention of consciousness in the world, and it is expressed through myth.

However, the identification of the knowledge of being with an event of 'participation' is present not only in the archaic mentality but also in the philosophical one. Platonism and Neoplatonism are the major philosophical systems that developed and promoted various

---

* See: P.A. Schilpp (ed.), *The Philosophy of Karl Jaspers*, New York: Tudor Publishing Company, 1957.

† See: Susan Greenwood, *The Anthropology of Magic*, Oxford: Berg, 2009.

conceptions of participation. In general, the understanding of being as participation means that every being (resp. every situation) is connected with other beings (resp. with other situations) and that it remains open to them in order to achieve its re-integration into them and also, with them and through them, to achieve its re-integration into the unique cosmic reality from which all beings have emanated.

As I mentioned in Part One, there are two general forms of 'participation': the one is passive, and the other is active. The passive form of participation refers primarily to those elements that beings have inherited from their common source and continue preserving them. Thus, this form of participation emphasizes the dependence or interdependence of beings. The active form of participation refers primarily to the beings' attempt to create a situation that will allow them to transcend their current situation. Thus, this form of participation emphasizes identification within the framework of common activities; 'identification' is a process whereby a being assimilates an aspect, property, or attribute of another being and is transformed wholly or partially.

Within the framework of systematic philosophy, the knowledge of being is necessarily dependent on the use of a specific method (i.e. a series of steps taken to acquire knowledge). In general, there are two kinds of philosophical methods: the 'a priori'* methods and the 'a posteriori'† methods. The common characteristic of the 'a priori' methods is that they are founded on initial assumptions that are usually arbitrarily conceived and postulated (in the form of axioms) and from which are deduced series of syllogisms that lead to the final conclusions in a consistent manner. The term 'consistency' means logical coherence among parts. From the viewpoint of 'a priori' methods, the more consistent a philosophy is the more chances it has to impose itself. However, usually, the logical structures that are created according to 'a priori' methods exhibit cracks in their supposedly solid bodies.

Some of the 'a priori' methods were developed in ancient times and continued being developed in medieval times, and some others were developed in modern times. Most Presocratic philosophers followed 'a priori' methods, and, in particular, they were postulating a first cause, or primary matter, which was supposed to be the

---

*   *A priori* is Latin for 'from the former' or 'from before'.

†   *A posteriori* is Latin for 'posterior to'.

essence of reality (e.g. water according to Thales, fire according to Anaximander, air according to Anaximenes, etc.), and from which all partial realities were supposed to follow. However, even though the Presocratic philosophy is characterized by a remarkably logical pattern of development, it is also characterized by a peculiar sense of scientific (cosmological/ ontological) dogmatism.

The Sophists and Socrates were the first philosophers who extricated philosophical thought from the intellectual shackles of the Presocratic philosophers' scientific dogmatism. The Sophists, starting from the lack of agreement among their predecessors, arrived at the epistemological standpoint that the perceiving mind is an important factor in the process of knowing and, hence, that knowledge depends on the particular knower. As we read in Plato's dialogues *Symposium*, *Theaetetus* and *Meno*, Socrates developed his own method of 'maieutics' (midwifery), which is based on the idea that the truth is latent in the mind of every human being due to innate reason but has to be 'given birth' by answering intelligently proposed questions. In fact, in Plato's *Symposium*, Socrates repeated the words of Diotima, a wise woman, according to whom the soul of men is pregnant and it wants to give birth, but the delivery cannot be done. Socrates argued that the role of the philosopher is to help in the delivery as a midwife and that what is delivered is light that is defined as 'logos'. Apart from their differences, the Sophistic epistemology and the Socratic epistemology share an important attitude: they both turn the interest of the philosophical minds away from Presocratic cosmological speculation and focus philosophical research on the human being.

'Knowledge' is explained as 'dialectic' by Plato in the central books of his *Republic*. Plato's dialectic displays two complementary processes of inquiry: the 'ascending' process of inquiry and the 'descending' process of inquiry. According to the ascending process of inquiry, consciousness starts from sensible objects (where the source of belief is sense perception) and ascends to higher levels of conceptual knowledge, which is conversant with the ultimate realities. According to the descending process of inquiry, consciousness starts from the knowledge of the ultimate realities and descends to the different levels of application, or manifestation, of those ultimate realities in the sensible world. In other words, through the ascending process of inquiry, the philosopher's consciousness moves from the phenomena to the ideas, which are participated by the phenomena and of which the phenomena are imitations, whereas, according to the descending process of inquiry, the philosopher's consciousness moves from the knowledge of ideas to the interpretation of phenomena.

Aristotle's philosophy expresses methodical quests that are similar to the methodical quests of Plato's philosophy. Aristotle wrestles with the problem of establishing a universal science of being qua being, which could interpret all partial realities. According to Aristotle's *Categories*, the study of being in general (being qua being) crucially involves the study of substance, and, additionally, in his *Metaphysics*, Aristotle argues for the ontological priority of substance. Aristotle explains that metaphysics is the study of being as being, i.e. a general theory of being. However, 'being', as Aristotle pointed out in the third book of his *Metaphysics*, is "said in many ways". For instance, consider the following analogy: there are business tables and statistical tables. A business table is a table in the sense of an open, flat surface supported by legs or by a base, whereas a statistical table is a table of statistical data. Hence, since there is not a single sense of 'table' which simultaneously applies to a business table and a statistical table, there is not a general science of tables. In other words, tables do not constitute a single kind, and, therefore, there is not a single science whose objects would be all objects that are correctly called 'tables'. If the level of ambiguity that characterizes the term 'table' in the previous example characterized also the term 'being', then Aristotle's general science of being would be impossible. Aristotle admits that the term being is said in many ways, but he argues that it is not merely ambiguous. According to Aristotle, the various senses of 'being' have an ambiguity "in relation to one" ("pros hen"), i.e. they are related to a single central sense. For instance, let us consider the term 'health': it does not have a single definition that applies uniformly to all cases, e.g. there are many different things that can be called 'healthy': organisms, diets, exercise, geographical locations, etc., but not all of these are healthy in the same sense; yet, these various senses have something in common: they all refer to one central thing (i.e. health) that is actually possessed only by some of the things that are called healthy (namely, by healthy organisms), and these are said to be healthy in the primary sense of the term. Other things can be characterized as healthy only to the extent that they are adequately related to things that are healthy in this primary sense of the term. The situation is the same, Aristotle argues, with the term being. 'Being' has a primary sense as well as related senses whereby it applies to other things, to the extent that they are adequately related to things that are 'beings' in the primary sense of the term. The beings in the primary sense are substances, whereas the beings in other senses are the qualities, quantities, etc. that belong to substances. For instance, consider a white horse: a horse is a substance, i.e. a being in the primary sense, and the color white (a quality) is a being only in a secondary sense because it qualifies some substance.

However, before embarking on the study of substance, Aristotle, in his *Metaphysics*, argues that, first of all, philosophy must address the most fundamental principles (namely, the axioms) that are used in all reasoning. Thus, first of all, philosophy must concern itself with the principle of non-contradiction, according to which "the same attribute cannot at the same time belong and not belong to the same subject and in the same respect"*. Hence, it is clear that Aristotle's method is a particular application of the 'a priori' philosophical method.

The ascending and the descending phases of Plato's dialectic were reversed by Plotinus and Neoplatonism in general. According to Plotinus' *Enneads*, the One, which is identified with the transcendent Good of Plato, should not be conceived as 'sheer unity' in the Parmenidean sense and neither as 'barrenness of being' or even 'absolute nothingness'; instead, the Plotinian One should be understood as the base unity of all multiplicities. In other words, the Plotinian One is nothing because it is everything, and it is no-one-thing and non-being because any sense of thingness would be a prostitution of its genuine nature. The Plotinian One is the point where all themes merge. In fact, the Plotinian conception of the One is the foundation of the so-called 'apophatic' theology, and it has exerted significant influence on the Hesychasts' exposition of Christianity, which I studied in Chapter 3.

In the Middle Ages, Aristotelian philosophy was, to some extent, crystallized by Thomas Aquinas, the major representative of the scholastic philosophy. According to Thomas Aquinas, knowledge starts from the world of the senses, which is the realm of the ratio inferior (e.g. natural science), and is completed in the mental world

---

*   Aristotle, *Metaphysics*, 1005b19.

and the supernatural, which is the realm of the ratio superior[*]. Aquinas argued that, in the world of the senses, all entities depend on something that transcends them and that this situation can be realized by careful observers through the contemplation of sensible objects. Thus, he acknowledged the central part played by sense perception in human cognition.

In the 16th century, Francis Bacon articulated a systematic study of the empirical method (induction), which was gradually developed by Italian scientists during the Renaissance. Bacon's method is based on a double empirical and logical standpoint. In his *Novum Organum Scientiarum*, induction implies ascending to axioms, as well as a descending to works, so that from axioms new particulars are derived and from these new axioms. In fact, induction starts from sensible data and moves, through natural history (providing sense-data as guarantees), to lower axioms or propositions, which are derived from the tables of presentation or from the abstraction of notions. It must be mentioned that, by the term 'experience', Bacon does not refer to everyday experience, but he presupposes that his empirical method corrects and extends sense-data into facts, which go together with his setting up of tables[†] (tables of presence and of absence and tables of comparison or of degrees, i.e. degrees of absence or presence). However, Bacon's empirical method does not end here, since Bacon assumes that from lower axioms more general ones can be derived by induction. Moreover, from the more general axioms, Bacon strives to reach more fundamental laws of nature, which lead to practical deductions as new experiments or works.

Descartes understood the significance of Bacon's new scientific method and used it in order to attack and transcend Scholasticism. Descartes formulated the analytical geometric method. In a famous passage in his replies to Mersenne's objections to the *Meditations*, in discussing the distinction between analysis and synthesis, Descartes remarks that analysis is the best and truest method of instruction, and it was this method alone that he employed in his *Meditations*. In his *Discourse*, Descartes showed how the arithmetical operations of addition, subtraction, multiplication, division and the extraction

---

[*]   See: Etienne Gilson, *Thomism: The Philosophy of Thomas Aquinas*, trans. L.K. Shook and A. Mauer, Toronto: Pontifical Institute of Medieval Studies, 2002.

[†]   See: Michel Malherbe, "Bacon's Method of Science", in M. Peltonen (ed.), *The Cambridge Companion to Bacon*, Cambridge: Cambridge University Press, 1996, p. 85.

of roots can be represented geometrically. In general, within the framework of analytic geometry, problems can be broken down into simpler problems involving the construction of individual straight lines, thus leading to an analytical approach to geometry. Hence, Descartes' *Geometry* is based on the use of algebra, which was called an "art of analysis". By reducing geometric problems to equivalent algebraic ones, Descartes made a major contribution to mathematics. Furthermore, Descartes' analytic geometry had great philosophical significance, too. For, by reducing geometric problems to algebraic ones, Descartes constructed a form of 'a priori' geometric philosophical method whose first principle was not an object of the external world, but it was the conscious experience itself. Descartes moves away from objects that are external to consciousness and turns his attention to the conscious experience itself, and, through the algebraic representation of geometric problems, he throws light on the structure of problem-solving in its general form[*].

The next major philosophical shift from the world to the human being was due to Kant. Kant was significantly influenced by David Hume's empiricism, which was formulated within a spiritual environment determined by the processing of Bacon's empirical method by British philosophers. Kant's epistemology is a 'critical', or, rather more precisely, a straddling, position between an 'a priori' philosophical method and an 'a posteriori' philosophical method. Kant argues that human beings are 'propositional animals' and that knowledge always appears in the form of judgments, which are essentially propositional cognitions. However, according to Kant, not every judgment gives us genuine knowledge. In an analytical judgment, the predicate merely elucidates what is already contained in the subject (e.g. 'body is an extended thing'). Only synthetic judgments give us genuine knowledge. For, in a synthetic judgment, the predicate extends our knowledge about the subject, instead of merely elucidating the subject (e.g. 'all bodies have specific gravity'). But not all synthetic judgments give us genuine knowledge. In fact, some synthetic judgments are derived from experience, and, therefore, they are lacking in necessity (reason does not compel their acceptance as it compels the acceptance of a mathematical proposition) and also they are lacking in universality (since one

---

[*]   See: Stephen Gaukroger, *Cartesian Logic: An Essay on Descartes's Conception of Inference*, Oxford: Clarendon Press, 1989.

cannot argue, because some objects of a class have certain qualities, that all have them). Judgments lacking in necessity and universality, namely, a posteriori judgments, do not give us genuine knowledge. If it is to qualify as genuine knowledge, a synthetic judgment must be a priori, i.e. it must be necessary and universal. Synthetic a priori judgments have their source in reason (not in sensation or perception).

Analytic judgments are always a priori, since such judgments are purely explicative and can be deduced from the principle of non-contradiction, without any reference to empirical data. But they do not give us genuine knowledge (since they are tautologies). Synthetic a posteriori judgments add to our knowledge, but the knowledge they yield is uncertain and problematic because it depends on experience. Apodictic certainty is possessed only by synthetic a priori judgments. Thus, Kant studied the following question: how are synthetic a priori judgments possible in mathematics and the foundations of physics, or, in other words, how are pure mathematics and pure physics possible?

For instance, let us consider the case of geometry. Kant argues that there can only be one explanation of our *a priori* knowledge of the properties of space. According to Kant, the spatial properties of the world must be contributed by the knowing subject. In other words, the world *as it is in itself* is not made up of objects arranged in space; it is only the world *as it appears to us* that is spatial, since space is only our way of representing the world to ourselves. According to Kant, space is a form of intuition (i.e. perception). Additionally, following a similar reasoning, Kant argues that time, too, is a form of intuition. Hence, in Kantianism, space and time are only features of the phenomenal world (the world as it appears to us), whereas the noumenal world (the world of things as they are in themselves) is a-spatial and a-temporal.

Furthermore, Kant argues that causal relations have a subjective origin, in the sense that they are projected into the world by the experiencing consciousness. Hence, causation, like time and space, is a feature of the phenomenal world, and not of the world that is external to consciousness. However, for Kant, the forms of intuition are features of our faculty of sensibility (the passive faculty that receives sense-impressions), whereas causation is one of the twelve categories, or 'a priori' concepts, imposed on sense impressions by the understanding (i.e. the active faculty of reason).

Kant finds that there are twelve kinds of pure concepts or categories of the understanding based on reason; these are arranged in four groups of three each as follows: The first group expresses the categories of quantity: totality, plurality, unity. It includes the following judgments: (1) the universal judgment (e.g. all dogs are animals), (2) the particular judgment (e.g. some fruits are sweet), and (3) the singular judgment (e.g. Isaac Newton was a natural scientist). The second group expresses the categories of quality: reality, negation, limitation. It includes the following judgments: (1) the affirmative judgment (e.g. electrical energy is a form of potential energy), (2) the negative judgment (e.g. the intentionality of consciousness is not extended), and (3) the infinite judgment (e.g. the intentionality of consciousness is unextended). The third group expresses the categories of relation: inherence and subsistence (or substance and accident), causality and dependence (or cause and effect), community/reciprocity between the active and the passive. It includes the following judgments: (1) the categorical judgment (e.g. the body is heavy), (2) the hypothetical judgment (e.g. if temperature increases, then entropy increases), and (3) the disjunctive judgment (e.g. energy forms are either potential or kinetic). The fourth group expresses the categories of morality: possibility and impossibility, existence and non-existence, necessity and contingency. It includes the following judgments: (1) the problematical judgment (e.g. this may be hot), (2) the assertory judgment (e.g. this is hot), and (3) the apodictic judgment (e.g. every effect must have a cause). These twelve rules function like a filter between our minds and the external world.

Kant's epistemology is a source of criticism toward the two major paths that modern philosophy has followed, namely, idealism and positivism. According to the terminology of modern philosophy, idealism is a philosophy exclusively founded on the inner experience of consciousness (which was exalted by Descartes), whereas positivism (which is derived from Enlightenment scholars such as Henri de Saint-Simon, Pierre-Simon Laplace, Auguste Comte, etc.) is a philosophy founded exclusively on the following principles: research can be proved only by empirical means (not argumentations), research should be mostly deductive (i.e. deduction is used to develop statements that can be empirically tested), and knowledge should be judged by logic and ideally should be true for every segment of space-time. According to Kant's epistemology, the difficulty of establishing empiricism-positivism is due to the fact that the mind is not a mere *tabula rasa*, which passively receives knowledge of the world through the senses, and the difficulty of establishing rationalism-idealism is due to the fact that logic alone cannot give rise to knowledge because knowledge presupposes both concepts and the empirical data supplied by the senses. Thus, according to Kant, theoretical knowledge (which is characterized by self-sufficiency with respect to the form of its object and, ideally, with respect to the object's existence, too) can only be of the world as it appears, and not of the world as it is in itself.

However, even though Kant argues that we cannot have theoretical knowledge of things-in-themselves, he argues that we can have practical knowledge of them. In the second edition of his first *Critique* (Bix-x), Kant argues that, "so far as reason is to be in these sciences", something within them must be a kind of a priori knowledge, and this a priori knowledge must be related to its object in two ways: either merely to *determine* its object and its concept (which must be given from elsewhere), or also *to make it actual*; the former is "theoretical knowledge of reason", and the latter "practical knowledge of reason". Whereas the goal of theoretical reason is to assess how things are, practical reason decides how things ought to be and what persons should do. However, while practical reason decides what to do, it cannot remake reality in an arbitrary manner; instead, the successful practical agent must take into account truths about the world.

For instance, let us consider free will. When one considers his actions as constituents of the phenomenal world, then he is obliged, endorsing a positivistic standpoint, to regard them as produced by objective deterministic laws, whereas, when he considers those same actions as they are in the noumenal world, he is not so obliged. Thus, according to Kant's philosophy, one can have practical knowledge of that freedom which he should postulate in order to account for his inescapable sense of himself as a responsible moral agent.

Post-Kantian philosophers followed different interpretations of Kantianism. In particular, the fact that Kant's epistemology gives priority to the logical form of experience over the real content of experience* inspired philosophers such as Johann Gottlieb Fichte,

---

* By the term 'schema', Kant means the procedural rule by which a category is associated with a mental image of an object. According to Kant, it is produced by the imagination through the pure form

Friedrich Wilhelm Joseph Schelling and Georg Wilhelm Friedrich Hegel to develop some parts of Kant's teachings in a monistic sense. In particular, Hegel's dialectic is characterized by its identification of the speculative thought process with the process of being. Hegel's logic is a philosophy of being as revealed trough abstract thought. The starting point of Hegel's dialectic is the concept of pure, absolute, indeterminate being, which he conceives as a process, as dynamic. According to Hegel's dialectic, the evolution of this dynamic principle takes place through the following three stages: (i) the stage in which it affirms itself as thesis; (ii) the stage of antithesis (negation, limitation), which is a necessary corollary of the previous stage; (iii) the stage of synthesis (return to itself, union of opposites), which follows necessarily from stages (i) and (ii). In the first stage, absolute being is the pure idea, or the universal reason (the subject-matter of logic); in the second stage (of otherness), absolute being becomes nature (the subject-matter of natural philosophy/science); in the third stage (of return), it is spirit, i.e. the realized absolute idea, the ground of appearance (the subject-matter of the philosophy of spirit, which includes ethics, politics, art and religion).

The dialectic that was formulated by Hegel is both a method of philosophical research and a model of a process according to which reality evolves and tends toward its integration. This dual application of the term dialectic by Hegel has contributed to the ambiguity of the Hegelian term dialectic and of 'Hegelianism' in general, and, additionally, it is responsible for the 'prophetic' mentality (i.e. a tendency to understand dialectic as an oracle) that characterizes Hegel and the philosophers who have been inspired by his dialectic. Thus, for instance, 'scientific materialism' (both 'dialectical materialism' and 'historical materialism*') has not clarified if it is a

---

of time. The category of quantity is expressed in the schema of time-series. The category of quality is expressed in the schema of time-content. The categories of substance, causality, and reciprocal action are expressed in the schema of time-order (permanence, succession, and simultaneity). The categories of possibility, actuality, and necessity are expressed in the schema of time-comprehension.

* Dialectical materialism is the world outlook of Marxism-Leninism, and historical materialism is the extension of the principles of dialectical materialism to the study of social life. Karl Marx followed Hegelianism in a reversed manner: in the context of Hegel's philosophy, the process of thinking, under the name of 'the Idea', is the creator of the real world, whereas, in the context of Marx's philosophy, the material world takes primacy over the forms of thought (Karl Marx, Second German Edition of Volume I of *The Capital*). Marx formulated his materialist conception of history in the 1859 preface to his book *A Contribution to the Critique of Political Economy*, Moscow: Progress Publishers, 1977.

general philosophical method or if it refers to particular objective processes that it tries to interpret. Similarly, the various forms of positivism, and especially Comte's positivism, are problematic because, even though they attempt to follow only an 'a posteriori' method, they make the mistake of depending for the development of their philosophical work on an 'a priori' model of human progress ("the law of the three stages"*), which is derived from the teachings of the 13th century scholar Gerardo di Borgo San Donnino. Therefore, Comte's positivism managed to influence epistemology, but it failed to stand as a general method of philosophical work (arguably, being able to offer only a general method of mysticism). In fact, Comte attempted to transform 'positive science' into a form of 'positive religion', a non-theistic religion of man and society, with its own calendar of saints (such as Adam Smith, Frederick the Great, Dante, Shakespeare, etc.).

Positivism gave birth to Neopositivism, which was nurtured by the thought of the philosophers who represented the so-called "Vienna Circle". The "Vienna Circle" was an association of philosophers gathered around the University of Vienna in 1922, chaired by Moritz Schlick; among its members were Gustav Bergman, Rudolf Carnap, Herbert Feigl, Richard von Mises, Otto Neurath, Friedrich Waismann, etc.

The Vienna Circle Manifesto states that its scientific world-conception is based on empiricism-positivism (i.e. the thesis that statements are cognitively meaningful only if they can be falsified or verified by experience) and on the method of logical analysis. Moreover, Otto Neurath, in his book *Physicalism*, delineated the general principles of positivism and its conceptual bases as follows: (i) the construction of a universal system that would comprehend all of the knowledge furnished by the different fields of science (this principle is known as the "unity of science[†]"); (ii) the rejection of metaphysics, i.e. he characterized all propositions not translatable

---

* According to the law of the three stages, in its development, humanity passes through three successive stages: the theological (during this phase, man believed whatever he was taught by tradition, and fetishism played a significant role), the metaphysical (it was a transitory phase that involved the justification of universal rights on the basis of the sacred, and, during this phase, people started reasoning and questioning although no solid evidence was laid), and the positive (the phase of questioning authority and religion and of following science). See: Mike Gane, *Auguste Comte*, London: Routledge, 2006.

† See: Rudolf Carnap, *The Unity of Science*, London: Kegan Paul, Trench, Teubner and Co., 1932/1934.

into verifiable scientific sentences as cognitively insignificant propositions[*].

The Vienna Circle Manifesto acknowledged the influence of the analytic philosophy of Ludwig Wittgenstein[†] on the philosophical program of Neopositivism. Indeed, analytic philosophy helped philosophers develop useful partial methods that allow them to clarify the proper use of particular (usually verbal) expressions. In other words, analytic philosophy can help philosophers overcome the confusion that is caused by imperfect and hence misleading analogies between particular uses of a given expression and other expressions. On the other hand, analytic philosophy runs the risk of repeating, in a more technical manner, the unsuccessful attempt by Kant to define the presuppositions of the presuppositions of philosophy, which can continue forever (ad infinitum).

Henri Bergson[‡] has criticized analysis as follows: analysis is always analysis ad infinitum and can never reach the absolute. According to Bergson, whenever philosophers follow the method of analysis, they divide the object of analysis according to the viewpoint that they have personally chosen, and then they translate the divided fragments into symbols whereby and wherein a specter of the original object of analysis can be reconstructed. But, Bergson continues, these symbols distort the corresponding parts of the original object of analysis, since they are intellectual abstractions, and, therefore, they ignore the original object's uniqueness and otherness.

The ideal of positivism was the total formalization of knowledge. Formal systems emphasize that no step of reasoning can be taken without a reference to an exactly formulated list of axioms and rules of inference (even the most obvious logical statements, such as 'if A implies B, and B implies C, then A implies C', must be either formulated in the list of axioms and rules explicitly, or deduced from it). In general, a theory T is called a 'formal theory' if and only if there is an algorithm that allows us to decide whether a given text is a correct proof in terms of the principles of T, or not. In other words,

---

[*] See: K.H. Müller, "Neurath's Theory of Pictorial-Statistical Representation", in T.E. Uebel (ed.), *Rediscovering the Forgotten Vienna Circle*, Dordrecht: Kluwer, 1991.

[†] See: Ned Block (ed.), *Perspectives on the Philosophy of Wittgenstein*, Oxford: Blackwell, 1981.

[‡] Henri Bergson, *The Creative Mind: An Introduction to Metaphysics*, trans. M.L. Andison, New York: Carol Publishing Group, 1992 (originally published in 1946).

if one is going to publish a 'mathematical text' calling it 'a proof of a theorem in theory T', then we must be able to decide mechanically whether the given text is really a correct proof according to the standards of proving accepted in theory T (i.e. according to the axioms and the rules of inference of the theory T). The Austrian mathematician and logician Kurt Gödel, who participated in the Vienna Circle from 1926 until 1928, proved that these hopes were naïve.

Gödel's incompleteness theorem of 1931 proved that, within any logically consistent system for mathematics, there will be some statements about numbers that are true but that can never be proved. He began with the statement 'this statement cannot be proved' (a version of the ancient "liar paradox"*). If the statement is false, then that means that the statement can be proved, suggesting that it is actually true, thus generating a contradiction. Then Gödel translated the previous statement into 'symbolic logic', using a code based on prime numbers (strings of prime numbers play the roles of natural numbers, operators, grammatical rules and all the other requirements of a formal language). Like its natural language equivalent, the resulting mathematical statement is true[†] but unprovable, i.e. it remains necessarily undecidable. Kleene has summarized and explained the results of Gödel's research work as follows: no effectively generated theory capable of expressing elementary arithmetic can be proved to be both consistent and complete; in other words, any consistent, effectively generated formal theory that proves certain basic arithmetic truths contains an arithmetic statement that is true but not provable in the theory[‡].

Gödel's proof that one cannot establish the consistency of any formalization of elementary number theory leads to the conclusions that logic is not a self-sufficient system and that the total formalization

---

* The "liar paradox" was developed by Epimenides, a 6th century B.C. Greek philosopher. Its most basic version is: 'This sentence is false'. The paradox of it is that, if it is true, it therefore must be false, and, if it is false, its falsehood affirms its truth.

† The word 'true' is used disquotationally here: the Gödel sentence is true in this sense because it asserts its own unprovability and it is indeed unprovable. According to the 'disquotational theory of truth', asserting that a statement is true is completely equivalent to asserting the statement itself (see: Craig Smoryński, "The Incompleteness Theorems", in J. Barwise (ed.), *Handbook of Mathematical Logic*, Amsterdam: North-Holland, 1982).

‡ S.C. Kleene, *Mathematical Logic*, London: Dover, 2002, p. 250.

of knowledge is impossible, and it corroborates L.E.J. Brouwer's mathematical philosophy of intuitionism. Rolin Wavre, a noted modern logician, philosopher and disciple of Brouwer, delineates the intuitionist school of mathematics by arguing that traditional logic can accomplish nothing more than conforming discourse to rules, but language itself is incapable of providing scientists with the genuine understanding of the facts of contemporary mathematics[*]. In other words, the truth of contemporary mathematics is a meta-linguistic question. On the other hand, mathematical intuition guarantees the autonomy of mathematics as an object of science.

Pragmatism and Bergsonism tried to formulate new, more successful, 'a posteriori' philosophical methods, but they encountered difficulties in applying their 'a posteriori' methods, too. William James, the major representative of pragmatism, agued that truth, namely, the agreement between reality and its image within consciousness, is not a given, but it is "made"[†] in the course of human experience due to the activity of consciousness, so that consciousness can induce change in reality due to the reference. This perception is shared by all philosophies of action. For instance, let us recall Marx's eleventh thesis on Feuerbach: "Philosophers have hitherto only interpreted the world in various ways; the point is to change it". Pragmatism has thrown light on particular psychological aspects of the philosophical work, but it cannot stand as a general 'a posteriori' method. If we follow pragmatism as a general 'a posteriori' method, then, ultimately, philosophy ceases to be a scientific activity and a purpose itself, and it becomes self-contradictory and self-defeating, since, due to pragmatism, the adoption of the conclusions of philosophy lacks logical and scientific justification, and, therefore, the conclusions of philosophy become meaningless. Furthermore, just as relativism leads to a contradiction by adhering to at least one absolute proposition (that all propositions are relative), so too pragmatism is pragmatically self-defeating, because, due to its dependence on and embracing of the established cultural practices and mentalities in each segment of space-time, pragmatism cannot operate as a progressive force.

---

[*]   Rolin Wavre, "Is There a Crisis in Mathematics?", *American Mathematical Monthly*, Vol. 41, October 1934, pp. 48ff.

[†]   William James, *Pragmatism*, Cambridge, MA: Harvard University Press, 1979 (originally published in 1907), p. 104.

The philosophy of Bergson, which exerted great influence on the development of pragmatism, has to overcome its own problems. According to Bergson, the only reality is duration, in which there is no juxtaposition of events, and, hence, there is no mechanistic causality. Thus, for Bergson, duration offers the experience of freedom. Bergson argues that duration can be conceived through intuition. Intuition, in Bergson's sense, is an 'a posteriori' method, but it has only one difference from the 'a priori' methods: its object, i.e. the inner experience, is identified with consciousness itself. Here we can see that Bergson's method of intuition is a form of reversed Cartesianism: Bergson formulates his anti-rationalist and anti-Cartesian theses in a rationalistic and Cartesian manner. This is the primary antinomy of Bergsonism.

Bergson's most important contribution to philosophy is his argument that the real object of philosophy transcends comprehensive analytic knowledge and that, in contrast with Kant's argument for the impossibility of the knowledge of noumena, this object is accessible to consciousness. In his book *The Creative Mind*, Bergson argues that philosophy does not consist in choosing between concepts and in taking sides, since these antinomies of concepts and positions result from the habitual way our intelligence works[*]. Endorsing a pragmatic approach to human intelligence, Bergson argues that the habitual way our intelligence works is guided by needs, and, therefore, the knowledge it gathers is relative since it is not disinterested. In the fourth chapter to *Matter and Memory*, Bergson contrasts his method of intuition to habitual intelligence. Habitual intelligence gathers knowledge through what Bergson calls "analysis", that is, the dividing of things according to perspectives taken, and comprehensive analytic knowledge then consists in re-composition of a thing by means of synthesizing the perspectives. But, even though this synthesis helps us satisfy needs, it never gives us the thing itself; it only gives us a concept of things. In other words, according to the habitual working of intelligence, synthesis is merely a development of analysis. On the other hand, Bergson's method of intuition reverses the habitual working of intelligence. In his book *The Creative Mind*, Bergson calls intuition "sympathy"[†], and, in *Time and Free Will*, Bergson explains that sympathy consists in

---

[*]   Bergson, *The Creative Mind*, pp. 157-176.

[†]   Ibid, p. 159.

putting ourselves in the place of others*. In other words, Bergsonian intuition consists in entering into the being rather than going around it from the outside. It is exactly this 'entering into', that, according to Bergson, gives us absolute knowledge.

There are significant similarities between Bergson's intuitive 'a posteriori' method and Husserl's phenomenological 'a posteriori' method. The concept of phenomenology was first used by Hegel, and, in that case, it consisted in a method of conceiving the itinerary of the spirit. For Edmund Husserl†, whose philosophical starting point is a form of Cartesianism combined with scholastic views, phenomenology is a method according to which the researcher focuses on the essential structures that allow the objects that are taken for granted in the "natural attitude" (which is characteristic of both our everyday life and ordinary science) to "constitute themselves" in consciousness.

Phenomenology is characterized by subjectivism in the sense that phenomenological inquiries are initially directed, in Cartesian fashion, toward consciousness and its presentations. On the other hand, phenomenology is not characterized by any psychological or mentalistic forms of subjectivism, since the subject-matter of phenomenology is not the realm of psychological ideas affirmed by empiricism but rather the ideal meanings and universal relations with which consciousness is confronted in its experience. Husserl explicitly opposed the attempts made by Carl Stumpf and Theodor Lipps to reduce logic to psychology. Husserl's phenomenology does not preclude legitimate psychological investigation, and its opposition to psychologism is a polemic only against the presumptuous claims of psychology to supersede logic and phenomenology.

The phenomenological method comes from a position prior to reflexive thought, called pre-reflexive thought, which consists of a turn to the very things. At that moment, the phenomenologist holds a phenomenological stance, which enables him to keep himself open enough to live that experience in its wholeness, preventing any

---

* Henri Bergson, *Time and Free Will: An Essay on the Immediate Data of Consciousness*, tr., F.L. Pogson, Montana: Kessinger Publishing Company, 1910.

† See: Herbert Spiegelberg, *The Phenomenological Movement*, 3rd revised and enlarged edition, The Hague: Nijhoff, 1982; Elisabeth Ströker, *Husserl's Transcendental Phenomenology*, Stanford: Stanford University Press, 1993.

judgment from interfering with his openness to the description. The phenomenologist is not concerned with the particular elements of the object under investigation, but with the given object's ideal essence, which is hidden by and shines through the particulars. Husserl used the Greek term "epoché" (suspension of judgment) to refer to the purification of experience of its factuality. The phenomenological method involves an initial suspension of judgment regarding the factuality (whether physical or psychical) of the presentations of consciousness. Epoché, i.e. the phenomenological bracketing of the factual aspects of our experiences, is a methodological attitude that allows consciousness to investigate the essential constitution of experience. For instance, pure mathematics systematically brackets the factual aspects of our experience of space and quantity and focuses attention on ideal relations*. In his preface to *Ideas Pertaining to a Pure Phenomenology — First Book: General Introduction to a Pure Phenomenology*, Husserl argues that phenomenology, like mathematics, is "the science of pure possibilities", which "must everywhere precede the science of real facts". By bracketing factuality, phenomenology exerted important influence on existentialism, and, in fact, it became the method of existentialism.

The phenomenologist is focused on the ideal entities with which he is confronted after he has bracketed factuality. Husserl argues that these ideal objects are not Platonic universals, and he refuses to assign to them any ontological status beyond the mere fact that they are envisaged. Like Alexius Meinong, Husserl invokes the theory of intentionality in his interpretation of the objects of phenomenological inquiry. Moreover, Husserl distinguishes between intentional and non-intentional units of consciousness: the former have intentional content (they always represent something as something), whereas the latter have not (e.g. pain). Thus, according to phenomenology, intentionality is an intrinsic trait of the subjective processes of consciousness whereby the subjective processes of consciousness refer to objects. The objects of phenomenology are intentional objects. The important thing for phenomenology is not the ontological status of ideal objects but the fact that such objects may be investigated in their interrelations and that the conclusions of such descriptive analysis are coercive and communicable. Then ideal objects possess

---

* See: Stefania Centrone, *Logic and Philosophy of Mathematics in the Early Husserl*, Dordrecht: Springer, 2010.

the only kind of objectivity that is necessary or desirable in order for the phenomenologist to gather genuine knowledge.

The next major step in the development of the phenomenological method took place when it was applied in the investigation of those elements of reality whose knowledge is prior to the knowledge of the essence of reality, i.e. when it was applied in the investigation of the elements that constitute the structure of reality. By the term 'structure', we mean an intimate reality that is organized and re-organized by itself and that is determined by its own order, which also constitutes the core of the given structure. The method of structuralism[*] is the final stage of phenomenology's attempt to cope with the problems that emerge from the philosophical investigation of the intimate meaning of reality. Closely related to the project of investigating the intimate meaning of reality is Gadamer's method of hermeneutics, which is an attempt to clarify the presuppositions of understanding[†]. In his book *Truth and Method*, Hans-Georg Gadamer argued that people have a "historically effected consciousness", that they are embedded in the particular history and culture that shaped them, and, therefore, understanding is always interpretation. In particular, understanding means to use one's own preconceptions so that the meaning of the object can really be made to speak to him[‡]. Furthermore, according to Gadamer, 'understanding' is not so much an action of one's subjectivity, but mainly it is the placing of oneself within a process of tradition, in which past and present are fused[§].

From the synthesis between structuralism and hermeneutics follows the philosophical method that invokes the kairicity of consciousness on the basis of which we can interpret both ontological reality and the intentionality of consciousness, which imposes its

---

[*] The term 'structuralism' itself appeared in the works of French anthropologist Claude Lévi-Strauss (Claude Lévi-Strauss, *Structural Anthropology*, trans. C. Jacobson, New York: Basic Books, 1963). Lévi-Strauss's structural analysis of myth is based on his structural theory of human mental processes: on one hand, mythical stories are fantastic and unpredictable, i.e. the content of myth seems completely arbitrary, but, on the other hand, the myths of different cultures are surprisingly similar. Thus, Lévi-Strauss proposed that universal laws must govern mythical thought and resolve this seeming paradox, producing similar myths in different cultures. In other words, according to Lévi-Strauss, even though each myth may seem unique, it is just one particular instance of a universal law of human thought (Lévi-Strauss, *The Raw and the Cooked*).

[†] H.G. Gadamer, *Truth and Method*, London: Sheed and Ward, 1975, p. 263.

[‡] Ibid, p. 358.

[§] Ibid, p. 258.

own structures on ontological reality in order to utilize ontological reality. The potential and the advantages of the method of kairicity become clear when we realize that the method of kairicity marks a shift from static descriptions of the actions of consciousness to the dynamic imposition of the intentionality of consciousness upon ontological reality. Furthermore, the method of kairicity, which I defend in this book, is not susceptible to the contradictions that, as I mentioned earlier in this section, characterize the prophetic type of theories that are rooted in the Hegelian dialectic, because the intention of the method of kairicity is to gather knowledge about consciousness and ontological reality simultaneously instead of substituting one for the other. As a criterion of reality and action, kairicity stems from consciousness, but, since it is not intended to offer philosophical 'legitimacy' to arbitrary idealistic action, it is activated only when it is possible to be applied on objective reality. Additionally, the method of kairicity is based on the ontological position that objective reality is activated for consciousness when consciousness assigns meaning and significance to objective reality. Even though reality is multidimensional, it becomes significant for consciousness only when it becomes 'updated' in relation to the intentionality of consciousness. Therefore, the knowledge of reality that is based on the method of kairicity is in agreement with both the nature of consciousness and the nature of reality.

TIPHARETH: KAIRICITY

Bergson managed to transcend the antithesis between realism and idealism by showing that the antithesis between consciousness and reality is reducible to the antithesis between intuition and intellect. According to Bergson, intuition and intellect may be combined to produce a dynamic knowledge of reality. In particular, Bergson argues that real time cannot be analyzed mathematically, since the measurement of time consists in an attempt to break or disrupt time. In other words, in order to try to understand the flow of time, the intellect forms concepts of time as consisting of defined moments or intervals, and, therefore, the attempt to intellectualize the experience of duration reduces to a falsification of this experience. The intellectual representation of time is related to space because it is conceptualized as an ordered arrangement of defined events, whereas the flow of real time can only be known by intuition. Furthermore, according

117

to Bergson, scientific principles are intellectual, and metaphysical principles are intuitive. However, Bergson argues that science and metaphysics can be combined to produce knowledge that is both intellectual and intuitive, and it is exactly this kind of knowledge that can unify divergent perceptions of reality.

Like Bergsonism, Hegelianism is another attempt to transcend the antithesis between realism and idealism. Even though, as I mentioned in previous sections, Hegel's attempt to transcend the antithesis between realism and idealism is problematic, it had significant impact on existentialism and structuralism. Existentialism is based on the thesis that consciousness attributes meaning to the reality of the world. Structuralism corroborates Gaston Bachelard's argument that there is a dynamic continuity between knowing consciousness and known object[*].

The antithesis between realism and idealism is not only a major problem in the history of philosophy, but it is also a major problem in the history of science. Apart from the real objects of which the natural scientist has direct knowledge, there are (for, instance, at sub-atomic level) behaviors that oblige modern physics to use concepts that are formulated in a subjective manner. Such terms as ions, photons, gravitons, etc. do not correspond to any indisputable form of reality; they exist within a system of nominalistic character and they are used for the formulation of hypothetical explanations of possibilities that underpin phenomena and behaviors. Niels Bohr, who made foundational contributions to understanding atomic structure and quantum mechanics, is reported to have said to Werner Heisenberg, who was another great pioneer of quantum physics: in the field of atomic and sub-atomic physics, "language can be used only as in poetry", since, like poets, physicists are not concerned so much with the description of facts as with the creation of images[†]. Moreover, in the same spirit, Alfred Whitehead, who co-authored the epochal *Principia Mathematica* with B. Russell, has argued that nature is always in a state of becoming and that the reality of the natural world is the natural becoming itself[‡].

Moreover, the synthesis between realism and idealism has been promoted by cybernetics. The term cybernetics comes from a Greek

[*]   See: Mary Tiles, *Bachelard: Science and Objectivity*, Cambridge: Cambridge University Press, 1984.

[†]   Quoted in: Jacob Bronowski, *The Ascent of Man*, Boston: Little, 1974, p. 340.

[‡]   Alfred Whitehead, *Science and the Modern World*, New York: Macmillan, 1944, p. 106.

word meaning 'the art of steering', and it is about having a goal and taking action to achieve that goal. Cybernetics as a concept in society has been used by Plato in order to refer to government. Norbert Wiener, a pioneering Harvard University mathematician, coined the term cybernetics around 1948 in order to denote the study of "teleological mechanisms". In general, by the term cybernetics, we refer to the interdisciplinary study of the structure of regulatory systems.

Within the framework of cybernetics, epistemologists focus on the observer in addition to what is observed. Lynn Segal[*] and Ernst von Glasersfeld[†] have explained that, according to modern cybernetics, scientific laws should not be considered as discoveries, as one, for instance, might discover an island in an ocean, but they should be considered as inventions by which scientists explain regularities in their experiences. In addition, they have pointed out that, according to modern cybernetics, persons interact with reality, and hence they construct and reconstruct reality.

In general, by the term 'truth', we mean the set of all presuppositions that constitute the terms under which the knowledge of reality (i.e. its representation in consciousness) is in agreement with the nature of reality, i.e. it corresponds to the presence of reality. Even though the history of philosophy and the history of science indicate that both realism and idealism have definitely failed to stand as general theories of truth, some aspects of realism as well as some aspects of idealism tend to approach truth. The endorsement of realistic views is encouraged and philosophically 'legitimized' by the awareness that the world is different from consciousness. In fact, if the world were not different from consciousness, then the latter would not try to know the world. In other words, if the world did not differ from consciousness, then the knowledge of the world would be exhausted in the self-knowledge of the conscious mind. On the other hand, the endorsement of idealistic views is encouraged and philosophically 'legitimized' by the awareness that, from a certain viewpoint, the structure of the world is not fundamentally different from the structure of consciousness. In fact, if the structure of the world were absolutely different from the structure of consciousness, then it would be absolutely impossible for consciousness to obtain

---

[*]   Lynn Segal, *The Dream of Reality*, New York: Norton, 1986

[†]   Ernst von Glasersfeld, *The Construction of Knowledge*, Salinas, CA: Intersystems, 1987.

even partial knowledge of the world. Therefore, the structure of the world and the structure of consciousness are not *identical* to each other, but they are *united* together. Reality consists of both the world and the conscious mind, which is consciousness of the world and consciousness of self. The reality of the world is different from the reality of consciousness only with respect to the degree of their integration and perfection.

The continuity between the reality of the world and the reality of consciousness is experienced by consciousness as a subjective energy, and its consequences are objectivated through the creative action of consciousness. Within this framework, the purpose of kairology is to find the 'kairic points' of reality, namely, those points which are decisively important for the evaluation and the utilization of the reality of the world and of the reality of consciousness by consciousness.

If existence means duration, then the goal of the consciousness of existence is the preservation of the existence of a given being under the best possible terms. Hence, the intentionality of consciousness operates as an impulse to participate in the world (since consciousness assimilates the world) and as pure self-knowledge. These functions take place at three different levels, namely: instinct, experience and reason.

At the level of instinct, everything shows that the level of conscious activity is minimal. In fact, at this level, instinctive forces dominate or ignore every kind of conscious activity. At the level of instinct, the two basic instincts, namely, those of survival and reproduction, dominate existence, and, in fact, they are identified with existence. Instinct is a highly condensed 'logical' behavior whose correctness has been verified by the practice of an unlimited number of generations, and which reflects the 'logic' of organic nature. Instinctive activity is characterized by a high level of assurance due to the accumulation of unlimited experiences by the species. In fact, instinctive activity is an *a priori* integral procedure whose purpose is always to be confirmed.

All problems or difficulties that instinctive activity may encounter are related to the manner in which existence adapts to given conditions. In this case, adaptation takes place according to the method of 'trial and error'. Jean Piaget, the pre-eminent developmental psychologist of the twentieth century, has pointed out that, through trial and error experimentation by handling objects, the concept that the external world is not part of the self or an extension manifests.

At the level of experience, the intentionality of consciousness is expressed through the operation of the senses. The senses are oriented toward the external world, to which they connect existence. Experience is about the person finding himself in some situation, and being aware of it. In other words, an experience is an event participated in or lived through. The early use of the word experience was *'knowledge* gained by repeated trials'. And that it comes from Latin *experiri*, which means to try, or to test. The word is composed from *ex* ('out of') + *peritus* ('tested'/ 'from trial'). At the level of experience, the level of conscious activity is higher than at the level of instinct, but consciousness is rather pathetic; for, according to the empiricist philosophers, consciousness is originally a "tabula rasa", i.e. blank slate, on which experience 'writes', thus filling the mind with ideas, and only at a second stage consciousness recalls those ideas that seem useful to it in order to act on various occasions. However, both Kant and Gestalt Psychology have pointed out that the conscious mind plays a much more active role in perception than the one thought by empiricists.

Gestalt Psychology[*] was founded by Max Wertheimer (1880—1943). Wertheimer noted that we perceive motion where there is nothing more than a rapid sequence of individual sensory events. This argument is based on observations he made with his stroboscope at the Frankfurt train station and on additional observations he made in his laboratory when he experimented with lights flashing in rapid succession (like the Christmas lights that appear to course around the tree, or the fancy neon signs in Las Vegas that seem to move). Wertheimer called this effect "apparent motion", and it is actually the basic principle of motion pictures. According to Wertheimer, apparent motion proves that people don't respond to isolated segments of sensation but to the whole (*Gestalt*) of the situation.

At the level of reason, reason plays an active role. By the term 'reason', Kant and his followers, mean a pre-existent (*a priori*) structure within the framework of which there are various functions of categories, which, when they are adequately activated, can connect isolated segments of sensation (i.e. empirical data) into a whole, thus allowing the formulation of synthetic statements

---

[*] See: Wolfgang Köhler, *Gestalt Psychology*, New York: Liveright, 1992.

and leading to a creative transcendence of the level of experience. Following Kant's philosophical legacy, Gestalt psychologists have shown, through various experiments, that the conscious mind does not respond to isolated segments of sensation but to the whole (*Gestalt*) of the situation and have argued that, in perception, there are many organizing principles called Gestalt laws. Examples of such laws are the following: the law of closure: if something is missing in an otherwise complete figure, we will tend to add it (e.g. a triangle with a small part of its edge missing, will still be seen as a triangle, and also we shall 'close' the gap); the law of similarity: we shall tend to group similar items together, to see them as forming a whole (*Gestalt*), within a larger form; the law of proximity: things that are close together are seen as belonging together. Thus, the conscious mind perceives and thinks in nonlinear ways and it actively influences perception. Furthermore, Gestalt Psychology has shown that, in perception, the method of trial and error coexists with intuition. Finally, in every operationally significant discussion about reason and rational knowledge, one should always keep in mind the following two remarks: (i) as I argued in Chapter 3, 'reason' should not be identified with 'logic' (since, according to the classical Greek conception of reason, logic and experience may be combined to produce knowledge based on the knower's spiritual participation in the idea of the object of knowledge); (ii) as I mentioned earlier in this chapter, Bergson has pointed out that intuition and intellect may be combined to produce a dynamic knowledge of reality.

By now, I have already explained the unity between the structure of the world and the structure of consciousness. As a result of the unity between the structure of the world and the structure of consciousness, the correspondence between reality and consciousness takes a new form, which is different from the one that has been proposed by Aristotle and Thomas Aquinas. In the philosophical systems of Aristotle and Thomas Aquinas, the correspondence between reality and consciousness assigns a pathetic role to consciousness. Within the framework of Aristotle's and Aquinas' correspondence theory of truth, the action of external objects on consciousness provides consciousness with the 'raw material' of knowledge that will be elaborated by the higher faculties of consciousness into conceptual knowledge. On the other hand, the unity between the structure of the world and the structure of consciousness implies that the correspondence between reality and consciousness is not static (as in Aristotelianism and in Thomism) but dynamic, and, furthermore, consciousness is not the field on which external objects act, but consciousness exerts its intentional influence on reality. The imposition of intentional consciousness on reality shows the latter's submissiveness to man.

Truth is created by the contact between consciousness and reality. Truth is the consequence of the contact between consciousness and reality, and it implies the ontological autonomy of consciousness and the possibility of the reconstruction and the utilization of reality by the intentionality of consciousness. However, the reconstruction and the utilization of reality by the intentionality of consciousness are not the outcome of arbitrary idealistic action, but they are the outcome of kairic action.

By the term 'kairic action', I mean that the human being uses its reason in order to improve its existential conditions in the world. In practice, the kairic activity of the human being consists in the following four-fold dialectical process:

- first, consciousness aims at acting on the reality of the world in order to transcend the established state of the world and improve the conditions under which existence is confirmed;

- second, consciousness aims at acting on the reality of the world in such a manner that it will not cause uncontrolled turbulence, which could ultimately put the continuity of existence in danger;

- third, when the turbulence that is caused by the action of consciousness on the world tends to get out of control, then consciousness tries to reduce the negative effects of its action by taking new action that balances its previous action, thus averting both the total elimination of the previous state of the world and the emergence of a totally unknown new order of things;

- fourth, the action of consciousness on the reality of the world aims at forming the necessary conditions that will allow consciousness to continue acting on the reality of the world in the future.

The four-fold dialectic of kairicity, which I have just delineated, is completely opposite to every fatalistic and mechanistic approach to human life and justice, such as the principle of Karma, which is the most characteristic example of the fatalistic and mechanistic attitudes that underpin the major Asian spiritual traditions. Moreover, whereas the traditional doctrine of Karma (known as Svakarmavada, i.e. individual Karma theory) does not take into account the effects of the deeds and influences of others on the individual's fate, other than the individual's own merits and demerits, the four-fold dialectic of kairicity takes into account the entire spectrum of social dynamics and thus protects man against pathological introversion and narrow-minded individualism.

From the viewpoint of the kairic action of consciousness, history is the fullest expression of man's potential. In fact, humanity tries to intensify the confirmation of its presence in the world by becoming more and more aware of its presence in the world. However, due to the kairic action of consciousness, the continuity of historical becoming is not completely substituted by the discontinuity that is caused by the action of consciousness on the world; the continuity of historical becoming is reconstructed by the imposition of the intentionality of consciousness on time. As a conclusion, instead of being defeated in his struggle against a necessary historical becoming, man overcomes natural necessity due to his freedom, which allows him, through kairic activity, to reconstruct the world.

YESOD: CONSCIOUSNESS

The analysis of the Kairological Qabalah's Tree of Life makes clear that consciousness is not merely a framework within which the accumulation of experiences takes place, but it is an alive and structured presence that has all the characteristics of a being, namely: substance, structure, temporal and spatial activity. Moreover, consciousness is continuously restructured, determining the laws of its activity, of its intentionality and of its integration in the world. Thus, consciousness is the fullest expression of the reality of the human being.

MALKUTH: BRAIN

John Searle has argued that consciousness is a biological

characteristic of human and certain animal brains, but conscious mental states and processes have a peculiar characteristic that is not possessed by other natural phenomena, namely, subjectivity. According to Searle, due to subjectivity, the conventional methods of biological and psychological research cannot be applied in the study of consciousness[*]. Thus, Searle argues that consciousness is a higher state of the brain, in the sense that consciousness is founded on the brain, but it transcends the brain.

The existence of values[†] causes the consciousness of existence, in the sense that, through values and due to values, the human being (as opposed to every other biological being) is not necessarily determined by the 'physical objectivity', but it can exist in a manner that implies that the human being can control and change the physical conditions of its existence, instead of being pathetically controlled by them. It goes without saying that the existence of the human being takes place in the physical realm (through the natural functions of the nervous system). But the fact that the human being is capable of decisively intervening in the fields of its natural energies and impulses implies that the thing that substantiates the personal mode of existence of the human being is not nature itself but it is an 'existential otherness' toward the common nature of the human beings, and this existential otherness makes the human subject a unique existence. This existential otherness and this freedom from nature are the core of the personal substance of the human subject.

In Christianity, the writings of the Greek Church Fathers have always stressed the unity of body and soul. With respect to this issue, Jean-Claude Larchet has pointed out that the Greek Church Fathers emphasize a balance in understanding the constitution of the human being, in the sense that, according to the Greek Patristic thought, the two substances of the human being (i.e. body and soul) are "distinct without being separated and united without being confused"[‡]. For instance, according to Symeon the New Theologian[§], the soul is

---

[*]   John Searle, *The Rediscovery of the Mind*, Cambridge, Mass.: MIT Press, 1992, pp. 90, 93.

[†]   According to R. Polin, by the term value, we mean "the centre of interest" toward which consciousness is directed whenever it is engaged in a practical activity (see: J.J. Kockelmans (ed.), *Contemporary European Ethics*, New York: Anchor Books, 1972).

[‡]   J. C. Larchet, *Thérapeutique des Maladies Mentales: L' Expérience de l' Orient Chrétien des Premiers Siècles*, Paris: Les Éditions du Cerf, 1992, p.29.

[§]   Symeon the New Theologian (949—1022 A.D.) was a Byzantine Christian monk and poet who is

united with the body in a fusion without admixture or confusion.

Furthermore, paraphrasing Maximus the Confessor, Larchet has written that every action and every movement of the human being is simultaneously an act of his body and his soul*, i.e. a coincidence of action and movement, as Maximus the Confessor has stated elsewhere, which is ideally achieved by "one who brings the body into harmony with the soul [ho harmosamenos to soma pros ten psychen]"†.

The Greek Church Fathers teach that, even though, as a result of the Fall of Man, which is mentioned in the book of *Genesis*, humankind and the world were reduced in a condition of existence marked by illness and imperfection, human beings were still subject to God's grace and were not wholly separated from Him. In other words, man was never deprived of the potential for perfection. This understanding of man's Fall runs contrary to any idea of "original sin", the total deprivation of human nature after the Fall. Timothy Ware (Bishop Kallistos of Diokleia) has explained that, even before the Fall, humans were *potentially* (not *actually*) perfect, in the sense that the Forebears of humanity were endowed with the image of God from the start, i.e. with a *potential perfection*, and that "they were called to acquire the likeness [of God]", i.e. *actual perfection*, by their own efforts combined with God's grace‡. This striving for perfection was not eliminated by sin, but, rather, it emerged as something even more significant in man's consciousness, as man had deviated from the path toward ensured perfection established by God.

For the Greek Church Fathers, 'Paradise' is a symbolic image of that state of existence in which the human mind is united with the source of the meaning of life, namely it is firmly oriented toward the Divine Archetype§. Thus, 'life in Paradise' does not signify a static condition of life, but it signifies a dynamic course toward man's

---

venerated as a saint in Eastern Orthodox Church.

* J. C. Larchet, *La Divinisation de l' Homme Selon Saint Maxime le Confesseur*, Paris: Éditions du Cerf, 1996, p.30.

† St. Maximus the Confessor, "Peri Theologias kai tes Ensarkou Oikonomias tou Hyiou tou Theou, Pros Thalassion" (Regarding theology and the incarnate oeconomy of the Son of God, to Thalassios), in *Philokalia ton Hieron Neptikon* (Philokalia of the Sacred Neptic Fathers — hereafter, *Philokalia*), Athens: Ekdotikos Oikos "Aster", 1975, Vol. 2, p.90.

‡ Timothy Ware, *The Orthodox Church*, second edition, London and N.Y.: Penguin Books, 1993, p. 219.

§ The Bible contains many anthropomorphic expressions, and the Greek Church Fathers teach that these anthropomorphic expressions should not be taken literally, but symbolically.

existential perfection. In Paradise, the Forebears of humanity were not endowed from the start with all possible wisdom and knowledge, i.e. their perfection was not a realized one but a potential one. Thus, their Fall is not a penalty imposed on them by God according to some legalistic formula, but it is the result of their failure to realize their potential. As Protopresbyter John S. Romanides[*] has pointed out, drawing on the theology of Theophilus of Antioch[†] and Irenaeus of Lyons[‡], the destiny of man was for him to progress toward perfection and, more specifically, toward divinization, and not to remain in his original state, not because he was made flawed in nature and morally deficient, but because moral perfection presupposes total freedom[§].

Thus, in contrast with various legalistic versions of Christianity that developed in the context of medieval Western theology, and also in contrast with the grotesque descriptions of afterlife by various Asian schools of mystical belief, the Greek Church Fathers teach that human nature was never totally deprived of God's grace after the Fall, and, moreover, that Christian soteriology has nothing to do with any legalistic notion of man's need to justify his sin before a wrathful, judgemental Creator.

As it has been pointed out by Protopresbyter John S. Romanides, according to the first theologians of the Church who dealt with the subject of the Fall of Man, the Fall was not a judicial matter but the failure of man to attain perfection and particularly divinization, because man 'missed the mark', i.e. the ultimate aim of existence, and he fell into the hands of the archon of death (Satan)[¶]. From this viewpoint, 'Satan' is simply the archetype of existential failure, and, of course, contrary to many Evangelicals' and Jesuits' views, Satan should never be interpreted as God's 'prosecuting attorney'.

---

[*] Protopresbyter John S. Romanides was Professor of Dogmatic Theology at the University of Thessaloniki, Greece, from 1968 until 1982 and, for long time, represented the Greek Orthodox Church to the World Council of Churches.

[†] Theophilus of Antioch was a 2nd century Bishop of Antioch and prominent Christian apologist. He is a saint in both Eastern and Western Christianity.

[‡] Irenaeus of Lyons (2nd century — 202) was Bishop of Lugdunum (now Lyons, France). He was a Greek from Smyrna in Asia Minor. He is a saint in both Eastern and Western Christianity.

[§] J.S. Romanides, *To Propatorikon Hamartema* (Ancestral Sin), Athens, 1957, p. 126 (in Greek). For an English translation of this book, see: J.S. Romanides, *The Ancestral Sin*, trans. G.S. Gabriel, Ridgewood, New Jersey: Zephyr Publications, 2002.

[¶] Romanides, *To Propatorikon Hamartema*, p. 112.

The early Greek Church Fathers had received their initial training in the Greek philosophical scholarship, whereas the early Latin Church Fathers had received their initial training in the Roman legal scholarship. This cultural difference corresponds to a significant difference between the Greek cosmo-conception and the Latin one. The Greek cosmo-conception is based on philosophy, whereas the Latin cosmo-conception is based on law. Therefore, the Greek Church Fathers exposed and interpreted Christianity in terms of the Greek philosophical tradition and language, emphasizing divine eros and the divinization of man, whereas the Latin Church Fathers exposed and interpreted Christianity in terms of the Latin legal tradition and language (Roman law), emphasizing sanctified forms of rational organization of human life and obedience to authority.

In the context of the Greek Church Fathers' spirituality, the narration of the *Genesis* is a story of human struggle for progress and existential perfection, and the Incarnation of the Divine Word is the historical manifestation of the Archetype of Perfect Man, i.e. Jesus Christ, in order to guide and inspire man in his struggle for progress and existential perfection.

8

THE INCARNATE LOGOS AND THE ESOTERIC
SIGNIFICANCE OF THE NUMBER THIRTY-THREE

WHY is man's relationship with God so important? To answer this question, it is useful to reformulate it as follows: what is at stake when man chooses his attitude toward the idea of God? The answer to the previous question is self-knowledge. God is the most trustworthy mirror in which man can see his true self, because God is the absolute, transcendental unity.

Apart from God, no other being or thing is *naturally* a total unity, since every being or thing in the world is characterized by contradictions and change. As Michel Foucault has pointed out, nothing in man, not even his body, is sufficiently stable to be used as the basis for self-recognition or for understanding other men*.

Therefore, given that God is the most stable existential mirror in which man can see himself, there is a significant dialectical relationship between one's conception of humanity and his conception of the Deity.

The Christianization of the Roman Empire, and mainly the Christianization of the Greek world, which played a decisive role in the history of Christianity in general, is intimately related to the classical philosophers' quest for a viable and fulfilling personal relationship between man and the Deity.

---

* Michel Foucault, *Language, Counter-Memory, Practice*, ed. D.F. Bouchard, Ithaca, N.Y.: Cornell University Press; Oxford: Blackwell, 1977, p. 153.

FROM THE GREEK PHILOSOPHICAL CONCEPTION
OF THEORETICAL LIFE TO THE INCARNATE LOGOS

In his *Physics*, V, 265a, Aristotle writes that God is the direct object of the universal love that characterizes the eternal natural beings (i.e. the celestial spheres), which imitate the perfectness of the divine mode of living through their harmonious motion. The classical Greek sees the 'cosmos' as a reality in which dwells the Word of God. Thus, according to classical Greek philosophy, it is only through his participation in the cosmos that man can actualize his divine potential. In the context of classical Greek philosophy, participation in the cosmos leads to socialization and to individualization, too, because the human being lives as a member of a harmonious whole and simultaneously it turns inside, into its own psyche, in order to actualize its personal divine potential. As the previous awareness of individuality becomes deeper and more intense, the Greek individual gradually moves toward an existential crisis, because it encounters the tragedy of existence: the Greek individual does not know exactly how it can preserve *divine justice* (which is the necessary existential presupposition of every being and every reality) whilst simultaneously experiencing the divine element that dwells in its own self as *freedom of will*. In other words, the Greek individual seeks the perfect harmony between the preservation of divine justice (which underpins socialization) and the actualization of free will (which underpins individualization).

According to classical Greek philosophy, 'theory' and 'theoretical life' are two terms that describe the best ideal in life. In the context of classical Greek philosophy, theoretical life means love for wisdom, i.e. the life of the philosopher, where wisdom is the object and the result of the operation of the philosophizing consciousness, which contemplates the cosmos and, together with the gods, experiences the pleasures of the mind. Aristotle, who places God, as the ultimate source of significance in the world, at the top of his metaphysical system, argues that the communication between man and God takes place through the perfection of the human mind and through the mental alertness that is caused by mental pleasure*.

On the other hand, the concept of theory (contemplation), which was coined by the classical Greek intellectuals, proved to be the

---

* Aristotle, *Nicomachean Ethics*, 1177a, and *Metaphysics*, 1072b.

limit of the development of the classical Greek thought. The classical Greek thought realized that the highest pleasure is 'theoretical life', i.e. the orientation of the mind toward the infinity of the Deity, but it also realized that, without the finite and corruptible body, the human being cannot experience its mental life, and, therefore, the classical Greek thought realized that there was a tragic chasm between the 'absolute' and the 'partial'. In the context of Aristotle's matter-form analysis of living things, form is predicated of matter as subject, and the very nature of the soul (or mind) as "form of the body" and "end of the body" requires that the soul exist only in conjunction with the body. Thus, the more the mind was moving toward the absolute and was realizing that, in order to be united with the absolute, it had to transcend the corruptible and the partial, the more painfully the classical Greek intellectuals were experiencing the awareness of the weak and corruptible character of human nature.

According to Aristotle's *Nicomachean Ethics*, 1177b11, man cannot live continuously in a state of pure theory, but only in rare, happy moments of his life, since the human being is a hylomorphic compound (compound of soul and body) and, for this reason, man mainly lives in accordance with the terms of 'human life' and not in accordance with the terms of 'theoretical life'. In other words, due to his soul and with his soul, man turns toward and is attracted to mental pleasures, but, as a mortal being, i.e. because of the weak and corruptible character of his life, he lives in human societies and is engaged in practical pursuits. Thus, the more intense the experience of the pleasures of the mind is, the more intense the pain of death (i.e. the separation of soul and body) becomes.

When Diagoras of Rhodes (5th century B.C.), an Olympic winner in boxing, was celebrating the victories of his sons in Olympic games, the public shouted to Diagoras: "mortal Diagoras, you will not climb Olympus"; in this way, the public expressed its admiration and respect for Diagoras, but simultaneously it pointed out that there was a limit to Diagoras' victories and pleasures. In general, the classical Greek intellectuals realized that, on the one hand, man can be existentially vindicated, because, through knowledge and through his reason, he can be united with the first principle of the cosmos, i.e. with God, who is pure spirit, but, on the other hand, when man encounters the reality of the natural world, he realizes his weaknesses and the limits of his ability to impose his intentionality on the natural world. In the third book of his *Nicomachean Ethics*,

Aristotle stresses that choice is the deliberate desire of things in our power, but our power is not absolute vis-à-vis natural necessities. Hence, the human spirit cannot find tranquility in the midst of a life that is irrational (since life urges us to pursue a better life that eventually appears to be totally transcendental to our present state of life) and fragmented between 'theoretical' and 'practical' life.

Classical Greek philosophy discovered and analyzed the life of the spirit, but it proved to be unable to secure the unity of that life, which appeared to be fragmented between 'theoretical' and 'practical' life. In particular, in his *Nicomachean Ethics*, 1178b, Aristotle argues that "happiness is some form of contemplation", but "man's nature is not self-sufficient for the activity of contemplation". The classical Greek thought arrived at its limits, i.e. it arrived at awarenesses whose consequences it could not handle. In order to find a creative outlet, the classical Greek thought needed a Logos* (Word) Who would be spiritual (and hence totally free from the logic of the material world) and *simultaneously* He could unite the material world with Himself. Thus, the classical Greek thought found the outlet that it was looking for in the Christian faith, since the latter is founded on the doctrine of the incarnation of the Divine Logos.

Justin Philosopher and Martyr† continued to hold Greek philosophy in high esteem after his conversion to Christianity. In particular, in his *Dialogue with Trypho*, II, 1, Justin writes the following: "philosophy is, in fact, the greatest possession, and most honorable before God, to whom it leads us and alone commends us; and those who have bestowed attention on philosophy are truly holy men". In addition, in *Dialogue with Trypho*, VIII, 1, Justin writes that he had found in Christianity "the only sure and profitable philosophy". Similarly, in his *Stromata*, IV, Clement of Alexandria argues that Greek philosophy proceeds from the same God who gave the Old and the New Testaments and that it was God's Providence that raised up philosophers among the Greeks and prophets among the Jews and the barbarians.

---

* In pre-Socratic philosophy, 'logos' means the principle governing the cosmos, the source of this principle, or human reasoning about the cosmos. In Stoicism, 'logos' means the active, material, rational principle of the cosmos; nous. Biblical Judaism understands 'logos' as the word of God, which itself has creative power and is God's medium of communication with man. In Christianity, 'logos' refers to the creative word of God, which is itself God and incarnate in Jesus (it is also called Word).

† Justin (103—165 A.D.) was an early Greek apologist and martyr. He is venerated as a saint by many Christian denominations including the Orthodox Church and the Roman Catholic Church.

The New Testament has offered exactly what the classical Greek philosophers had been looking for: the manifestation of the Absolute *within* the historical, material world. According to the New Testament, God, in Christ, became a human being. In *John* 12:45, Jesus Christ says that, if one wants to know what God is like, he should study the person and words of Jesus Christ. Similarly, in *Luke* 24:53, Jesus Christ is portrayed as the perfect example of a life lived according to God's will. Furthermore, in *Hebrews* 1:1-3, the Apostle Paul writes that Jesus Christ is the complete expression of God in human body.

In the language of modern psychology, Christ is the *archetype*, the Divine Archetype, of the human being as the latter is restored to its proper and God-ordained path to perfection and divinization (deification). Speaking of Christ as the Archetype of restored man, Gregory the Theologian* has written in his *First Oration: On Easter and His Reluctance*†: "[Today] I am glorified with Him..., today I am quickened with Him,...let us honor our Archetype". Moreover, in his *Homily in Transfigurationem Domini* (*Patrologia Graeca*, Vol. 7, 552C), John of Damascus‡, speaking of the deification of man, refers to the divine image in man as it is "mingled" with Christ the "Archetype". The idea of Christ as the restored human, the new or second Adam, taking on the flesh of man, effecting a new creation, and setting human beings once more on the path toward deification and perfection, is poetically expressed in one of the *Theotokia* (hymns to the Virgin Mary, appointed in the *Octoechos*, the service book containing hymns for the eight modes [tones] of the weekly liturgical cycle of the Greek-Orthodox Church) for Sunday Matins in the second mode: "Most blessed art thou, O Virgin Theotokos; for through Him Who was incarnate of thee..., Adam has been restored [*anakekletai*, or, literally, 'recalled' to new life]".

The Greek Church Fathers managed to decodify Christ's Gospel,

---

* Gregory the Theologian (also known as Gregory of Nazianzus) was a 4th century A.D. Archbishop of Constantinople and philosopher, and also he is widely considered as one of the most accomplished rhetorical stylists of the early patristic era. He is a saint in both Eastern and Western Christianity.

† See: Philip Schaff and Henry Wace (eds), *A Select Library of Nicene and Post-Nicene Fathers of the Christian Church*, Grand Rapids, MI: Wm. B. Eerdmans, 1991, Vol. 7, p. 30.

‡ John of Damascus was a Syrian Christian monk and priest, who died at his monastery, Mar Saba, near Jerusalem, in 749 A.D. His fields of interest included theology, philosophy, music and law. He is a saint in both Eastern and Western Christianity, and the Roman Catholic Church recognizes him as a Doctor of the Church.

i.e. to understand the Christ Mystery, by interpreting the expression 'Son of God' as the manifestation of God's love in history. In other words, according to the Greek Fathers, the 'Son of God' is God's extension in this world, i.e. the 'Son of God' is the incarnate manifestation of God's love in this world. Hence, Jesus Christ is the channel through which God's love for the world became manifest in the world. Jesus Christ makes humans children of God through the incarnation of God's love in the context of the Christ Mystery. The Greek Fathers emphasize that God was manifested in Christ as a way of life, and, therefore, Christ revealed to humans that they are potential gods and showed to them how they can live as gods. Thus, Hesychasm, which is the most influential Eastern Roman tradition of Christocentric mysticism, emphasizes an esoteric understanding of Christianity focused on the psychological cure and deification of the human being.

GEMATRIA

Pythagoras, one of the most important ancient Greek mathematicians, formulated the famous Pythagorean Theorem (the square of the hypotenuse of a right-angled triangle is equal to the sum of the squares of the other two sides) and studied the connections among music, letters and numbers. Kieren Barry has argued that, from several methodic observations of the 'sacred' geometry to be found in nature, and influenced by the use of 'sacred' numbers in the Orphic Mysteries, Pythagoras developed the idea that number theory leads to a profound understanding of the nature of the universe*. This Pythagorean tradition, namely, the correspondences between numbers and letters, exerted significant influence on Qabalism.

In the context of the (Jewish and non-Jewish) Qabalah, the term 'Gematria' refers to a system of assigning numerical values to letters. For instance, the numerical value of the Tetragrammaton (the Ineffable name of God in Judaism) is 26. In particular, the Tetragrammaton (Yehovah) consists of the following four Hebrew letters, which are characterized by the following correspondences:

---

* Barry, *The Greek Qabalah*, p. 28.

- Yod = 10 (Fire)

- He = 5 (Water)

- Vau = 6 (Air)

- He = 5 (Earth).

Furthermore, the number 26 corresponds to the Middle Pillar of the Qabalistic Tree of Life:

- First sephirah: Kether: 1

- Sixth sephirah: Tiphareth: 6

- Ninth sephirah: Yesod: 9

- Tenth sephirah: Malkuth: 10

With the sum of these values: 1+6+9+10 = 26.

The following table shows the numerical values of the 22 Hebrew letters, which, as we saw in Figure 2, correspond to the 22 paths of the Tree of Life. A standard textbook for these Gematria values during the Renaissance was Agrippa's *Three Books of Occult Philosophy* (1532), Book II, Chapter xix. The 'final' figures for Kaph, Mem, Nun, Pe and Tzaddi are counted as such when these letters come at the end of a word. The Gematria value of the word may be taken at this higher value, but it may also be counted low.

Table 3: The Gematria Values of Hebrew Letters

Letter	Value	Final	Value	Name	Transliteration
א	1			aleph	A
ב	2			beth	B
ג	3			gimel	G
ד	4			daleth	D

Letter	Value	Final	Value	Name	Transliteration
ה	5			he	H
ו	6			vau	V
ז	7			zayin	Z
ח	8			cheth	Ch
ט	9			teth	T
י	10			yod	I
כ	20	ך	500	kaph	K
ל	30			lamed	L
מ	40	ם	600	mem	M
נ	50	ן	700	nun	N
ס	60			samekh	S
ע	70			ayin	Aa
פ	80	ף	800	pe	Ph
צ	90	ץ	900	tzaddi	Tz
ק	100			qoph	Q
ר	200			resh	R
ש	300			shin	Sh
ת	400			tau	Th

In Hebrew Numeration, Yod was the number ten, called the Decad by ancient Greek philosophers and especially by the Pythagoreans. The Decad was called the numerical symbol of the universe. Additionally, if we consider the Decad and the Tetractys of Pythagoras from the viewpoint of the Qabalah, and according to the numerical values of the Hebrew letters, we shall find that the important symbolic number seventy-two is produced: Yod, Y, alone is ten; Yod, He, YH, is ten and five, that is fifteen; Yod, He, Vau, YHV, is ten, five and six, that is twenty-one; Yod, He, Vau, He, YHVH, is ten, five, six, five, that is twenty-six. The total is seventy-two, the number of steps of the Ladder of Jacob which, according to Biblical legends, reached from earth to heaven; upon each step, says the *Talmud*, was an Angel bearing one of the names of God.

These names are derived from the words and letters of the nineteenth, twentieth and twenty-first verses of the fourteenth chapter of the book of *Exodus*, and to each name is added the angelic title of AL or AH as a termination. Moreover, the number seventy-two is the numeration of the name Chesed (Cheth, Samekh, Daleth: 8+60+4=72), i.e. of the fourth sephirah of the Qabalistic Tree of Life.

Furthermore, Gematria helps one to understand the mystery that is hidden in the age at which Jesus Christ started his earthly ministry and in the age at which Jesus Christ was exalted to the "Right Hand" of God the Father. *Philokalia* (Greek for 'love of the beautiful'), which is the most well-known and influential book on Orthodox Christian mysticism, includes a text in which Maximus the Confessor explains the Christology that is hidden in the number thirty-three (33).

According to the New Testament, Jesus Christ started his earthly ministry when he became 30 years old. When adequately understood, the number thirty (30) presents Lord Jesus Christ as the Creator and Preserver of time and nature as well as of the world of ideas, because of the following reason: the number seven alludes to the Creator of time, because time is divided in weeks and each week has seven days, and because, according to Moses' cosmogony, the creation of the world was completed in seven days; the number five alludes to the Creator of nature, because there are five senses; the number eight alludes to the Creator of the intelligible world, or the world of ideas, because the intelligible world transcends the sensible (temporal) world, and the latter is symbolized by the number seven; the number ten alludes to the Preserver of the world, because, according to the Bible, God gave ten Commandments for the moral perfection of mankind and because the first letter of the name of the Incarnate Logos in Greek, namely, ΙΗΣΟΥΣ (JESUS), is the tenth letter of the Greek alphabet. Thus, if we add the numbers five, seven, eight, and ten, we get the important symbolic number thirty. If we add the number three, i.e. the number of the Holy Trinity, to the number thirty, we get the number thirty-three, which symbolizes the Exaltation of Jesus Christ.

To explain the meaning of the Christian Trinitarian formula, one can use the following metaphor about a poet, e.g. T.S. Eliot: the poetry of T.S. Eliot is his 'logos', or word; Eliot's word proceeds from Eliot's 'nous' (mind); and Eliot's word gives to its readers the 'spirit' of Eliot, i.e. a special feeling of participation in the personal world of Eliot. The spirit of Eliot remains with the readers of Eliot's word even when they do not have his poems in front of them. By analogy, 'God the Father' is the Nous, or Mind, of God, 'God the Son' is the Logos, or Word, of God, and the 'Holy Spirit' is the Spirit of God. However, in the case of the Holy Trinity, the Nous of God (Father), the Logos of God (Son), and the Spirit of God (Holy Spirit) are not attributes or functions of a being, but they are three Hypostases (modes of being) of the same Divine Nature.

John of Damascus, in his essay entitled *An Exact Exposition of the Orthodox Faith*, defines 'nature' as the principle of motion and repose, and, on this ground, he identifies nature of subject with its substance. However, he adds that, according to some pre-Christian philosophers, such as Aristotle, in contrast to substance, which is simple being, nature is substance that had been made specific by essential differences so as to have, in addition to simple being, being in such a way. According to John of Damascus, hypostasis not only possesses common as well as individual characteristics of the subject, but also exists in itself, whereas nature does not exist in itself, but is to be found in hypostasis. Thus, Orthodox Christianity emphasizes the personhood of God. The hypostatic modes of existence of God imply that God's nature does not constrain Him, i.e. God's existence is characterized by absolute freedom, and, therefore, the Divine Word can become man without compromising His Divine Nature, since He is not constrained by his Nature. By analogy, since, according to the Bible, man is the image of God, personhood (i.e. the reality of the human being and the existential otherness of each and every man) takes primacy over the impersonal, natural mode of being. Thus, the freedom of personhood transcends the law of Karma (i.e. the Asian doctrine of cause and effect).

PART THREE

ESOTERIC FRATERNITIES, MORALITY
AND POLITICS FROM THE PERSPECTIVE
OF THE KAIROLOGICAL QABALAH

IN the following chapters, using the arguments that I have put forward and the concepts that I have studied until now, I analyze the ethos of the major Western esoteric fraternities and currents, placing special emphasis on the moral and political dimensions of Western esotericism. Even though the most important Western esoteric societies are focused on man's moral development, many contemporary esotericists have a very sketchy knowledge of moral philosophy, and they are mainly attracted by other, rather fanciful, aspects of Western esotericism.

Without sufficient knowledge of moral philosophy and of the debates that take place among the different 'schools' of moral philosophy, esotericists cannot understand the extent to which and the manner in which esotericism is related to moral philosophy, and, therefore, they think that morality is exhausted in elementary teachings about piety and good manners and that esotericism becomes meaningful and interesting when it excites imagination through occult speculations and 'exotic' spiritual 'cocktails'. Moreover, even though politics is one of the noblest expressions of man's moral consciousness and of his determination to creatively undertake his historical responsibilities, many Western esoteric fraternities, especially after the 19th century, seem to ignore the critical interdependence between politics and spirituality, and they even forbid political discussions within their assemblies. It is for all the above mentioned reasons that, often, especially in the era of the so-called advanced modernity, many Western esoteric currents and societies, even though they may continue to attract new members and maintain an air of compelling charm, in essence, fall into spiritual insignificance and preserve atavistic attitudes.

I have structured this part as follows: in Chapter 9, I study the rituals and teachings of Freemasonic Orders (e.g. Symbolic Masonry, the Order of the Holy Royal Arch, the Ancient and Accepted Scottish Rite, the Royal Order of Scotland, the Baldwyn Rite, etc.), Rosicrucian Orders and the Illuminati as well as the spiritual structure of Western esotericism in general, trying to throw light on great moral teachings contained in them; in Chapter 10, I analyze the relationship between Western esotericism and morality through a methodic and systematic study of all the problems of moral philosophy; in Chapter 11, I analyze the political dimension of Western esotericism in relation to the general problem of human autonomy and to the kairicity of human consciousness.

9

THE RITUALS AND TEACHINGS
OF WESTERN ESOTERIC FRATERNITIES

AMONG humanities scholars, the history and the ethos of Western esoteric fraternities was a heavily under-researched area throughout the twentieth century. However, the 1970s marked the dawn of a new era in the academic study of Western esoteric fraternities. In the 1970s, a specific research institute was established at the University of Amsterdam, in whose development Wouter Hanegraaff (Professor of History of Hermetic Philosophy and Related Currents) has played a decisive role, and other similar institutes were established at the Sorbonne in Paris by Antoin Faivre, and the University of Exeter in England, led by Nicholas Goodrick-Clarke (Professor of Western Esotericism).

Within the Introduction, I explained the difference between my perspective of Western esotericism and Antoin Faivre's one. Furthermore, the Kairological Qabalah, which I propose in this book, opens a new way of thinking about Western esotericism, and it is intended to transform Western esotericism into an additive and creative research program and to liberate it from the intellectual shackles of Gnosticism.

At the University of Sheffield, the Centre for Research into Freemasonry and Fraternalism was established in the academic session 2000—2001 as the first centre in a British university devoted to scholarly research into Western esoteric fraternities and especially into Freemasonry. This research centre is a pioneer in its field, but it is strongly focused on the British conception of Freemasonry and is intellectually anchored on the United Grand Lodge of England's Freemasonic doctrines. At the University of Exeter, the Exeter Centre for the Study of Esotericism is an interdisciplinary research organization and offers MA, MPhil and PhD Programs in Western Esotericism. Even though this research centre makes substantial contribution to the scientific study of Western esotericism, its perspective of esotericism is intellectually anchored on Gnosticism, Neoplatonism, Hellenistic schools of mysticism, classical Qabalism and Theosophy, and, therefore, it has long avoided to tackle the following foundational issue: the previous bodies of Western esoteric traditions can elucidate particular domains of the Western man's esoteric life, and, therefore, every attempt to define Western esotericism only in terms of Gnosticism, Neoplatonism, Hellenistic schools of mysticism, classical Qabalism and Theosophy discounts or ignores altogether the integrity of those domains of the Western man's esoteric life that its premises do not encompass. In other words, every attempt to define Western esotericism only in terms of Gnosticism, Neoplatonism, Hellenistic schools of mysticism, classical Qabalism and Theosophy is unable to give rise to an additive research program of Western esotericism, which could keep pace with the history of philosophy and the history of science.

Furthermore, several esoteric fraternities have created their own research organizations or research groups, which are concerned with the production of scholarly works related to the culture of the corresponding esoteric fraternity. For instance, the United Grand Lodge of England has created a reputable research lodge called "Quatuor Coronati", the Southern Jurisdiction of the Scottish Rite of Freemasonry, in the U.S.A., has created the Scottish Rite Research Society, the Grand Orient of France encourages and sponsors Masonic research that contributes to the study and promotion of its own Masonic doctrines, the Societas Rosicruciana in Anglia and the Societas Rosicruciana in Scotia encourage methodic and systematic research in Western esotericism, the Theosophical Society, the Anthroposophical Society and the Lucis Trust develop their own systematic research programs in esotericism, etc. Even though the previous organizations do an excellent job in order to promote their own cosmo-conception, they have two important defects: first, what they treat as 'secret' and 'sacred' knowledge is nothing more than basic lessons taught to undergraduate university students of humanities and natural sciences around the world, and, second, they do not help their members to obtain a global knowledge of the history of philosophy, but they tend to keep their members fixated on specific philosophical schools, usually connected with Neopythagoreanism, Neoplatonism and Gnosticism.

Finally, I should mention that conspiracy theorists methodically undermine every creative attempt to study Western esoteric fraternities. Conspiracy theorists play a double role: on the one hand, they speculate on people's ignorance and insecurities, and, thus, they earn a lot of money (e.g. many conspiracy-theory books are best-sellers); on the other hand, they serve the interests of corrupt social elites, because they diffuse confusion, fear and misleading information among the masses, thus undermining people's capabilities of analyzing, criticizing and acting in rational and effective ways. Conspiracy theorists make people see reality through specific 'keyholes' that are created and controlled by the industry of conspiracy theory itself, and, therefore, conspiracy theorists manipulate people's imagination and transform people from potential creators of reality into pathetic viewers of reality.

In this chapter, I study major Western esoteric fraternities from the perspective of the Kairological Qabalah. Based on the Kairological Qabalah, I articulate an interpretation of such major Western esoteric fraternities as Freemasonry, Rosicrucianism and the Order of the Illuminati, and I explain which elements of the previous Western esoteric fraternities' teachings and rituals I deem significant in the era of advanced modernity and in the light of the arguments that I put forward in the previous chapters. My interpretation of the previous Western esoteric fraternities helps one to develop a dynamic, eclectic, critical and creative attitude toward the different esoteric schools, to see that each esoteric school is a wave in the ocean of esotericism and to discard atavistic attitudes.

THE MASONIC LEGACY: SYMBOLIC MASONRY AND THE HOLY ROYAL ARCH

In its broadest sense, Symbolic, or Speculative, Masonry is an initiatory organization that uses symbols and allegories related to Operative Masonry in order to teach morality and transmit moral virtue, to dramatize philosophical ideas and to forge fraternal relations among its members. However, beyond the previous general definition of Symbolic Masonry, each particular Body of Symbolic

Masonry has its own 'landmarks' and ethos. Thus, for instance, the United Grand Lodge of England, the Grand Orient of France, the International Order of Co-Freemasonry Le Droit Humain, the Swedish Order of Freemasonry, and other Orders of Symbolic Masonry comply with the previous general definition of Symbolic Masonry, but each one of them has different landmarks and/or initiatory customs than the rest. In other words, like the market of construction companies, which is pluralistic and competitive, the market of symbolic construction companies, i.e. of Symbolic Masonic Orders, is pluralistic and competitive, too.

In the British Museum, there is an old document from around 1390 that gives some rules and regulations, or, as they are known among Freemasons, 'Charges'. This document is called the *Regius Poem*[*], and it is admitted to be the oldest genuine record of Masonry known. The Charges contained in the *Regius Poem* indicate that Masonry was not only a technical activity, but simultaneously it was organized in such a manner that it safeguarded and promoted a specific civil ethos. Thus, from the very beginning, Masonry was a civilizing force founded on the culture that underpinned the creation of the first medieval towns in Western Europe. The fact that Masonry has a cultural core, which transcends the technical activities of Operative Masons, led to the creation and survival of Freemasonry as a symbolic system, namely as a cultural phenomenon, after the decay of the guild system.

In Scotland, historians found several trustworthy historical sources on lodges of stonemasons (i.e. Operative Masons). Lodges were geographically-defined units controlling the operative trade on the basis of their statute law. On 28 December 1598 and also on 28 December 1599, William Schaw (1550—1602), who, in 1583, was appointed the King's Master of Works[†] (by King James VI of

---

[*]   For the complete original text, see: *Constituciones Artis Geometriae Secundum Euclydem*, with introductory remarks by H.J. Whymper, London: Spencer & Co., Great Queen Street, 1889. The modern English translation was made by Roderick H. Baxter, Past Master of Quatuor Coronoti Lodge, No. 2076, under the auspices of the United Grand Lodge of England, and it is reproduced by: A.G. Mackey, *Encyclopedia of Freemasonry*, new and revised edition, New York and London: The Masonic History Company, 1914. See also: S.H. Sheperd, *The Landmarks of Freemasonry*, Whitefish, MT: Kessinger Publishing, 1997.

[†]   On 21 December 1583, James VI appointed him principal Master of Works in Scotland for life, with responsibility for all royal castles and palaces. See: *Register of the Privy Seal of Scotland, 1581—1584*, Vol. 8, No. 1676, 1982, pp. 276-277.

Scotland), drew up the documents that today are known as the First and the Second Schaw Statutes, and they include instructions to Scottish stonemasons' lodges on practical matters concerning Operative Masonry. However, the Schaw Statutes include also instructions that have a cultural and particularly moral character; for example: "that they be true to one another, live charitably together as becometh sworn brethren and companions of Craft"; and: "that they observe and keep all the good ordinances set down before concerning the privileges of their craft as set down by their predecessors of fond memory".

Furthermore, historians are now certain that Scottish operative lodges began, in the 17th century, to admit non-operative members as "Accepted", i.e. honorary or gentlemen, Masons, and that, by the early 18th century, the Accepted Masons had gained the ascendancy*. The lodges in which the Accepted Masons had gained the ascendancy became symbolic, or 'speculative', lodges, while others continued practicing Operative Masonry. The speculative, or symbolic, Scottish lodges eventually combined to form the Grand Lodge of Scotland in 1736.

In addition, historical researchers have found several references to the Scottish stonemasons' lodges having a Mason's Word and secret modes of recognition, thus establishing a system of mutual trust among travelling Operative Masons: through their secret Word and secret modes of recognition, Operative Masons could gain work or sustenance whenever they were visiting the area of another lodge[†].

According to the Emulation Ritual, which is one of the most widely practiced rituals of Symbolic Masonry (known also as the 'Craft') in England and in many other countries, in the Entered Apprentice Degree Ceremony (Initiation), the Worshipful Master, i.e. the chief administrator, of the Lodge, exhorts the newly initiated Brother to practice "every domestic as well as public virtue", and in particular to be directed by prudence, chastened by temperance, supported by fortitude and always guided by justice. Hence, a Freemason's itinerary is inextricably linked to the meticulous study of notions and questions that belong to the field of moral philosophy. In the Fellow-Craft Degree Ceremony, the Emulation Ritual defines Freemasonry as follows: "A peculiar system of morality, veiled in

---

[*]   See: John Hamill, *The Craft: History of English Freemasonry*, London: Aquarian Press, 1986.

[†]   Ibid.

allegory and illustrated by symbols". Furthermore, according to the Emulation Ritual, the working tools of a Master Mason are: the Skirret, which "points out that straight and undeviating line of conduct" laid down in the Bible, the Pencil, which is a symbol of moral accountability, and the set of Compasses, which is a symbol of Divine Justice.

The Third Degree of Symbolic Masonry, namely, that of a Master Mason, was first conferred in 1726, in London, in the Society for Music and Architecture. In 1730, we find the first reference to the Hiramic legend, which is the mythological framework of the third degree. However, according to the Graham Manuscript, in 1726, Freemasons were still using the legend of Noah and his three sons, and not the Hiramic legend.

Figure 5: A Square and a Set of Compasses
Joined Together with the Letter G.

(The single most identifiable symbol of Freemasonry: the Square teaches the members of the 'Craft' that they must square their actions by the square of virtue with all humankind; the set of Compasses exemplifies a Mason's wisdom of conduct, i.e. the strength to exercise rational control over our desires and passions; the letter G stands for geometry.)

The first record we have of the Hiramic legend being introduced in Freemasonry occurs in 1730, when Samuel Prichard published *Masonry Dissected*, and he referred to Hiram as Grand Master Hiram. Moreover, in his book *Masonry Dissected*, Prichard narrates both the Masonic legend of Noah and the Hiramic legend. In 1738, when the 'Grand Lodge of London and Westminster' changed its name into the 'Grand Lodge of England', its Constitution was rewritten by the Reverend Dr James Anderson. Thus, in 1738, Anderson published *The New Book of Constitutions of the Antient and Honourable Fraternity of Free and Accepted Masons, Containing Their History, Charges, Regulations, &c. Collected and Digested By Order of the Grand Lodge from their old Records, faithful Traditions and Lodge-Books, For the Use of the Lodges*. In his Constitutions of 1738, Anderson wrote that, after the Temple of Jerusalem was completed, "their joy was soon interrupted by the death of their dear Master, Hiram Abiff, whom they decently interred in the Lodge near the Temple according to ancient usage".

The name "Hiram Abiff" does not appear as such in the Bible, but there are three references to people named Hiram that are present:

1. Hiram King of Tyre is credited in *2 Samuel* 5:11 and *1 Kings* 5:1-10 for having sent building materials and men for the original construction of the Temple in Jerusalem; thus, according to the Emulation Ritual's Hiramic legend, Hiram King of Tyre was one of the three Grand Masters of the Craft during the building of King Solomon's Temple.

2. In *1 Kings* 7:13-14, Hiram is described as the son of a widow from the tribe of Naphtali who was the son of a Tyrian bronze worker, contracted by Solomon to cast the bronze furnishings and ornate decorations for the Jerusalem Temple. From this reference, Freemasons often refer to Hiram (with the added Abiff) as "the widow's son". Hiram lived or at least temporarily worked in clay banks (*1 Kings* 7:46-47) in the plain of the Jordan between Succoth and Zarethan/Zeredathah.

3. Hiram (often spelled Huram, Hebrew), a craftsman of great skill sent from Tyre. In *2 Chronicles* 2:13-14,

we read that King Solomon of Jerusalem sent a formal request to King Hiram I of Tyre for workers and for materials to build a new temple; King Hiram responded as follows: "And now I have sent a skilful man, endued with understanding, of Huram my father's, the son of a woman of the daughters of Dan; and his father was a man of Tyre, skilful to work in gold, and in silver, in brass, in iron, in stone, and in timber, in purple, in blue, and in fine linen, and in crimson; also to grave any manner of graving, and to devise any device; that there may be a place appointed unto him with thy skilful men, and with the skilful men of my lord David thy father". In the original Hebrew version of 2 *Chronicles* 2:13, the phrase translated above as "Huram my father's" (or Huram my master craftsman) is "Huram Abi". The Masonic term "Hiram Abiff" is derived from the Hebrew term "Huram Abi", and it is the name of a Freemasonic archetype. In particular, John L. Cooper III, Grand Secretary of the Grand Lodge of Free and Accepted Masons of California, has argued that the Hiramic Legend is allegorical and that Hiram Abiff is a symbol of devotion to duty[*].

According to the Emulation Ritual, the Master Mason, in his raising in the Third Degree, participates in the enactment of the drama of the assassination of Hiram Abiff by three Fellow Crafts who, after the completion of King Solomon's Temple, conspired in order to obtain the secrets of the Third Degree. In particular, according to the Master Mason Degree Ritual, when Hiram Abiff finished his devotions, he moved toward the South entrance, where he was opposed by the first of those impious Fellow Crafts, who was armed with a heavy Plumb Rule and demanded the secrets of a Master Mason, warning Hiram Abiff that he would die if he refused to comply with those ruffians' request. Hiram Abiff refused to divulge the secrets of a Master Mason without the consent and co-operation of Solomon King of Israel and Hiram King of Tyre, and he added that patience and industry would, in due time, entitle every worthy Mason to a participation of the secrets of a Master Mason. The "ruffian" aimed a violent blow at Hiram Abiff, but he only glanced on Hiram Abiff's

---

[*]   J.L. Cooper III, "Who Was Hiram Abiff?", *The Alberta Freemason*, Vol. 75, No. 6, June 2010.

right temple. When Hiram Abiff recovered from the shock, he moved toward the North entrance, where he was opposed by the second "ruffian", who was armed with a Level. After Hiram Abiff gave a similar answer to the second "ruffian", the latter "struck him a violent blow on the left temple". Hiram Abiff, "faint and bleeding", moved toward the East entrance, where he was opposed by the third "ruffian", who was armed with a Maul. After Hiram Abiff gave a similar answer to the third "ruffian", the latter "struck him a violent blow on the forehead", which was fatal.

The above-mentioned Hiramic allegory implies that, due to the death of Hiram Abiff, the genuine secrets of a Master Mason are lost and cannot be communicated to any Freemason, since, "without the consent and co-operation" of the three Grand Masters (Solomon King of Israel, Hiram King of Tyre, and Hiram Abiff), they could never be divulged. However, in the context of English Freemasonry, the mythological content of the Order of the Holy Royal Arch restores the genuine secrets of a Master Mason, and, therefore, the United Grand Lodge of England (UGLE) considers the Royal Arch to be the completion of the Third Degree.

The earliest reference to the Royal Arch in the minutes of a Lodge is found in Ireland, in 1752, while the oldest record of an admission is that of 22 December 1757 when three brethren were "raised to the degree of the Holy Royal Arch" in Fredericksburg, Virginia. The general business of the Order of the Holy Royal Arch is transacted in assemblies described as Royal Arch Chapters. According to the UGLE Constitution, each and every Royal Arch Chapter must be attached to a Lodge of Symbolic Masonry, but the Supreme Grand Chapter of Royal Arch Freemasons of Scotland is a completely autonomous organization, and, furthermore, it controls a number of other Masonic degrees that are not controlled by the Grand Chapter of Royal Arch Freemasons of England in its jurisdiction.

The Third Degree of Symbolic Masonry is focused on the notions of 'death' and 'loss'; but that which was 'lost' in the Third Degree is 'found' in the Royal Arch. Harry Mendoza, Past Grand Officer of the Grand Chapter of the UGLE and Past Master of the Quatuor Coronati Lodge, No. 2076 (UGLE), has argued that, when Symbolic Masonry refers to the Lost Word (i.e. the loss of the genuine secrets of a Master Mason), the term 'loss' does not mean that something was misplaced, but it should be interpreted as a failure "to keep something in mind", and, similarly, the term 'found' (i.e. the restoration of the genuine secrets of a Master Mason) should be interpreted as a discovery of "something for the first time"*.

The ceremony of 'exaltation' to the Order of the Holy Royal Arch is based on the legend of the rebuilding of King Solomon's Temple after the Babylonian Captivity. In fact, the main body of the Royal Arch Ritual is based on the following two separate stories:

1. The true Biblical story describing the Jews' return from Babylon and the building of the Temple of Jerusalem (thus, the emblem of Royal Arch Masonry is the letter T, standing for the Latin word Templum, over H, standing for the Latin word Hierosolymae, as shown in Figure 6).

2. The ancient Royal Arch didactic legend describing the discovery of the Vault, the Altar and the Sacred Word[†]. According to the English Royal Arch's allegorical narrative, Jewish captives returning to Jerusalem, after the Babylonian Captivity, discover an underground chamber while constructing the Second Temple of Jerusalem. Within this chamber, they discover the true name of God, namely, YEHOVAH. The symbolic meaning of this discovery has been explained by Harry Mendoza as follows: what was lost by King Solomon and most of his successors for the next four centuries was the genuine metaphysical secrets of Judaism and, more particularly, the belief that Yehovah was the one and only true God of Israel. What was found by the time the captives returned to Jerusalem was an even broader awareness than the one which was lost: the exiles re-discovered the truth that Yehovah was the one and only true God of Israel, and, additionally, they discovered that Yehovah was not merely the God of a specific nation, i.e. Yehovah was not only the God of Israel among different 'national' deities, but He was the one and only universal

---

* Harry Mendoza, *Fifty Royal Arch Questions Answered*, September 1994, p. 12.

† In the 5th century A.D., Philostorgius, writing of the rebuilding of the Jerusalem Temple, refers to the discovery of the Vault, and this is the earliest framework of the Royal Arch legend. Nine hundred years later, in the 14th century, Nicephorus Callistus (*Ecclesiastica Historia*) refers to a similar legend. For more details, see: *Ars Quatuor Coronoatorum*, Vol. lxix, p. 43.

God*. Thus, after the Babylonian exile, the Israelites developed a new, much deeper and more universal, awareness of monotheism.

Figure 6: T over H, the Characteristic Symbol of the Holy Royal Arch

At this point, it is useful to mention that monotheism was not originally developed by the Hebrews and that the Hebrews were not the only monotheistic nation in the ancient world. At the zenith of ancient Egyptian civilization, Pharaoh Amenhotep IV (reigned for approximately 16 years: 1352—1336/1334 B.C.), known also as Akhenaten (meaning Effective Spirit of Aten), attempted to change the polytheistic religion of Egypt into a monotheistic one by promulgating the monotheistic worship of Aten, the Sun-God. Aten means bright disk, and, thus, the falcon-headed picture of Ra-Harakhti (the previous Egyptian religion's solar deity) was replaced by the symbol of a solar disk whose rays ended in human hands some of which were holding the holy ankh, the symbol of life. In contrast to the old Egyptian religion's solar deity, which was representing the physical Sun, Aten was a symbol of the Trans-cosmic One, the One life-giving source, which creates and preserves the cosmos through its light. Moses, the most important prophet in Judaism, was initiated into the mysteries of the Egyptian monotheism, and, when the Egyptians decided to abandon Akhenaten's monotheistic religion and return to polytheism, Moses preserved and expanded the monotheistic tradition among the Hebrews. Thus, Judaism became the strictest and most effective custodian of monotheism in the ancient world. Moreover, in the

---

* Mendoza, *Fifty Royal Arch Questions Answered*, pp. 12-13.

Hebrew Bible, the manifestations of God's Glory are often described as light or fire, and one of the Hebrew names for God is Adonai, which comes from the root 'ada', which means radiant.

In ancient Greece, in the context of the Orphic Mysteries, there was a monotheistic religious dogma, and, in contrast to Homer's popular polytheistic beliefs, the Orphic hymns celebrated the One and Universal God. According to Iamblichus and Porphyry, even though Pythagoras was making references to several gods, he was teaching that there is only one God and that the various different gods mentioned in the Greeks' popular polytheistic religion are powers or energies of the One God. In the same spirit, Plutarch, one of the most influential Platonist philosophers, believed in one, unitary, trans-temporal God, with different names for the Deity's different aspects.

Why is monotheism so important for the spiritual development of humanity? Monotheism leads to the ontological liberation of God from the cosmos, and, therefore, in the context of monotheism, the Divine Reason is free from cosmic laws. In the context of integral monotheism, God's mode of existence is freedom. As I mentioned in Chapter 3, Maximus the Confessor, in his explanation of the Christian monotheistic doctrine, pointed out that the essential autonomy of God from the natural cosmos implies that God relates to the natural cosmos only under terms dictated by God's own free Will, and, therefore, the laws that govern the natural cosmos (Creation) do not govern the Divine Mind (i.e. the ultimate Cause of Creation) Itself. Hence, since God is the mirror in which we see ourselves, and since the qualities and the nature of the God with Whom we empathize determine our way of thinking about ourselves and about our existential perfection, the God of monotheism is the perfect archetype of human emancipation and spiritual perfection. If man is mirrored in a God who is essentially and totally free from the Creation (physical universe), then he develops a sense of autonomy vis-à-vis natural necessity.

Given that the mythology of the Order of the Holy Royal Arch is focused on monotheism, it was a wise decision on behalf of the United Grand Lodge of England to declare that that the Order of the Holy Royal Arch is the completion and perfection of pure ancient Freemasonry. The Preliminary Declaration to the *Book of Constitutions* of the United Grand Lodge of England (UGLE) states the following: "By the solemn Act of Union between the two Grand Lodges of

Freemasons of England in December 1813, it was 'declared and pronounced that pure Antient Masonry consists of three degrees and no more, viz., those of the Entered Apprentice, the Fellow Craft, and the Master Mason, including the Supreme Order of the Holy Royal Arch'".

THE TEMPLARS' LEGACY AND THE SPIRITUAL
ITINERARY OF THE KNIGHTS KADOSH

The period 1740—1800 saw the rise of a host of new Masonic Rites and degrees on the European Continent, which were composed by Freemasons to whom the UGLE Masonic traditions were not enough, and, therefore, they devised ceremonies that enlarged and expanded the scope of the Masonic domain that had been structured and determined by the UGLE. Of the degrees that appeared, many were credited by various European and American Freemasons with a Scottish title and/or origin, even though none was literally connected to Scotland. The rituals of these Scots degrees are varied, but one chief idea underlies most, if not all, of them: the discovery in a vault by Templars of the long-lost and ineffable Word, during the search for which they had to work with the sword in one hand, and the trowel in the other. This same symbolism of the sword and the trowel is mentioned in the celebrated oration delivered in 1737 in the Provincial Grand Lodge of England in Paris by Chevalier Ramsay, who traced the origins of Freemasonry to the time of the Crusades. Moreover, the symbols of the sword and the trowel are mentioned in the ritual of the Royal Order of Scotland (which, according to popular assertions, is senior to every other Masonic system, with the exception of the Craft), in which the candidate takes his oath with a sword in one hand and a trowel in the other*.

In the 1760s, a Rite of Perfection of 25 degrees was being practiced both in Continental Europe and the Americas, and, toward the end of the 18th century, the Rite was increased to 33 degrees and was called Ancient and Accepted Scottish Rite (AASR). The AASR was restructured and took a solid form in 1801, when the Supreme Council of the Thirty-Third Degree for the United States of America was founded in Charleston, South Carolina. In 1802, the

---

* See: A.E. Waite, *Secret Tradition in Freemasonry*, Whitefish, MT: Kessinger Publishing, 1992 (originally published in 1937).

new Supreme Council 33° appointed Comte de Grasse-Tilly as the Sovereign Grand Commander of a Supreme Council for the Antilles for life and authorized him, through a special patent, to spread the AASR in both Hemispheres. The AASR was introduced by Comte de Grasse-Tilly into France (1804); from France it passed into Italy (1805), Spain (1811) and Belgium (1817). In 1819, a patent was granted to the Duke of Sussex (the first Grand Master of the United Grand Lodge of England) to form a Supreme Council in England, but he failed to act upon it, probably due to his keen desire to see the UGLE maintain its 'purist' policy, according to which pure Ancient Masonry consists only of the degrees of the Entered Apprentice, the Fellow Craft, and the Master Mason, including the Supreme Order of the Holy Royal Arch.

The 33 degrees of the Ancient and Accepted Scottish Rite (AASR) are the following:

1°   Entered Apprentice,

2°   Fellow Craft,

3°   Master Mason,

4°   Secret Master,

5°   Perfect Master,

6°   Intimate Secretary,

7°   Provost and Judge,

8°   Intendant of the Buildings,

9°   Elect of Nine,

10°   Elect of Fifteen,

11°   Sublime Elect,

12°   Grand Master Architect,

13°   Royal Arch of Enoch,

14°   Scotch Knight of Perfection (Grand Elect Perfect and Sublime Mason),

15°   Knight of the East or of the Sword,

16°   Prince of Jerusalem,

17°   Knight of the East and West,

18°   Knight of the Pelican and Eagle and Sovereign Prince Rose Croix of Heredom,

19°   Grand Pontiff,

20°   Venerable Grand Master (of the Symbolic Lodges),

21°   Patriarch Noachite or Prussian Knight,

22°   Prince of Libanus,

23°   Chief of the Tabernacle,

24°   Prince of the Tabernacle,

25°   Knight of the Brazen Serpent,

26°   Prince of Mercy,

27°   Commander of the Temple,

28°   Knight of the Sun,

29°   Knight of Saint Andrew,

30°   Grand Elected Knight Kadosh or Knight of the Black and White Eagle,

31°   Grand Inspector Inquisitor Commander,

32°   Sublime Prince of the Royal Secret,

33°   Sovereign Grand Inspector General.

The Degrees 1°—3° are not worked by the Supreme Council 33°, because they are the three Degrees of Symbolic Masonry, and, therefore, the first three Degrees of the AASR belong to the jurisdiction of the Grand Lodge of Symbolic Masonry. With the exception of the Degrees 18°, 30°, 31°, 32° and 33°, which are worked in full, most of the Degrees 4°—33° are conferred by name only.

In the 30th Degree (Grand Elected Knight Kadosh*) of the Ancient and Accepted Scottish Rite of Freemasonry, the candidate is shown a double-cleated ladder that consists of seven ascending steps and seven descending steps. The seven ascending steps symbolize the hierarchy of the liberal sciences (Grammar, Rhetoric, Logic, Arithmetic, Geometry, Music, and Astronomy), through which abstract thought and systematic knowledge of the universe become possible. The seven descending steps symbolize seven moral virtues, through which man can turn his mind to his fellow-humans, 'down here' (in this world), in order to promote humanity's prosperity; these seven virtues bear the following Hebrew names: Tsedakah, which means justice and charity, Schor Laban, which means goodness and innocence (literally this Hebrew phrase translates as white ox in English), Mathok, which means gentleness and mildness, Emounah, which means trust in truth, Hamal Saghia, which means Great Work and emphasizes the moral significance of practical work, Sabbal, which means moral weight and responsibility, and Ghemoul Binah Thebounah, which means that prudence leads to wisdom. Furthermore, the ritual of the 30th Kadosh is strongly Templar in tone, and the candidate is pledged to honor the memory of Jacques de Molay, the last Grand Master of the Crusading Order of the Knights Templar, by figuratively punishing crime and protecting innocence.

The "Poor Fellow-Soldiers of Christ and of the Temple of Solomon" (Latin: *Pauperes commilitones Christi Templique Solomonici*), commonly known as the "Knights Templar", the "Order of the Temple" (French: *Ordre du Temple* or *Templiers*) or simply as "Templars", were among the most famous Crusading Orders. When the Holy Land was lost,

---

*   In Hebrew, Kadosh means 'holy' or 'consecrated'.

support for the Order faded. Rumors about the Templars' secret initiation ceremony created mistrust, and King Philip IV of France, deeply in debt and jealous of the Templars' financial prosperity and power, took advantage of the situation. In 1307, many Templars in France were arrested, tortured into giving false confessions, and then burned at the stake. King Philip IV had Jacques de Molay, the 23rd and last Grand Master of the Knights Templar, burned at the stake in Paris, in March 1314. Moreover, under pressure from King Philip IV, Pope Clement V disbanded the Order in 1312. Since at least the 18th century, Freemasonry has incorporated Templar symbols and rituals in a number of Masonic Bodies, mainly using the Order of the Temple as a symbol in order to teach moral lessons about the significance of being committed to noble goals, about fortitude and about the need for a new-era humanistic crusade.

According to the widely respected Masonic historian John Hamill, the fabrication of the Masonic Degree of Knights Templar took place in France in the 1740s. Ladislas de Malczovich was one of the first Masonic researchers who supported this theory in a paper given at the Quatuor Coronati Lodge No. 2076 (UGLE) and published in *Ars Quatuor Coronatorum*, Vol. 5, 1892. The earliest references to Masonic Knight Templar activity in the British Isles are to be found in Ireland around 1764/5. However, the first record of a Masonic Knight Templar being made is in the Minutes of the Saint Andrew Royal Arch Chapter in Boston, Massachusetts, in 1769. The earliest known records of Masonic Knight Templar activity in England were minuted at Portsmouth in 1777. In general, these Masonic Templar rituals have been worked under the authority of existing warrants of Royal Arch Chapters as appendant degrees and were not organized Masonically in a rigorous manner. The first English Grand Conclave of Masonic Knights Templar was formed in 1791, it comprised of seven independent Encampments, and Thomas Dunckerley was installed as Grand Master. A candidate for installation into Masonic Knighthood must be of the Christian faith, a Master Mason and a Royal Arch Mason.

The Masonic Degree of Knights Templar commemorates the actions of a group of knights (namely, Hugues de Payens, Godfrey de Saint-Omer, Payen de Montdidier, Archambaud de St. Agnan, André de Montbard, Geoffrey Bison, two men recorded only by the names Rossal and Gondamer, and probably Count of Champagne himself) who were granted a place of habitation on the Temple

Mount by Baldwyn II King of the Latin Kingdom of the Holy Land in 1118. The Temple Mount had a mystique, because it was above the ruins of King Solomon's Temple. The mission of the monastic and chivalric Order of the Templars was the protection of the Christian pilgrims. According to the Ritual of the Masonic Degree of Knights Templar, the candidate for installation is admitted in the character and garb of a pilgrim, undergoes, symbolically, a period of pilgrimage and warfare, and he assumes the vows of a Crusader. Furthermore, he receives instructions about the role that penance and meditation play in Christian Knighthood, and, ultimately, he is received, armed and proclaimed a Knight Templar. Additionally, according to the Ritual of the Masonic Degree of Knights Templar, the sacred symbols of the Order are the Lamb, the Dove and the Cock: the first symbolizes the Paschal Lamb; the Dove symbolizes the Almighty Comforter, who descended like a Dove on Christ at His baptism; the Cock is the monitor of the Order, because, as his crowing heralds the morn, so the Templars' consciousness must be alert and morally responsible.

In England, the Masonic Knights Templar are governed by the Great Priory of the "United Religious, Military and Masonic Orders of the Temple and of Saint John of Jerusalem, Palestine, Rhodes and Malta, in England and Wales and Provinces Overseas". Furthermore, the Grand College of the "Holy Order of the Royal Arch Knight Templar Priests" controls more than 30 degrees, of which most are conferred on the candidate 'by name'; it is the final degree only which is worked in full, that of Holy Royal Arch Knight Templar Priest*. According to the Ritual of the Holy Royal Arch Knight Templar Priest, the candidate is conducted to seven pillars, placed in the form of a triangle, at each of which is stationed a Pillar Officer. The Pillar Officers have the following words referring to the attributes of the Lamb of God, who, according to the *Book of Revelation*, opened the seven seals, thus revealing the various Spirits of God:

Pillar I: Faith,

Pillar II: Hope,

Pillar III: Mercy,

---

* This degree has its origins in Ireland, where records exist of workings in the late 18th century.

Pillar IV: Utterances to preach the Word,

Pillar V: Salvation,

Pillar VI: Perseverance to the pure in heart,

Pillar VII: Life for all of them that endure to the end.

After passing the seventh Pillar, the candidate is led before the Tabernacle's Preceptor and is proclaimed a priest forever after the Order of Melchizedek, a great king and priest mentioned in the 14th chapter of the Book of *Genesis*. Whereas, in the Old Testament, priests were such because they were born into Aaron's family (i.e. they were priests by natural birth), priesthood after the Order of Melchizedek, who is an archetype of Christ, implies that we are priests because we are spiritually (re)born into God's family (i.e. we are priests by spiritual birth). Thus, in *1 Peter* 2:9, the Apostle Peter calls all Christians "a royal priesthood".

However, the Ancient and Accepted Scottish Rite (AASR) maintains its own distinct Masonic Templar traditions and ritual. In the context of the 30th Degree of the AASR, the Knights Templar are used as a symbol in order to teach lessons about fortitude, zeal, commitment to noble ideals, and the protection of human rights. Thus, a Grand Elected Knight Kadosh is supposed to be a Crusader of Humanism.

It is important to notice that one of the most important and oldest mottos of the 30th Degree of the AASR is: "Nec proditor Nec proditus innocens foret", which means that neither the betrayer not the betrayed can be innocent. The Order of the Knights Templar was betrayed by some of its members, by its political head, namely King Philip IV of France, and by its ecclesiastical head, namely Pope Clement V. However, the Order of the Knights Templar itself had betrayed the ancient pure Christian ethos, which it was supposed to safeguard, because the Knights Templar gave in to the temptations of excessive violence and excessive wealth. Not only did the Templars conducted a ruthless religious war and looted several areas in the Eastern Roman Empire (Byzantium) and the Middle East, thus acting in contrast to Christ's pacifism, but also they accumulated huge financial wealth by trading money*, thus becoming forerunners of capitalism, which also contradicts the pure Christian ethos.

In his book *A Contribution to the Critique of Political Economy*, Karl Marx correctly pointed out that the primary formation of capital was neither due to the ownership of land nor due to the medieval guilds, but it was due to the wealth that was accumulated through usury and commerce. Capitalism is founded on the thesis that money has an intrinsic virtue on the basis of which it can multiply by itself. The previous thesis was officially adopted by the Roman Catholic Church in the 15th century. Capitalism appeared in the historical foreground as a peculiar form of trade organized by the Fugger family in Germany; the Fugger family was a historically prominent group of European bankers who were members of the fifteenth and sixteenth-century mercantile patriciate of Augsburg.

It goes without saying that money was already in existence in ancient and early medieval societies. But, in those societies, money could not be transformed into 'capital', because, for those people, financial wealth as such had no intrinsic value, and also those people were creating personal, as opposed to financial, bonds with the land and/or with their trades. The previous economic regime changed and capitalism was born when people believed that, next to the traditional use-value of money, there was an additional dimension of money, namely, the exchange-value of money. In the context of Platonism and Aristotelianism, people refuse to accept that money, or financial wealth in general, has an intrinsic value, and they treat money only as a use-value for the sake of humanity's well-being. In the context of capitalism, the exchange-value of money acquires increasing importance versus the use-value of money, and the trade of money tends to become an end in itself and a means by which the banking-financial subsystem of the economy tends to dominate the entire economic system, instead of operating as a servant of the productive forces of the economy.

The highly influential British social philosopher and economic historian Richard Henry Tawney[†], in his historical study of

---

* The Order of the Knights Templar created an international banking network, became a banker of monarchs for their mortgages and was offering loans to finance wars through the Order's Paris headquarters.

† R.H. Tawney, *The Acquisitive Society*, London: Bell, 1921; Ibid, *Equality*, London: Allen & Unwin, 1931.

capitalism, has delineated and methodically analyzed the manners in which a capitalist economy had come to acquire its autonomy from morality and the manners in which industry and property had become detached from any principle of function and purpose, thus giving rise to various phenomena of social sickness and nihilism. Against such a society, Tawney proposed the principles of functional property and common social purpose.

Those who can understand the esoteric teachings of Freemasonry know that the 30th Degree of the AASR uses the history of the Knights Templar neither in order to teach the 'merits' of usury and holy war nor in order to promote the trade of defunct chivalric titles, but in order to urge Freemasons to contemplate on moral values and human rights and in order to transform Freemasons into fully conscious Crusaders of Humanism.

The 31st Degree of the Ancient and Accepted Scottish Rite is called Grand Inspector Inquisitor Commander and is conferred in a Supreme Tribunal wherein the candidate is charged to oversee the observation of Freemasonic justice, and, in the course of his induction, is introduced to representatives of the following great law givers of the past (according to the 1987 edition of the Thirty-First Degree Ritual published by the Supreme Council of Scotland): Alfred the Great, King of Saxon England, who was a wise legislator, and he established an efficient and fair judicial system; Socrates, the famous ancient Athenian philosopher, whose life and teachings imply that a true and worthy Judge is an example of obedience to the Laws; Confucius, who taught the Chinese that "Justice is equity" and that a just polity renders to every man that to which he is entitled; Minos, who counseled the ancient Cretans to act so that men might praise their moderation, their determination, their equity and their integrity and also to feel that they are morally accountable toward their contemporaries and the future generations, too; Zoroaster, whose words became a law to the ancient Persians and who taught that the best servant of God is a person whose heart is upright and has a liberal attitude toward all men; Moses, the great law giver of Israel, who was initiated into the ancient Egyptian Mysteries, and he gave the Israelites their Moral Law.

Finally, according to the 31st Degree Ritual, the Master of Ceremonies, counsels the candidate to focus his mind on the real Christian justice by quoting the following statements by Jesus Christ: "For if ye forgive men their trespasses, your heavenly Father will also forgive you. But if ye forgive not men their trespasses, neither will your Father forgive your trespasses" (*Matthew* 6:14-15). "For with what judgment ye judge, ye shall be judged: and with what measure ye mete, it shall be measured to you" (*Matthew* 7:2). "And if thy brother sin against thee, go, show him his fault between thee and him alone: if he hear thee, thou hast gained thy brother" (*Matthew* 18:15). "Judge not according to the appearance, but judge righteous judgment" (*John* 7:24). "If thy brother sin, rebuke him; and if he repent, forgive him. And if he sin against thee seven times in the day, and seven times turn again to thee, saying, I repent; thou shalt forgive him" (*Luke* 17:3-4). "Blessed are the merciful: for they shall obtain mercy" (*Matthew* 5:7).

The 32nd Degree of the Ancient and Accepted Scottish Rite is called Sublime Prince of the Royal Secret and counsels charity and tolerance toward all mankind. This is exemplified by a symbolic pilgrimage in search of truth, when the candidate is conducted around the Camp of Chivalry were the respective points mark Confucius, Zoroaster, Buddha, Moses, Hermes Trismegistus, Plato, Jesus of Nazareth, and Mohamed. Here within the Consistory, the candidate is able to realize the moral content of the renowned religions and philosophies of the world, and he is taught that the pillars of the symbolic Temple that Freemasons try to erect are Liberty, Justice, Reason and Love. This is the essence of the 'Royal Secret', which is communicated to the candidate in this degree.

Figure 7: The Emblem of the Thirty-Third Degree of the Ancient and Accepted Scottish Rite. A double-headed eagle (a traditional image of chivalry and sovereignty) carrying a dagger in its claws; on a ribbon is written "Deus Meumque Jus", i.e. "God and my Right"

The 33rd (ne plus ultra) Degree of the Ancient and Accepted Scottish Rite is called Sovereign Grand Inspector General, and the members of this degree have to endure a test that demands great courage and are charged to encourage charity and fraternal love throughout the Order and to protect the Order against its enemies and especially against the Papacy's Knights of Malta. According to the 33rd Degree legends (19th century editions of the Thirty-Third Degree Ritual published by the Southern Jurisdiction of the United States), "the Knights Kadosh or K.H. were originally called Knights Templar", and, after the dissolution of the Order of Knights Templar, by King Philip IV of France in concert with Pope Clement V, the Templars' rich possessions were given to the Knights of St. John of Jerusalem, now called Knights of Malta. Thus, according to the 33rd Degree legends, since the Knights of Malta have refused to surrender those possessions which were wrested from the Knights Templar by cruelties and injustice, the Knights Kadosh have bound themselves to restore justice.

The Supreme Council 33° is set up in purple, skeletons, skulls and cross-bones are painted above, and, in the North, is a human skeleton standing upright, holding in the left hand the white banner of the Order and in its right a dagger ready to strike. The Very Puissant Sovereign Grand Commander is dressed in a robe of crimson bordered with white, he wears a royal crown on his head and has a sword in his right hand. The skeletons and skulls serve to remind of the massacre of the Knights Templar (the ancestors of the Knights Kadosh) by King Philip IV of France, who delivered them to the cruelest tortures. The swords indicate that the Knights Kadosh and the members of the 33rd Degree mourn their loss and simultaneously they are ready to avenge their loss.

However, in the 33rd Degree Ceremony lies a much deeper philosophical message, which leads to a new way of thinking about the Hiramic legend of Symbolic Masonry. Through the Masonic stories and legends about the Knights Templar, those who are truly initiated in the 33rd Degree of the Ancient and Accepted Scottish Rite become aware of the danger that Law (e.g. in the case of King Philip, the persecutor of the Templars), Possession of material wealth (e.g. in the case of the wealth possessed by the Order of the Temple) and Religion (e.g. in the case of Pope Clement V, who issued an edict officially dissolving the Order of the Temple) can become three catastrophic forces, three symbolic assassins (ruffians) of the

Archetypal Man (alluded by the Craft's mythical Hiram Abiff), i.e. of the man who tries to ascend to higher levels of consciousness and achieve 'Godship'.

Jesus Christ set a clear and eternal example of how the deified man, i.e. the man who is united with the Deity, approaches Law, Possession and Religion:

- *Jesus Christ's teaching about Law:* "The Sabbath was made for man, and not man for the Sabbath" (*Mark* 2:27). Additionally, he said: "A new command I give unto you: That ye love one another" (*John* 13:34). "And one of the scribes came, and heard them questioning together, and knowing that he had answered them well, asked him, What commandment is the first of all? Jesus answered, The first is, Hear, O Israel; The Lord our God, the Lord is one: and thou shalt love the Lord thy God with all thy heart, and with all thy soul, and with all thy mind, and with all thy strength: this is the first commandment. The second is this, Thou shalt love thy neighbour as thyself. There is none other commandment greater than these" (*Mark* 12:28-31).

- *Jesus Christ's teaching about Possession of material wealth:* "Verily I say unto you, It is hard for a rich man to enter into the kingdom of heaven. And again I say unto you, It is easier for a camel to go through a needle's eye, than for a rich man to enter into the kingdom of God" (*Matthew* 19:23-24). The Apostle Paul observes that "the love of money is the root of all kinds of evil" (*1 Timothy* 6:10). David W. Miller emphasizes that "it is the love of money that is the obstacle to faith, not the money itself"[*]. Although Jesus never condemns material wealth as evil *per se*, he consistently addresses the danger of material possessions as a hindrance to full and sincere compliance with the New Law of Christ, which is Love. Moreover, Basil the Great (4th century A.D.), one of the most influential Greek Fathers of the early Christian

---

[*]   D.W. Miller, "Wealth Creation as Integrated with Faith: A Protestant Reflection", Muslim, Christian, and Jewish Views on the Creation of Wealth, April 23—24, 2007, Habsburg Center Auditorium.

Church, who is recognized as a Doctor of the Church in both Eastern Orthodoxy and Roman Catholicism, in his sermon *To the Rich* (*Patrologia Graeca*, Vol. 31, 277C—304C), states that man's ultimate existential goal is deification and not economic success and that, if wealth is owned by a man, its only proper use is as a means to existential perfection (salvation). For Basil the Great, the previous statement means using wealth in accordance with Christ's commandment to love one's neighbor as oneself. In the same sermon, Basil the Great states that "it is right for those who are prudent in their reasonings to regard the use of money as a matter of stewardship, not of selfish enjoyment".

- *Jesus Christ's teaching about Religion:* First of all, Jesus said to humans: "Ye are Gods" (*John* 10:34), thus revealing that true Christianity is a mystical path toward man's deification, and that Christ is the manifestation of every worthy religion's purpose, namely, the deified man[*]. Furthermore, Jesus said about the true worship of God: "the hour cometh, when neither in this mountain, nor in Jerusalem, shall ye worship the Father...But the hour cometh, and now is, when the true worshippers shall worship the Father in spirit and in truth: for such doth the Father seek to be his worshippers. God is a Spirit: and they that worship him must worship in spirit and in truth" (*John* 4:21-24). Thus, as we read in *Revelation* 21:22, there is no temple in the New Holy City: "And I saw no temple therein: for the Lord God the Almighty, and the Lamb, are the temple thereof".

However, the above-mentioned moral, religious and political messages of the 33rd Degree of the AASR are often intentionally concealed and even suppressed or distorted, since many Supreme

---

[*] Whereas Jesus Christ taught the divinization of the human being, the Jews insisted on a phyletic theology of salvation, centred on the messianic destiny of the Jewish nation. Thus, John Chrysostom (ca.347—407), who is venerated as a saint and Doctor of the Church and is one of the most influential Greek Church Fathers, wrote, in his *First Homily Against the Jews*, that ethnocentric Jews have developed a profoundly misguided approach to the Bible, and, therefore, "they have the prophets but do not believe them; they read the sacred writings but reject their witness".

Councils of the 33rd Degree of the AASR around the world have rewritten their rituals on several occasions in order to avoid accusations of radical humanism, or because they have changed their spiritual identity.

According to old French rituals of the 33rd Degree of the Ancient and Accepted Scottish Rite, true Freemasonry is the actual revolution and the on-going conspiracy against religious/spiritual and political despotism. Thus, according to those 33rd Degree rituals, true Freemasonry has been voluntarily masqueraded and hidden behind emblems that Royals and religious elites use in order to rule society. In other words, those who delve into the history of the ne plus ultra degree of the Ancient and Accepted Scottish Rite realize that Royals and senior religious officers could not tolerate an institution that was harmful to their interests and was frightening them, and, therefore, some of them attempted to control Freemasonry through penetration, i.e. they joined Freemasonry; these are the people who have introduced several childish and sometimes even morally offensive traditions and practices into Freemasonry. Thus, old French rituals of the 33rd Degree of the Ancient and Accepted Scottish Rite reveal that several ridiculous and childish Masonic ritualistic systems are a shield that protects the real Masonic ethos against its enemies. Under the protective cover of childish chivalric and pseudo-Biblical narratives, the initiates of true Freemasonry can continue working in order to achieve the ultimate Masonic goal, seeking vengeance for the assassination of the innocent Grand Architect, i.e. of the Archetypal Man, by three ruffians that are known as Law, Possession and Religion. After the punishment of the previous three assassins by Freemasonry, humans will be free to restructure society, establishing the Masonic notion of Law, the Masonic notion of Possession and the Masonic notion of Religion, which can be found in the humanistic ethos of the Gospel of Jesus Christ, in the *Acts of the Apostles*, in the eschatological visions that are contained in John the Evangelist's *Revelation* and in several movements for human emancipation throughout the modern history of the West.

The Ancient and Accepted Scottish Rite contains chivalric degrees and several narratives about the Crusaders and especially about the Knights Templar, even though the missions of the medieval chivalric orders (including the Templars) and the authoritarian ethos of the medieval feudal elites are alien and detestable to the members of the true core of Freemasonry. The Ancient and Accepted Scottish Rite uses myths based on the building of King Solomon's Temple (such as the Hiramic legend), the Crusaders' symbols and the dramatic history of the Templars, because it views them as pedagogically effective and politically correct methods whereby the humanistic ethos of enlightened Freemasonic initiates can be inculcated to the neophytes. In the context of the Ancient and Accepted Scottish Rite, King Solomon's Temple is totally irrelevant to the Temple of the Jewish religion, because it is a symbol of the true Masonic Temple, which is the Temple of Humanism, whose Pillars are Liberty, Justice, Reason and Love. Furthermore, the ethos of the Masonic Knights Templar and especially of the Knights Kadosh is totally irrelevant to the ethos of the medieval Knights Templar. If true Freemasonry had to declare a Crusade, then that Crusade would be for the capture of those Holy Lands that are known as Liberty, Justice, Reason and Love.

THE ROSICRUCIAN LEGACY

Rosicrucianism is a very influential phenomenon in the history of Western esotericism. For instance, Rosicrucian legends have inspired a variety of works, among them the works of Michael Maier (1568—1622) of Germany, Robert Fludd (1574—1637) and Elias Ashmole (1617—1692) of England, Teophilus Schweighardt Constantiens, Gotthardus Arthusius, Julius Sperber, Henricus Madathanus, Gabriel Naudé, Thomas Vaughan, and others. Moreover, many Western esoteric fraternities and many Masonic degrees and orders are founded on Rosicrucianism.

The Society of the Rosicrucians in England (SRIA) is a Masonic esoteric Christian Order formed by Robert Wentworth Little (a clerk and cashier of the secretary's office at the United Grand Lodge of England) in 1865, following the reputed discovery of certain manuscripts in the archives of the United Grand Lodge of England. However, the oldest Masonic Order of Rosicrucians is the Societas Rosicruciana in Scotia (SRIS). The Rosicrucian Society of Freemasons has power to confer the following nine Degrees:

1°   Zelator,

2°   Theoricus,

3°   Practicus,

4°   Philosophus,

5°   Adeptus Minor,

6°   Adeptus Major,

7°   Adeptus Exemptus,

8°   Magister,

9°   Magus.

Moreover, senior members of the Rosicrucian Society of Freemasons (who have attained the Degree of Adeptus Minor or above) may join the elite Order of Eri, which is said to be derived from a very ancient Order in Ireland*, it is based on Celtic traditions, and it consists of the following three Degrees:

1°   Man-at-Arms,

2°   Esquire,

3°   Knight.

The Rosicrucian Societies of Freemasons (i.e. SRIA, SRIS and other Freemasonic societies that are called 'Societas Rosicruciana') are based on symbolism and traditions of a 17th century Society known as the Fraternity of the Rose and Cross, which in turn claimed its origin from a legendary, perhaps allegorical, person known as Christian Rosenkreutz. The earliest public notice of the Fraternity of the Rose and Cross appeared in 1614 in a pamphlet printed at Cassel

---

*   An ancient book entitled *The Annals of the Four Masters of Ireland* tells of the Knights of the Collar of Eri as instituted by King Eamhium and his eight princes over the armies of the provinces of Ulster, Munster, Leinster and Connaught. The ancient Irish Chivalric Order was comprised of Ollamhs, who were the teachers and hospitallers, the Brehons, who were the judges, the Cruimthears, who were the priests and attended to the religious and moral education of the people, the Bards, who were the historians and preserved the memory of the noble deeds of their ancestors, and the Heralds, who assisted in developing the Arts and Sciences.

in Germany, and entitled *Fama Fraternitatis*. It was a narrative of the founding of the Society of the Rosicrucians, and it was reprinted in 1615, together with a second pamphlet entitled *Confessio Fraternitatis*. These tracts were translated in English in 1652 by Thomas Vaughan, a mystic philosopher who wrote under the pseudonym Eugenius Philalethes.

According to the *Fama Fraternitatis*, Christian Rosenkreutz was a German doctor and alchemist who discovered and learned esoteric wisdom during his voyages to the East, supposedly in the early 15th century, and ultimately he returned to Europe and founded the Fraternity of the Rose and Cross with him as Head of the Order. Christian Rosenkreutz is an archetypal Renaissance freethinker and scientist. Frederick Leigh Gardner (1857—1930) has published a *Catalogue Raisonné* of Rosicrucian literature, which reviews a very voluminous literature concerned with the Rosicrucian legend and the mystical studies of the Rosicrucians. Moreover, many learned Masonic historians, such as Frederic Nicolai, Johann Gottlieb Buhle, and Thomas de Quincey, have asserted that Rosicrucianism has exerted decisive influence on the composition of the Rituals of Symbolic Masonry, when Speculative Masonry arose out of the Operative Masonry of the great Trade Guilds of Masons, who were the Cathedral and Church builders of the Western Middle Ages.

In the Adeptus Exemptus Degree Ceremony of the Societas Rosicruciana in Anglia (the Rosicrucian Society of Freemasons), the candidate is taught the following moral principles and duties (early 20th century editions): to love God and act justly with all men, to study nature, to teach as well as learn, to be merciful and to remember the Rose as a symbol of the Divine Spirit within man, and the Cross as a symbol of self-sacrifice and high endeavor. In the same spirit, in the Magister Degree Ceremony of the Societas Rosicruaciana in Scotia (early 20th century editions) the candidate is taught that the Rosicrucian Magisters are empowered to rule the members of the lower degrees of the Rosicrucian system and to supervise and evaluate their work, and that the Rosicrucian Magisters must first of all learn to be true Masters over their own lower self.

The Rose Cross symbol plays major role in other Freemasonic Orders, too. The 18th Degree of the Ancient and Accepted Scottish Rite is called Sovereign Prince Rose Croix of Heredom, and, in the English Masonic tradition, it is one of the most significant Christian Masonic degrees. It teaches that the Rose symbolizes "secrecy and silence" and also "Him Who is the Rose of Sharon and the Lily of the Valley", i.e. Christ, since, in the *Song of Solomon*, we find reference to the Savior under the mystical title of the "Rose of Sharon". Additionally, according to the 18th Degree of the Ancient and Accepted Scottish Rite, the Rosicrucians' Cross is a representation of the Cross of Calvary, red with the Savior's Blood.

According to the 18th Degree Ritual, the candidate is symbolically admitted in a Chapter of Princes Rose Croix of Heredom "at the ninth hour of the day", when the earth quakes, the rocks are rent, the veil of the Temple is rent in twain and darkness overspreads the earth, highlighting the Passion Narrative in Matthew's Gospel (27:50-51). In a series of highly mystical experiences, the 18th Degree Ceremony expresses the figurative passage of man through the darkest veil, accompanied and sustained by the three theological virtues, namely, Faith, Hope and Charity, and it teaches that, assisted by these virtues, the candidate will succeed in attaining the Rosicrucians' ultimate goal, which is that Word on which the eternal salvation of humanity depends.

Figure 8: The Prince Rose Croix Jewel.
A set of compasses surmounted by a rose and celestial
crown, a rose-cross is between the legs of the set of
compasses, and under it is a pelican pecking its breast to
feed its seven young (an ancient symbol of the Savior).

The 18th Degree of the Ancient and Accepted Scottish Rite consists in a synthesis between the Gospel of Jesus Christ and the 17th century Rosicrucian manifestos. Throughout the 15th, the 16th and the 17th centuries, the Rosicrucians were pioneering natural scientists who were mainly working in the contexts of alchemy and medicine in order to promote the spirit of science. In the Middle Ages, the labors of the alchemists and their utensils laid the foundations of modern Chemistry. The Rosicrucians were the boldest freethinkers and defenders of natural science in the 15th, the 16th and the 17th centuries. Jesus Christ was the greatest defender of moral truth, he boldly fought against the hypocricy and the tyranny of the Pharisees and Scribes, and he founded his moral teachings on man's direct participation in the Deity. Freemasonry in general and the 18th Degree of the Ancient and Accepted Scottish Rite in particular endorse both the Rosicrucians' struggle for the development of science and Jesus Christ's struggle for the humanization of religion through the doctrine of the deification of man.

The Royal Order of Scotland is an elite Masonic Order, it depicts Freemasonry in a purely Christian aspect, and it contains two degrees, namely: (i) the Heredom of Kilwinning, and (ii) Knighthood of the Rosy Cross. According to Masonic legends, this Order was instituted by Robert Bruce, King of Scotland under the title of Robert I, at Kilwinning, immediately after the Battle of Bannockburn in 1314, in order to commemorate the valor of a group of Knights Templar who had aided him in the great victory. Moreover, from the earliest written records of meetings, the Royal Order of Scotland claimed that the King of Scots was the hereditary Grand Master, and a seat in the East is kept vacant for him at all meetings of Grand Lodge.

According to the Ritual of the Heredom of Kilwinning, the Perpend-ashlar, which is present in every Masonic Lodge, is a symbol of the Son of Man, the Stone that was rejected by the Builders and has now become the Chief Stone of the Corner*, or "the most perfect pattern for Masons to try their Moral Jewels upon". According to the Ritual of the Knight of the Rosy Cross (1980s edition), the Rose is a symbol of Jesus Christ, "the lovely Sharon rose", and the Cross is a symbol of Jesus Christ's sacrifice for the redemption of humanity. Furthermore, according to this degree, three Knights of the Rosy

---

* See: *Psalm* 118:22, *Matthew* 21:42, *Acts* 4:11.

Cross form a complete Knighthood Lodge, because the number three alludes to their faith in the Christian Trinitarian Doctrine.

The 7th and ne plus ultra Degree of the Baldwyn Rite (a system of Masonic ceremonies with Time Immemorial status centred at Bristol) is called Knight of the Rose Croix of Mount Carmel, and it is similar to the 18th Degree of the Ancient and Accepted Scottish Rite. However, according to the Baldwyn Rite, candidates are received into the Camp of Baldwyn through 'Installation' as Knights Hospitaller and Knights Templar and as such present themselves for 'Perfection' in the Rose Croix Chapter (before attaining this, they are entrusted with the passwords of the following degrees: "Knights of the Nine Elected Masters", "Scots Knights Grand Architect and Scots Knights of Kilwinning", and "Knights of the East, the Sword and the Eagle").

THE ILLUMINATI'S LEGACY

The term Illuminati (plural of Latin 'Illuminatus', enlightened) usually refers to the Bavarian Illuminati, an esoteric society founded on 1 May 1776 by Adam Weishaupt[*] (1748—1830), who was the first lay professor of Canon Law at the University of Ingolstadt. The Order of the Illuminati was modelled on Freemasonry, and it was made up of freethinkers. Given that, by the middle of the 18th century, many Freemasonic Orders had been placed under the control of conservative social elites and Royal Houses and many Freemasons had developed a petit-bourgeois mentality, Adam Weishaupt attempted to politicize the humanistic morality of Freemasonry by creating a new esoteric society whose members would be capable of contemplating on the political ramifications of Freemasonic and Rosicrucian moral legends and teachings and of undertaking humanistic and libertarian political initiatives. According to the instructions for the Degree of Regent, if the Order of the Illuminati cannot establish itself in any particular place with all the forms and regular progress of its degree system, it must operate under a cloak of secrecy, and "the inferior Lodges of Freemasonry are the most convenient cloaks" for the Illuminati's grand object[†]. The degree system of the Order of the Illuminati is as follows: Novice, Minerval,

---

[*] Originally, Weishaupt had planned the Order to be named the "Perfectibilists"

[†] Weishaupt was initiated into the Masonic Lodge "Theodor zum guten Rath" at Munich in 1777.

Illuminatus Minor, Illuminatus Major, Illuminatus Dirigens, Epopt (or Priest of Illuminism), Regent (or Prince of Illuminism), Magus-Philosopher, and Rex (or Man-King).

Due to fierce disagreements between Weishaupt, who was the Chairman of the Illuminati's 'Areopagus' (peak administrative apparatus), and Adolph Freiherr Knigge, who was a very influential member of the Illuminati's 'Areopagus' and senior official of the Freemasonic Order of Strict Observance, and due to the fact that, in 1777, Karl Theodor, a proponent of Enlightened Despotism, became ruler of Bavaria and, in 1785, he banned all secret societies, including the Illuminati, the Order of the Illuminati was shattered in Bavaria. Adam Weishaupt had already resigned from his official position of power in the Order at an Illuminati congress convened in Weimar in 1784. The authoritarian Bavarian political regime that was established by Karl Theodor and the Jesuits conducted a vicious propaganda campaign against Adam Weishaupt and the Illuminati, and many Freemasons, mainly out of fear of being persecuted by political and religious authorities, denounced the Illuminati.

In his own defense of the Order of the Illuminati, Weishaupt explained that the proper candidate for the Order of the Illuminati is a person that has the following qualities[*]:

1. He "does not close his ear to the lamentations of the miserable";

2. He does not close his heart to "gentle pity";

3. He is "the friend and brother of the unfortunate";

4. He has "a heart capable of love and friendship";

5. He is "steadfast in adversity, unwearied in the carrying out of whatever has been once engaged in, undaunted in the overcoming of difficulties";

6. He "does not mock and despise the weak";

---

[*] Adam Weishaupt, *Apologie der Illuminaten*, 1786; Adam Weishaupt und A.F. von Knigge, *Illuminatus dirigens, oder schottischer Ritter*, 1794.

7. He is "susceptible of conceiving great designs, desirous of rising superior to all base motives, and of distinguishing himself by deeds of benevolence";

8. He "shuns idleness";

9. He "considers no knowledge as unessential which he may have the opportunity of acquiring, regarding the knowledge of mankind as his chief study";

10. "when truth and virtue are in question", he is "sufficiently courageous to follow the dictates of his own heart", "despising the approbation of the multitude".

Furthermore, in the Epopt Degree of the Order of the Illuminati, Adam Weishaupt exposed his revolutionary vision about the autonomy and happiness of mankind, and he clarified that "Morality shall alone produce this great Revolution".

According to the rituals of the Order of the Illuminati, the members of the Illuminatus Major Degree should obtain a deep awareness of the following issues: the extent to which men have failed to actualize their ontological potential; the extent to which and the manners in which civil institutions have degenerated into new kinds of despotism; the errors that lie in the means that have been hitherto employed by the sages; the abandonment of the world to "the yoke of the wicked"; the persecution and misfortune of the honest man in the present, corrupt polities; and the sacrifice of the better part of humanity to selfish interest. Furthermore, according to their ritual, the members of the Illuminatus Major Degree should promise to co-operate with the other members of the Order of the Illuminati in order to promote the spiritual and political emancipation of humanity.

The Epopt Degree of the Order of the Illuminati places the candidate under much more solemn and weighty obligations, and it urges him to work for the establishment of the "empire of reason", in the context of which political and spiritual prejudices and contradictions will be eliminated and all the people will be capable of undertaking their existential responsibilities and of governing themselves. Furthermore, according to the Illuminati's rituals and Weishaupt's directions, promotion to the Regent Degree presupposed that the candidate was "as much as possible free man and independent of all Princes" and also that the candidate had shown how ardently he wished for a change in the political system. In particular, according to Weishaupt's "Code of the Illuminati", the Epopts who were worthy to be promoted to the Regent Degree are persons that unite prudence with the liberty of thinking and acting, that know how to combine transcendence of wit with gravity and dignity of manners, and that their heart is entirely devoted to the Order's mission for the welfare of humanity. Thus, according to the Regent Degree Ritual, the initiator tells the candidate: "You are now strong enough to conduct yourself, be then in future your own guide...Be free; that is to say, be a man, and a man who knows how to govern himself, a man who knows his duty, and his inalienable rights...Here, take back the engagements you have hitherto contracted with us. To you we return them all".

On 31 January 1800, Thomas Jefferson[*], the principal author of the United States Declaration of Independence (1776) and third President of the United States of America, wrote to Bishop James Madison about Adam Weishaupt and about the Illuminati and Freemasonry. In his correspondence with Madison, Jefferson put forward the following arguments: Weishaupt was a humanist, he believed in the infinite moral improvement of mankind, and he wanted to develop people's capacity for self-government; Weishaupt's political views were touching closest to William Godwin's anarchist political philosophy, and, therefore, conservative religious and political authorities, using propaganda mechanisms and techniques, attempted to present Weishaupt's political principles as "a conspiracy against all government"; Weishaupt believed in the purity of the early Christian Church's ethos and wanted to restore it through the moral system of the Order of the Illuminati, since, according to Weishaupt, Freemasons had failed to do so and most Freemasonic Orders had lost touch with the genuine meaning of their rituals and were infiltrated by representatives of political and spiritual despotism; Weishaupt created a secret society in order to protect himself and other freethinkers against the tyrannical regime of Bavaria.

---

[*] See: *The Thomas Jefferson Papers*, The Library of Congress, Federal Edition.

THE LEGACY OF THELEMIC MAGICK

Aleister Crowley* (1875—1947), the founder of the occult system of "Thelema", in his books *Magick in Theory and Practice* (Book 3) and *Magick Without Tears* (Chapter 1), acknowledged and stressed the significance of morality by defining "Magick" as the science and art of bringing about change according to one's own will and by adding that any required change may be effected by exercising rational control over the forces that one uses. Furthermore, according to Crowley, "Magick" is the science of self-knowledge and the art of putting self-knowledge in action.

Aleister Crowley's moral system is a kind of extreme moral emotionalism, which led him to an indiscriminate rejection of Christian teachings and made him notorious throughout the Western world. Crowley's rejection of Christianity is heavily due to the fact that his understanding of Christianity was conditioned by the Plymouth Brethren, a conservative Evangelical Christian movement, which, in the 19th century, transformed the religion of Love into a system of moral policing and spiritual terrorism, and by the authoritarianism of the Papacy, which, in the Middle Ages, 'exiled' Christ to some obscure and inaccessible 'Heavens' and declared that the Bishop of Rome is God's delegated administrator for earthly affairs. When Crowley articulated his occult theory of Thelema and created his own Abbey of Thelema in Sicily, he had in mind only François Rabelais' conception of Thelema and Rabelais' Abbey of Thelema, and he was obviously unfamiliar with both Maximus the Confessor's Christocentric 'Thelemism' (to which I referred in Chapter 3) and the Eastern Roman Emprire's mystical Christianity (Hesychasm), which I explained in Chapter 3. In fact, many Hesychasts and generally many Greek Church Fathers would, in essence, subscribe to Crowley's criticism of those Christian communities which live under the fear of punishment and Hell, feel 'damned', refuse to undertake responsibility for their lives and fail to experience a divinizing communion with God.

In philosophical terms, Crowley's Law of Thelema ("Do what thou wilt") is an emotionalist moral theory. The very fact that Crowley's Thelema is based on moral principles and has its own

---

* Aleister Crowley, *The Book of Thoth*, York Beach, Maine: Weiser Books, 2000 (originally published in 1944).

moral criteria is important for the scope of this chapter, because it indicates that there is an inextricable link between occultism* and moral philosophy.

PRACTICAL ESOTERICISM: AN ISSUE OF MORAL PHILOSOPHY

As we read in Plato's *Apology of Socrates*, Socrates argued that "the life which is unexamined is not worth living"; life without moral thought has neither meaning nor value. It is only though moral thought that the intentionality of consciousness can be vindicated. Through moral philosophy, the activity of consciousness is organized by being centred on a specific choice that, by being generalized, becomes a moral criterion, i.e. a universal measure whereby one can judge the intentions and the acts of his own consciousness and of the others' consciousnesses. Therefore, every meaningful discussion about the 'eso', i.e. about the esoteric life of man, must explicitly address the following issues: the nature of moral consciousness, the value of moral consciousness, and the moral criterion.

---

* For a general study of occultism, see: N. Drury and G. Tillett, *The Occult: A Sourcebook of Esoteric Wisdom*, London: Grange Books, 1997; L. Spence, *An Encyclopaedia of Occultism*, New York: Dover Publications, 2003 (originally published in 1920).

10

WESTERN ESOTERICISM AND MORAL PHILOSOPHY

A TRUE adept of the Kairological Qabalah is a *homo creator* in the most authentic sense of that term, because, even though he recognizes that reality is not a projection of human consciousness, he is aware of the submissiveness of reality to the intentionality of human consciousness. Creativity brings man face to face with the need of making judgments and therefore with moral questions. The purpose of this chapter is to give clear and adequately researched answers to the following questions, which naturally emerge in esotericism: the nature of moral consciousness, the value of moral consciousness, and the moral criterion.

THE NATURE OF MORAL CONSCIOUSNESS

With respect to its nature, moral consciousness is not an entity that can be separated from the consciousness of existence. Moral consciousness and consciousness of existence have the same identical essence, or nature. Moral consciousness is the consciousness of existence that expresses approval or disapproval of the structure and the style of an action whose goal is to change a being's relation to the world or to other beings, according to the dialectic of kairicity, which I have already explained. Moral consciousness, as a special functional form of the consciousness of existence, should be distinguished from psychological consciousness. Psychological consciousness is the consciousness that perceives itself as an alive being, i.e. it operates as a witness; but moral consciousness makes evaluative judgments, i.e. it operates as a judge.

With respect to its structure and operation, moral consciousness is a unified being, but it is not homogeneous. With respect to its operation, moral consciousness is composed of the following three factors:

1. The sentimental factor: the sentimental elements that determine moral consciousness are revealed and expressed through action, i.e. when they are experienced by consciousness, because our deeds reveal the extent to which we comply with the values that, according to our perception, require respect from every conscious being. Sentimental elements of this type are respect, pride, indignation and guilt.

2. The intellectual factor: the intellectual elements that determine moral consciousness consist in determinate ideas that can be clearly distinguished from values and can be conceived as the logical causes of action.

3. The volitional factor: the volitional elements that determine moral consciousness refer to the firm decisiveness of consciousness to accomplish an action that may be associated with the execution of one's duty, or with the defense of one's rights, or with a procedure for restoring a disturbed order.

The previous three factors of moral consciousness are inseparable from each other, but the sentimental factor plays the predominant role in the formation of moral consciousness, since moral consciousness is more strongly affected by the sentimental factor than by the intellectual factor or the volitional one. For instance, an idea, i.e. an intellectual element of moral consciousness, may be ambiguous, and, therefore, it may not be able to lead moral consciousness to a clear decision, but, due to a clear sentimental orientation, moral consciousness may be able to clearly and correctly evaluate the situation in which it has to act. Furthermore, the volitional factor may be manifested in a weak manner, and, it may not be able to lead moral consciousness to a clear decision, but, due to a clear sentimental orientation, moral consciousness may be able to remain strong and lively and express itself in an intense manner.

THE VALUE OF MORAL CONSCIOUSNESS

With respect to its value, moral consciousness can be judged according to the stability or the instability of its manifestations. There are cases in which moral consciousness remains unvaried, but there are others in which moral consciousness exhibits variations in its operation. These changes in the state of moral consciousness have led skeptical philosophers (mainly Gorgias and Thrasymachus in ancient Greece, and Michel de Montaigne and Blaise Pascal in the modern era) to formulate negative evaluations of moral consciousness. However, the skeptical evaluations of moral consciousness have failed to recognize that, even though moral consciousness is subject to change, the changes that take place in the field of moral consciousness are not arbitrary, but they follow a series of progress. In fact, the history of civilization indicates that there is progress in the fields of moral ideas, institutions and moral sensitivity:

- Progress in the field of moral ideas: morality becomes more and more specialized, in the sense that its rules follow a continuous process of differentiation from religion and law; morality becomes internalized, in the sense that, as Kant has stressed, moral consciousness evaluates actions not only on the basis of their consequences but also on the basis of the agent's motives; morality becomes individualized, in the sense that, in addition to group rights (i.e. rights associated with social control), individual rights (i.e. rights associated with political and economic freedom) receive increasing emphasis, too; morality expands, in the sense that, apart from group rights, human rights (namely, "basic rights and freedoms that all people are entitled to regardless of nationality, sex, national or ethnic origin, race, religion, language, or other status"*) receive increasing emphasis.

- Progress in the field of institutions: humanity

---

* This is the basic definition of human rights according to Amnesty International.

continuously searches for new institutional frameworks within which there will be more justice. From this viewpoint, the abolition of slavery was a major step toward the institutional integration of societies, and the Universal Declaration of Human Rights was a major step toward the development of a global moral code.

• Progress in the field of moral sensitivity: some situations that were considered normal in the past (e.g. child abuse, torture, gender discrimination, despotic behaviors on behalf of political and religious elites, etc.) are unacceptable and morally condemned today. Moreover, today, even though violations of human rights continue taking place in the advanced Western world, the authorities that are engaged in such actions always try to find justifications and do not dare to commit human rights violations in a blatant manner.

The previous series of moral progress contribute to the refutation of the rationale of skepticism, but they cannot completely refute the skeptics' arguments. The history of mankind is characterized by both moral progress and moral regression; in fact, there are historical periods that are imprinted by morally negative and unacceptable situations that are caused by egopathic persons, such as Josef Stalin and Adolf Hitler*. Such negative personalities make it more difficult for historians and philosophers to identify patterns of moral development and to compare different historical periods with respect to the issue of moral progress, and they indicate the dual character of human nature, which exhibits both nobleness and misery.

Between the perception that stresses the progress of moral consciousness and the perception that stresses the instability of moral consciousness (and phenomena of moral regression), there is enough space in order to search for stable structural elements of moral consciousness that will enable us to argue that moral consciousness is characterized by structural stability. If we approach moral values in terms of their contents, then we realize that, in the history of civilization, different values have been placed at the top

---

*   See: Alan Bullock, *Hitler and Stalin: Parallel Lives*, New York: Vintage Books, 1993.

of the 'moral pyramid'; for instance: in ancient times, there was a transition from the value of 'bravery' to the value of 'education' and, from the value of 'education', to the value of 'sanctity'; in the Middle Ages, the ancient value of 'hospitality' was substituted by the value of 'chivalry'; in the French society of the 17th century, the value of 'chivalry' was substituted by the value of 'honesty'; in the American society of the 19th century, the value of 'chivalry' was substituted by the value of the 'self-made man'. However, 'courage', 'truthfulness', 'uprightness' and 'bravery', even though they can be interpreted in different manners, are values that exert predominant moral authority on men both in the past and in the present. Moreover, if we approach moral values in terms of the forms through which they are manifested, then we realize that, in every historical period, every society makes a fundamental distinction between 'good' and 'evil', i.e. between 'moral positivity' and 'moral negativity'.

The previous analysis indicates the structural stability of the operation of moral consciousness, i.e. the qualitative features of moral consciousness are recurrent. Moral consciousness is *affected* by social structure, but it is not *created* by social structure. Even though moral consciousness internalizes and reflects social values, and even though moral consciousness may be obliged to comply with social values, it can always judge and criticize social values, conceive the idea of a more just society and even revolt. Thus, moral consciousness seems to be innate*. In fact, moral consciousness imposes itself on history by operating as an innate quest for the 'good'. The sentimental, the intellectual and the volitional factors of moral consciousness together conceive the 'good' and determine the conditions under which it can be historically objectivated.

THE MORAL CRITERION

Every moral act is evaluated by means of a moral criterion. With respect to the moral criteria that they use, moral philosophies can be divided into the following three categories: moral emotionalism, moral sentimentalism and moral rationalism.

Moral emotionalism: Moral emotionalism can be distinguished

---

* For a detailed and in-depth inquiry into the innate character of moral consciousness, see: Evangelos Moutsopoulos, *He Poreia tou Pneumatos: He Axie (The Itinerary of the Spirit: Values)*, Athens: 1977, in Greek; C.D. Gruenber and E. Moutsopoulos (eds), *The Idea of Europe: Its Common Heritage and Future*, New York: PWPA, 1991.

into three types of theories: hedonism, eudemonism and utilitarianism. According to hedonism, the criterion of morality is the presence of a particular pleasure in consciousness, since pleasure itself enables consciousness to found its evaluative judgments on the unquestionable reality of the experience of the given pleasure. However, this simple and straightforward moral criterion has two important defects. First of all, through hedonism, consciousness is engaged in a continuous quest for pleasurable experiences that, by their own nature, do not last long enough. Thus, a hedonistic consciousness experiences the following contradiction: it searches for lasting pleasure in experiences that, by their own nature, do not last long enough, and, for this reason, ultimately, consciousness experiences pain instead of pleasure. The second defect of hedonism is that, because various pleasures may be contradictory to each other, it becomes extremely difficult, or rather impossible, for consciousness to place all pleasures in a unified, consistent hierarchy.

According to Plato's theory of pleasures[*], most pleasures are mixed, in the sense that they are simultaneously pleasurable and unpleasurable (i.e. mixed pleasure is just the middle state between pleasure and pain that only seems pleasurable by contrast to pain). On the other hand, pure pleasures are pleasurable in themselves, and they include pleasures that are related to the enjoyment of art and imply the cessation of sadness. This qualitative distinction between mixed and pure pleasures influenced Epicurus' eudemonism and the moral philosophies of Arthur Schopenhauer and John Stuart Mill.

Whereas Maine de Biran[†] (1766—1824) formulated an extreme, optimistic voluntarist philosophy, by substituting the principle of 'volo' for the Cartesian principle of 'cogito', Schopenhauer[‡] (1788—1860) formulated a negative voluntarist philosophy that stresses the self-destructive character of volition. According to Schopenhauer, volition is will-to-live, and, because life is intimately related to the desire for pleasures that prove to be temporary and, therefore, cause pain and sadness, it logically follows that the only way in which existence can be freed from pain and sadness is to be freed from

---

[*] Plato exposes his theory of pleasures in his dialogue *Philebus*.

[†] See: N.E. Truman, *Maine de Biran's Philosophy of Will*, New York: Macmillan, 1904.

[‡] See: Bryan Magee, *The Philosophy of Schopenhauer*, Oxford: Oxford University Press, 1997.

this life and to be oriented toward the contemplation of ideas, which are considered to be the only realities that have lasting value and the only adequate objectivation of the will. The idealism of Schopenhauer's philosophy is based on Platonism and primarily on Hinduism, since the ultimate goal of Hinduism is the attainment of the "eternal bliss" of Nirvana, which is the state of liberation from pain and individual existence. In this way, the intentionality of consciousness is directed toward the eternal and permanent, in which it is ultimately eliminated, and the only other worthy pleasure is that of art, which is experienced as a temporary liberation from the world of phenomena and volition.

The most important defect of Schopenhauer's philosophy and of the teachings about Nirvana is that they deprive the human being of the ability to creatively reflect on its life and, therefore, of the ability to realize what it really wants, since they teach the elimination of reason in spirituality. In order to be able to realize what it really wants, a person must reflect on itself, and, in order to be able to creatively reflect on itself, a person needs to be able to apply reason to the objects of its consciousness. But if a person is sunk in the abyss of its emotions, then it cannot creatively reflect on itself, and, hence, it cannot realize what it really wants. When people follow such emotional approaches to philosophy and faith, they cannot achieve self-awareness, and, therefore, they cannot make reliable commitments to the fulfillment of specific historical duties; after all, they perceive history as if it were a "valley of tears" or an illusion. Additionally, when historical becoming does not satisfy the powerful and all-pervading emotions of such people and urges them to endorse a reasonable attitude to life, their emotional inner world explodes in irrational manners and becomes a potential source of anti-social behavior and violence.

The transition from hedonism to eudemonism was mainly the result of Epicurus' attempt to find ways of prolonging the experience of pleasure. The philosophy of Epicurus* starts from the concept of pleasure and aims at finding a new element in this concept that will allow the creative transcendence of the temporary character of pleasure. According to Epicurus, this new element is the experience of security and serenity in pleasure. Epicurus argues that,

---

* See: Epicurus, *The Essential Epicurus*, trans. and introduction by E. O'Connor, New York: Prometheus Books, 1993.

if, as Plato has put it, we can assert that the consequence of pleasure is the cessation of sadness, then the ideal that we should pursue is the ideal of mental calmness that can be achieved through permanent pleasure. Thus, for Epicurus, we should avoid those pleasures that are temporary, mixed with pain and lead consciousness from the experience of scarcity to the experience of saturation, and instead we should pursue only those pleasures that bloom in mental calmness because only these pleasures are stable and intrinsically pleasurable. Epicurus teaches that pleasures are directly connected with desire, and, therefore, pleasures are evaluated by the same rule that is applied for the evaluation of desires. Epicurus approaches the problem of the moral criterion from a standpoint that is characterized by subjectivism and individualism. Hence, the most important defect of Epicureanism is that it stresses the importance of individual interest and ignores the importance of social interest.

In the modern era, the main representative of moral emotionalism was Jeremy Bentham[*]. Bentham stressed the importance of the quantity of pleasure, and, in fact, his moral philosophy consists in a "felicific calculus". According to Bentham, happiness can be gauged by a felicific calculus, and, as J.V. Orth has mentioned, Bentham believes that the following four circumstances determine the value of a pleasure: intensity, duration, certainty, and propinquity[†].

Bentham's arithmetic of pleasures implies that, for Bentham, the quality of pleasures ultimately reduces to their quantity or at least to their intensity, which is interpreted as the price assigned to them by consciousness. Even when Bentham tries to identify different factors that determine the value of a pleasure, he always characterizes pleasures in quantitative terms. Thus, the first defect of Bentham's moral philosophy is his arithmetic of pleasures, since it is unable to address qualitative issues. Furthermore, another problematic principle of Bentham's moral philosophy is his argument that one of the factors that determine the value of a pleasure is the number of persons affected by it; this principle leaves the following possibilities open: the social duties of a moral consciousness may be dictated by

---

[*] Jeremy Bentham, *An Introduction to the Principles of Morals and Legislation*, ed. J.H. Burns and H.L.A. Hart, London: Athlone Press, 1970 (originally published in 1789).

[†] See: J.V. Orth, "Jeremy Bentham: The Common Law's Severest Critic", *American Bar Association Journal*, Vol. 68, 1982, p. 714.

its individual interest, and this attitude is a form of mental egoism (i.e. one may accept that he has social duties, but he may define them according to his individual interests); even though Bentham argues that the same pleasure can be experienced by different subjects, the evaluation of each pleasure may always be a subjective question; and, finally, the protection of the general interest of society may lead to the sacrifice of individual interests. Thus, the second defect of Bentham's moral philosophy is that he identifies the general interest of society with the individual interest in a manner that makes his moral philosophy blurred and inconsistent.

John Stuart Mill[*] attempted to lead utilitarianism out of the dead end of Bentham's moral philosophy by arguing that utility as a moral criterion is of a qualitative nature, and not of a quantitative one. According to J. Stuart Mill, if one overlooks the qualitative dimension of pleasure, then he arrives at a moral theory "worthy only of swine"[†]. Mill proffers a distinction between higher and lower pleasures, and he argues that higher pleasures, including mental aesthetic and moral pleasures, must be preferred over lower pleasures. Thus, Mill formulated and defended the thesis that "it is better to be a human being dissatisfied than a pig satisfied"[‡]. Furthermore, Mill argues that, according to the previous principle, the general interest of society must be respected and get priority because of its intrinsic value and not because it may coincide with people's individual interests. According to J.S. Mill, the golden rule of utilitarian morality is to do as you would be done by and to love your neighbor. Hence, Mill's utilitarian morality implies that only a pleasure that is intrinsically noble is worthy to be experienced by the human being (i.e. it is worthy of human nature). Moreover, the foundation of Mill's utilitarian morality is the value of being human.

Indeed, Mill's utilitarian morality is an improvement of Bentham's utilitarian morality. However, Mill's utilitarian morality is characterized by contradictions that are intrinsic to utilitarianism in general. Mill argues that there is an empirical criterion for the qualitative evaluation of pleasures and that this criterion

---

[*]   See: Karl Britton, *John Stuart Mill*, Harmondsworth: Penguin, 1953; Roger Crisp, *Mill on Utilitarianism*, London: Routledge, 1997; Pedro Schwartz, *The New Political Economy of J.S. Mill*, London: Weidenfeld & Nicolson, 1972.

[†]   J.S. Mill, *Utilitarianism*, London: Parker, Son and Bourn, 1863, p. 332.

[‡]   Ibid, Chapter 2.

is unerringly manifested in the conscious minds of the most scientifically cultivated and knowledgeable people. Furthermore, according to Mill, if no other factors (such as restrictions, coercion, etc.) interfere, consciousness is attracted, and it should be attracted, to the noblest pleasures. Mill's point makes a logically illegitimate inference from 'is' to 'ought', from 'is desired' to 'is worthy of desire', and G.E. Moore* called it the "naturalistic fallacy". In fact, in practice, there are cases in which people seem to prefer a lower pleasure over a higher one, and also the judgment of the most scientifically cultivated and knowledgeable people cannot be assumed to be infallible. Furthermore, Mill's utilitarian morality leaves the following question open: since there is no criterion of morality other than pleasure, on what grounds can a specific pleasure claim superiority over all other pleasures?

Bentham had put forward the fallacious argument that, since each pursues his individual interest, therefore each pursues the general interest of society. Mill avoided this fallacy, and, to the contrary, he argued that the pursuit of the general good would require constant calculation of long term consequences, and that is hardly possible. According to Mill, individuals seek the general happiness only in the best state of society, where the educational system and the legislation secure the harmonization of individual interests, but we are clearly not in the best state. However, these observations and arguments contradict Mill's attempt to establish moral emotionalism.

In general, from the previous analysis, it follows that every type of moral emotionalism is unable to provide us with an acceptable criterion of morality: hedonism disbands the ego; eudemonism presupposes a distance between the person that has a given experience and the given experience itself (in order to achieve inner serenity); utilitarianism overemphasizes the notion of interest, thus leading to the overemphasization of the antithesis among interests and of the need to harmonize individual interests, which, ultimately, proves to be chimerical (within the framework of utilitarianism).

Moral sentimentalism: By the term 'sentiment', I mean an emotion endowed with a subjective evaluative judgment. The moral theories that belong to the 'school' of moral sentimentalism can be divided into three categories, according to the criterion on which they are based: the morality of sympathy, the morality of compassion and

---

*   G.E. Moore, *Principia Ethica*, New York: Prometheus Books, 1988 (originally published in 1903).

the morality of altruism. The main representative of the morality of sympathy was Adam Smith, who published *The Theory of Moral Sentiments* in 1759 and is recognized as the father of classical political economy.

Adam Smith defined 'sympathy' as the intuitive perception of the normative character of human behavior. Adam Smith's definition of sympathy can be understood through the following example: a soldier is killed during a battle in order to defend his officer whom, at a personal level, may hate. Moreover, Smith relates sympathy to approval. In fact, Smith argues that "to approve of another man's opinions is to adopt those opinions, and to adopt them is to approve of them"[*]. In addition, he argues that "to approve of the passions of another…as suitable to their objects, is the same thing as to observe that we entirely sympathize with them"[†].

According to Smith, sympathy, of which we must become worthy, must have the following characteristics: (a) it must be pure and unconditional (since, in the field of moral sentiments, ambiguous impressions reflect suspicious actions, but our actions must be pure); (b) it must be universal, i.e. experienced by everybody, or at least by the majority of the people. However, the following problem emerges: what should we do in case we do not know if others approve or disapprove of our actions? In this case, Smith argues, other persons' approval or disapproval of our actions can be substituted by our own judgment under the condition that we shall form our judgment according to the method of an impartial spectator of our actions, i.e. under the condition that we shall operate as impartial spectators of our actions.

Adam Smith's moral philosophy has the following defects: (a) Sympathy is not a necessary state and may vary from one consciousness to another and from one moral area to another. Thus, sympathy cannot be as universal as Smith wishes. (b) Sympathy may not always be in harmony with the most rational moral judgments, since moral consciousness can be influenced by non-rational forces. Thus, sympathy, as a criterion of morality, cannot lead to the formulation of moral judgments that are immune to criticism. (c) By arguing that the actor's own consciousness can substitute for the

---

[*] Adam Smith, *The Theory of Moral Sentiments*, ed. D.D. Raphael and A.L. Macfie, Oxford: Oxford University Press, 1976 (originally published in 1759), p. 17.

[†] Ibid, p. 16.

consciousness of a sympathizing spectator-judge if the first operates as an impartial spectator, Smith stresses that sympathy or antipathy must be eliminated in exactly those cases (i.e. moral deliberation and judgment) in which sympathy or antipathy is presupposed; this is a logical contradiction. The fundamental contradiction of Smith's moral theory is that it attempts to reduce sympathy to a sentiment, but it treats sympathy as an expression of moral rationality. In other words, Smith argues that sympathy is a moral sentiment, but, in essence, he interprets sympathy as a manifestation of the operation of moral reason.

The founder of the morality of compassion is Schopenhauer. Like every other philosophy of action, Schopenhauer's philosophy starts from the principle that effectiveness is the purpose and the vindication of action. According to Schopenhauer, the good of other people can become the motive of our action due to our compassion for others. Schopenhauer argues that compassion connects our suffering ego with other suffering egos and that the world is in principle a place of suffering. Within the framework of Schopenhauer's pessimism, suffering is the only thing that enables us to know the consciousness of another person. In this context, Schopenhauer's approach to moral life is one-dimensional and wrong: the perception that, at the level of morality, suffering is the only positive datum on which the knowledge of other persons' consciousness can be based is a psychological fallacy. Apart from its passivity, the human being is mainly characterized by activity and by the objectivations of its activity, i.e. by the things it creates, which express the totality of its sentimental world. Furthermore, compassion is a complex sentiment that cannot be easily controlled by reason, and, therefore, it can even underpin unjust actions.

The founder of the morality of altruism is Comte. Comte founded what in the early 1820s he called 'political science', subsequently dubbed 'social physics' and in 1838 called 'sociology', on the historicist 'law of the three stages'.

Comte argued that humanity was progressing from the theological state of monarchy, through the metaphysical state of democracy, to the positive state of scientism and industrialism. In particular, he asserted that scientists must "elevate politics to the rank of a science of observation"[*]. In this context, Comte proposes

---

[*]   Auguste Comte, *The Early Essays,* in R. Fletcher (ed.), *The Crisis of Industrial Civilization,* London:

the replacement of the worship of God by the worship of humanity, and he regards each individual as a substantiation of the concept of humanity. Additionally, Comte argues that our egoistic impulses coexist with social instincts of sympathy and that the latter can be divided into two categories: special social instincts (e.g. a connection between two persons, the adoration of socially superior persons by socially inferior persons, etc.) and general social instincts (e.g. goodness, ecumenical love, etc.). According to Comte, the fact that we live among other people and through other people is certain, and it implies that we have the following moral obligations: to secure solidarity among our contemporaries and continuity across generations. Thus, Comte believed that individuals had a moral obligation to "live for others", i.e. he identified eudemonism with the principle of duty.

As a consequence of his previous positions, Comte argues that every attempt to connect each person with the 'Absolute' (or God) directly is equivalent to an attempt to separate the individual from humanity, to which it belongs. In this context, Comte argues that every monotheism, and especially Christianity, leads to the domination of the principle of personhood, and the principle of personhood, in turn, leads to egoism. On the other hand, for Comte, the replacement of the worship of God by the worship of humanity, or of the "Great Being" (which is composed of all the beings that cooperated for the sake of their common existence and includes even the useful animals), inhibits egoism by inhibiting the development of personhood. At this point, it is clear that Comte failed to understand the difference between the terms 'individual' and 'person', and, therefore, he wrongfully attributed the negative characteristics of the first to the latter. John Zizioulas (Christian Orthodox Metropolitan of Pergamon and former President of the Academy of Athens), in explaining the meaning of personhood in Christian thought, has pointed out that God's personal mode of existence implies that God's substance does not constrain Him and that communion is not a constraining structure, but God's being is the consequence of a free person[*]. Being as communion, which is the essence of 'personhood', means that there is no such thing as absolute individual, conceivable in itself, and simultaneously the ontological category of communion

---

Heinemann, 1974, p. 134.

[*]   J.D. Zizioulas, *Being as Communion*, New York: St Vladimir's Seminary Press, 1985, p. 18.

comes from a concrete and free person. According to John Zizioulas, the person cannot exist without communion, but communion should never deny or suppress the person*. Hence, in contrast with Comte's assertions, 'personhood' is not equivalent with 'individualism' and does not lead to egocentrism. Finally, Comte's moral theory is self-contradictory because, even though it seems that Comte attempted to found altruism on positive science, and particularly on sociology, in essence, Comte founded altruism on the worship of humanity, i.e. on a sentiment.

From the previous analysis of moral sentimentalism, it follows that every form of moral sentimentalism leads to contradictions. Hence, in order to formulate a consistent moral system, we must combine the power of sentiment with the power of reason.

Moral rationalism: Moral rationalism includes the moral theories of Plato, the Stoics and Kant. Plato's moral theory is founded on the supreme idea-value of the 'good'. Plato evaluates a pleasure in accordance with the manner in which it is experienced by the human being. Moreover, in *Timaeus*, Plato stresses the difference between "prudent" and "imprudent" persons, and, in *Theaetetus*, Plato stresses the difference between ignorance and knowledge as judgment with an account. Plato agrees with Socrates' thesis that "no one errs willingly", and he argues that every diversion from rationally-grounded moral judgments is due to lack of an integral moral reason; if one's moral reason is integral, then moral reason imposes proper behavior on his moral consciousness. Descartes arrived at the same conclusion from a very different path, and, in the *Discourse*, he explained that his moral theory is founded on the notion of 'virtue' as a disposition of the will to choose in accordance with reason's judgments about the good and on the notion of 'happiness' as a state of mental well-being that is attained by acquiring all the virtues and in general all the other goods that we can acquire.

The main problem with the previous form of moral rationalism is that consciousness cannot always know with certainty whether it has captured all the data that describe and summarize each particular case, but moral reason can impose proper behavior on moral consciousness only if the latter has captured all the data that describe and summarize each particular case, and this happens rarely. Usually, consciousness does not have the necessary mental soberness

---

*   Ibid.

in order to capture all the data that describe and summarize each particular case. Furthermore, things become even more complicated if we accept Plato's argument that moral integration is achieved through love ('eros'). According to Plato's *Symposium*, within the framework of Platonic love, the lover transmits knowledge, and his beloved receives this knowledge and thus becomes a better person. However, according to Aristotle's moral theory, which is also founded on reason, moral integration does not presuppose a pathetic state in which one receives knowledge from his lover, but it is based on a state of equality, which corresponds to friendship, and on the mental soberness that underpins Aristotle's principle of the mean[*].

The moral theory of Stoicism[†] is founded on Zeno's principle of "living in agreement" (Arius Didymus, 63A), which was reformulated by Cleanthes as "living in agreement with nature" (Arius Didymus, 63B). Additionally, Chrysippus amplified this to "living in accordance with experience of what happens by nature". According to Stoicism, natural laws are manifestations of a universal reason, and nature itself is reason (Hegel made similar assertions by stressing that everything that is reasonable must be real and everything that is real must be reasonable). In this context, virtue is a continuous choice of living in agreement with the natural order of things, and passion is a form of reason that deviates from nature.

According to the Stoics, because reason is diffused throughout the entire universe ('cosmos') and the conscious minds of all human beings, it follows that all human beings are equal. This principle implies that slavery should be abolished, we should love mankind, and we should endorse a cosmopolitan attitude[‡]. The Stoics' love for mankind is impersonal; the Stoic philosopher has no personal family; instead, his family is the entire humanity. However, the Stoic ideal of morality is an essentially negative one. Epictetus has summarized the Stoic ideal of morality as follows: "All philosophy

---

[*]   In his *Nicomachean Ethics*, Aristotle argues that 'courage' means holding a mean position in one's feelings of confidence and fear; temperance is a mean with regards to pleasure; liberality or generosity is a mean with regards to giving money; magnanimity (i.e. "greatness of soul") is a mean between the excess of vanity, or "chaunotes", and the deficiency of smallness of soul, or "mikropsychia"; gentleness concerning anger is a mean between irascibility and spiritlessness, etc.

[†]   See: Brad Inwood, *The Cambridge Companion to the Stoics*, Cambridge: Cambridge University Press, 2003.

[‡]   See: Alasdair MacIntyre, *A Short History of Ethics*, London: Routledge and Kegan Paul, 1967, p. 107.

lies in two words: sustain and abstain". In his *Discourses* and *Enchiridion*, Epictetus starts from the distinction between those things in our power ('prohairetic' things) and those things not in our power ('aprohairetic' things), and he argues that the things that are in our power are only those that are our own work, and these are our opinions, impulses, desires and aversions, whereas the things that are not in our power are our bodies, possessions, glory and power. In this context, Stoicism cultivates apathy, which was described and summarized by Epictetus in his *Enchiridion*. By leading to apathy, the moral philosophy of Stoicism fails to understand the emotion and pulse of true love and the active ways in which one can express his solidarity to other people, instead of simply tolerating them and sustaining life. A radical reaction against the moral philosophy of Stoicism and against the morality of those Christian Church Fathers and theologians who mixed Christianity with Stoicism was put forward by Friedrich Nietzsche, who, in his *Daybreak: Reflections on Moral Prejudices*[*] (1881), argued that the morality of Stoicism and the Christian moral theories that were founded on Stoicism are moralities of weakness.

Kant developed a new approach to moral philosophy by shifting the debate about morality from actions to intentions. In fact, Kant adopted J.-J. Rousseau's thesis that nothing is absolutely good in this world or out of it except a good intention. To this thesis, Kant added that an intention is good when it is determined by respect for the moral law, i.e. by the consciousness of duty. Neither spiritual nor material goods are intrinsically good, because their value depends on the individual circumstances; for instance, the coolness of a criminal makes people hate him even more. On the other hand, a good intention is good not because its results are good but because it is good in itself, assuming, of course, that it is combined with adequate action. Thus, an act is moral if its sole motive is pure respect for the moral law.

According to Kant, the moral law is a categorical imperative, i.e. it commands unconditionally. In other words, Kant's morality rejects the sentimental morality of "the volunteers of duty", and it simply says: do this because it is your duty to do it. Kant's morality lays down the following fundamental principle: always act so that

---

[*]   Friedrich Nietzsche, *Daybreak: Reflections on Moral Prejudices*, trans. R.J. Hollingdale, Cambridge: Cambridge University Press, 1997 (originally published in 1881).

you can will that everybody shall follow the determining principle of your action. This is the ultimate criterion of morality, according to Kant. For instance, you cannot will that everybody should make lying promises, for, if everybody did, nobody would believe anybody and finally lying promises would prove to be self-defeating. A lying promise is a contradiction, and no rational being can really will a contradiction. Furthermore, no rational being can will to disregard the welfare of others, because if such conduct became universal, the given being itself might some day become the victim of inhuman behavior. Kant stresses that the rational will imposes upon itself universal laws.

Kant's moral theory has the following defects: (a) Kant's argument that nothing is absolutely good in this world or out of it except a good intention is wrong. There are, in fact, epistemological values, e.g. knowledge, which is preferable than ignorance. (b) Kant's argument that the moral law is a categorical imperative leads to oversimplification. For instance, it may be neither psychologically easy nor rational to be sincere when one asks you information about a person whom he wants to kill. Kant proposes the elimination of sensitivity and generally the elimination of the sentimental factor in moral life in order to make morality more powerful and consistent, but, ultimately, in this way, he deprives the human being of powerful motives that contribute to the development of moral life*. (c) Kant treats love as an experience that merely underpins respect. But love can be understood as a way of life and, more specifically, as that way of life which is characterized by selflessness.

THE MORAL CRITERION FROM THE
PERSPECTIVE OF THE KAIROLOGICAL QABALAH

From the analysis of the moral criterion that I conducted in this chapter, it follows that none of the previous moral theories can offer guarantees that it can capture the entire spectrum of moral life: pleasures express attraction to life; sentiments express inner vibrations, since they are ideas colored by emotions; and reason

---

* For this reason, the earliest Fathers of the Christian Church called discretion the greatest of all virtues. As we read in Abbot Moses' *Cassian* (Col. II), Antony the Great (born in Faylum about the middle of the 3rd century A.D.), a great legislator and organizer of monks, said that "there are people who, having used up all of their bodily powers in excessive asceticism, do not succeed in drawing near to God, since they lack discretion".

expresses the power of consciousness to control itself. However, all these partial principles can be combined into a kairological morality, which leads to kairic action and is a presupposition of kairic action. In other words, kairological morality is a synthesis of moral emotionalism, moral sentimentalism and moral rationalism. Kairological morality expresses the intentionality of consciousness, which, in turn, is expressed as an itinerary toward a better life and utilizes every aspect of morality in order to be confirmed.

11

THE POLITICAL DIMENSION OF WESTERN ESOTERICISM AND THE KAIROLOGICAL QABALAH

THE Kairological Qabalah implies that human history is creation. This means that social entities are objectivations of the intentionality and particularly of the kairicity of the citizens, but often citizens are not aware of the fact that their kairic activity is the cause of the institution of social organizations or even they do not want to know that their kairic activity is the cause of the institution of social organizations, since kairicity implies moral responsibility and excludes laziness. From the viewpoint of the Kairological Qabalah, esotericism must be inextricably related to politics, in the sense that it is through politics that man's spiritual achievements can be put in the service of humanity. Therefore, any attempt to radically disengage esotericism from politics is a kind of obscurantism and a negation of history.

POLITICIZED WESTERN ESOTERIC FRATERNITIES

As I argued in Chapter 9, the Order of the Illuminati was one of the most intellectually consistent and decisive attempts to combine esotericism with politics in an explicit and systematic way. However, apart from Adam Weishaupt's Illuminati, in the modern history of Europe and America, there are many other initiatory fraternities that have operated as incubators and/or vehicles of revolutionary and progressive political movements. The well-known British historian Eric Hobsbawm[*] has pointed out that, in the 18th and the 19th centuries revolutions in Europe, all revolutionary forces were structured as secret insurrectionary fraternities and that such fraternities derived or copied from Freemasonic models. The most famous and internationally influential of those insurrectionary fraternities was that of the "good cousins" or Carbonari.

The Carbonari, most probably, descended from Freemasonic or similar lodges in Eastern France via anti-Bonapartist French officers in Italy[†] and from the Illuminati of Naples under the guidance of the Illumnati of London[‡]. The Carbonari's initiation rituals were structured around the trade of charcoal-selling, hence their name ('Carbonari' means charcoal-burners); a lodge was called 'baracca' (a hut), a meeting was called 'vendita' (a sale), and an important meeting was called 'alta vendita'. The language of religion was extensively used by the Carbonari in order to express their emancipatory program for humanity.

In the context of the Carbonari's mystic rites, Christ was the lamb torn by the wolf, and clearing the 'wood' (society) of 'wolves' (tyrants) became the symbolic expression of the Carbonari's aim. At the conclusion of the Initiation Ceremony, the whole congregation (baracca) knelt, held daggers to their naked breasts, and they declared "the devotion of their whole lives to the principles of liberty, equality and progress, which are the soul and purpose of all the secret and public acts of the Carbonari". In 1814, the Carbonari wanted to obtain a constitution for the Kingdom of Naples by force. Prominent members of the Carbonari included: Giuseppe Mazzini (1805—1872, Italian politician, journalist and activist for the unification of Italy), Marquis de Lafayette (hero of the American and French Revolutions), Lord Byron (1788—1824, British poet) and Giuseppe Garibaldi (1807—1882, Italian general and politician considered as one of Italy's "fathers of the fatherland"). After the suppression of the revolutions in Naples and Piedmont, in 1821, the Carbonari throughout Italy were declared guilty of high treason. However, societies of a similar kind had been formed in France, and, ultimately, Paris became the headquarters of Carbonarism.

---

[*]   Eric Hobsbawm, *The Age of Revolution: 1789—1848*, New York: Vintage Books, 1996, p. 115.

[†]   Ibid, p. 115.

[‡]   P. Pieri, *Le società segrete e i moti degli anni 1820—1821 e 1830—831*, Milano, 1931, p. 60.

THE INTERPLAY BETWEEN POLITICS AND ESOTERICISM

In the context of culture, every being and thing in this world is embedded in a symbolic system, i.e. it exists inextricably united with its meaning. Peter Berger and Thomas Luckmann have pointed out that symbolic universes integrate different systems of significations and institutions in a symbolic totality[*], and, in effect, all human activity occurs within a symbolic universe. According to Berger and Luckmann, the symbolic universe is the system that is composed of all socially objectivated and subjectively real meanings[†], and it links man with humanity, thus allowing him to transcend the finitude of individual existence[‡]. As I have already argued, myth, namely, the spiritual core of beings and things, is the major determining factor of civilization. By changing the mythological foundation of a civilization, one can change the manner in which the members of the given civilization see themselves and the world, and, eventually, he can change civilization itself. Thus, as Zbigniew Brzezinski, former Director of the U.S. National Security Council under President Carter, has put it, ideas mobilize political action and hence shape the world[§].

In general, societies need to legitimize their institutions, i.e. to explain why their institutions are good and just. Archaic societies did that by believing that their laws were given to them by a supernatural ancestor or god or that they were the image of a cosmic order and so must be true. Capitalist societies legitimize their system (i.e. capitalism) through logic, by arguing that their system makes logical sense. The previous efforts are tautological, i.e. closed logical systems, since they legitimize a system through rules defined by the system itself. For instance, capitalist societies first define what logic is and then base their system on that logic, thus making it immune to fundamental criticism, i.e. they transform it into a political totem.

The four-fold dialectic of kairicity, which I defined in Chapter 7 and corresponds to the sephirah of Tiphareth of the Kairological Qabalah, is the ultimate foundation of man's autonomy. I

---

[*] P.L. Berger and T. Luckmann, *The Social Construction of Reality: A Treatise in the Sociology of Knowledge*, Garden City, N.Y.: Doubleday & Co., 1966, p. 88.

[†] Ibid, p. 89.

[‡] Ibid, p. 95.

[§] Zbigniew Brzezinski, *Out of Control: Global Turmoil on the Eve of the 21st Century*, New York: Collier Books, 1993, p. x.

defined the concept of autonomy in Chapter 3, explaining that a society is autonomous if and only if it creates its own laws and also is aware of this condition. In contrast, the members of heteronomous societies attribute the results of the kairic activity of their consciousness to some authority that is beyond criticism. Thus, heteronomous societies are characterized by the creation of political totems, i.e. regulations that are beyond criticism and hence unchangeable.

The existence of an autonomous society is directly dependent on the alertness of people's consciousness, i.e. on the awareness of the wisdom that lies in the Kairological Qabalah's Middle Pillar. Otherwise, people tend to forget the four-fold dialectic of kairicity, thus giving rise to a heteronomous society. For instance, the initial conditions of a society may be autonomy, usually in some form of direct democracy, like the town hall meetings during the American Revolution and the local assemblies of the Paris Commune (1871). However, a society that is initially autonomous may end up with a political system in which the citizens delegate their legislative power to a group of experts who remain in power, largely unchecked by official means, for a number of years (until the next election day). In contrast, the concept of political autonomy, which was originally developed in the 5th century B.C. Athens, implies that the people, the 'demos', voted constantly on matters of government and law, and the elected rulers, the 'archons', are mainly asked to enforce them. In other words, in the context of an autonomous society, the legislative power is constantly and actively accountable to the electorate.

Both market capitalism (also known as the bourgeois political economy) and state capitalism (also known as bureaucratic socialism, such as the form of socialism that was applied in the Soviet Union and the Maoist China) approach the economy as if it were the centre of the world, reduce all values to the concept of economic price and treat certain economic structures, institutions and processes as if they were natural necessities. Thus, both market capitalism and state capitalism are totemic systems and have nothing to do with human autonomy, because a society is autonomous if and only if political and economic reality is freely created and recreated by the people, i.e. if and only if democracy is the only political and economic 'orthodoxy' and the keystone of every political and economic entity.

For instance, the first decade of the history of the Euro and the economic crisis of 2009—2012 indicate that the Eurozone is a totemic society whose 'totem' is the rationalistic and bureaucratic economic system that was formally established by the Maastricht Treaty (signed on 7 February 1992) and primarily serves the interests of the Eurozone banking-financial elite and of the German political elite. On the other hand, a significant portion of the society of the United Kingdom, which has the oldest parliamentary system of government in the modern history of Europe and has defended liberal Europe against German imperialism, resists persistently the Eurozone super-state. Moreover, Jean-Jacques Rosa, a distinguished academic and an economic adviser to the French Prime Minister during 1997—1999, in his book *Euro Exit**, explains why and how European politicians and businessmen circumvented democratic consent in order to lock their societies into the Eurozone super-state.

A democratic society is a reflective society, and, therefore, it has to appeal constantly to the kairic activity and the kairicity-based opinion of all citizens. In 1693, William Penn (English philosopher and Founder of the Province of Pennsylvania), in his essay on the peace of Europe, developed a theory of collective security and, with amazing foresight, articulated in detail a model of European Union to ensure peace in the continent. Furthermore, Rosicrucianism promoted the idea of a European Union founded on the Rosicrucians' vision of humanist universalism. In contrast to the essence of democracy, to Penn's pacifistic European Union ideal and to Rosicrucianism's humanistic European Union vision, the Eurozone, which was created by the Maastricht Treaty in 1992, is a society whose deity is a monetary value, and it is characterized by the reign of a new 'nobility' of professional politicians, 'experts' and televised polls. The Eurozone's 'priesthood' is the European Central Bank, and its 'Holy Inquisition' is an army of technocrats who are always willing to rationalize and impose pan-European conformism to the 'Bulls' of the Eurozone's business and banking elite and to Germany's imperialist 'Europapolitik', which contradicts the principles of democracy and development. Thus, for instance, it is not coincidental that, during 2008—2011, the President of the European Commission, José-Manuel Barroso, undertook several initiatives in order to enlist as many Freemasonic Grand Lodges

---

* Jean-Jacques Rosa, *Euro Exit: Why (and How) to Get Rid of the Monetary Union*, New York: Algora Publishing, 2012.

as possible into the established European Integration Project, and he had several official meetings with Masonic delegations from different countries and different Masonic Orders.

Furthermore, many socio-economic elites use symbolic systems and spirituality as means for the consolidation of their power and authority. In other words, the social establishment tries to stifle and manipulate the kairicity of the collective consciousness. There is a significant yet elusive spiritual affinity among a Puritan Anglo-Saxon, a German Pietist, a Calvinist banker and a Muslim fundamentalist: all of them need and use God as the supreme guarantor of fairness in economic transactions, as the supreme guarantor of a system of policing social morals, and even as the supreme guarantor of processes by which the 'faithful' (to the rationality of the market or to Allah) can acquire and enjoy the wealth of the 'infidels' (e.g. of those who do not conform to the consecrated capitalist structures or of the non-Muslims, respectively).

Esotericism is potentially 'dangerous' for the social establishment, because it can function as a powerful underpinning of personal and social autonomy. Therefore, political and economic elites, traditionally, try to control esoteric fraternities, not necessarily by suppressing them, but mainly by placing the most influential esoteric societies under the patronage or the direct administration of persons who belong to the political and/or economic establishment and whose primary aim is to spread generalized conformism.

We can easily understand the relationship between esotericism and politics if, for instance, we consider the following facts about Freemasonry: the history of English Freemasonry is strongly related to the political conflicts between the Jacobites (who were supporters of the House of Stuart) and the Whigs (who were the liberal supporters of King George I) as well as to the religious conflicts between Roman Catholicism and Protestantism; the history of French Freemasonry is strongly related to the French Revolution; the Soviet and the Nazi regimes suppressed Freemasonry, since those totalitarian political regimes were afraid of Freemasons' teachings about freedom of consciousness; the bourgeois, traditionally, try to use Freemasonry as an instrument for the consolidation of the bourgeois ethos; many naïve Freemasons endorse a petit-bourgeois approach to Freemasonry and are commonly known as "fork and spoon Masons"*; and several Freemasonic administrative authorities develop rigidly traditionalist attitudes, claim a monopoly of Freemasonic 'regularity', tend to maintain feudal and authoritarian mentalities under the cloak of esotericism[†], and revise Masonic rituals in order to distort or even eliminate certain humanistic aspects of Freemasonry.

On the other hand, my Kairological Qabalah leads to a deeply anti-authoritarian approach to esotericism and invites and urges esotericists to continually reflect on social institutions, to deconstruct every political totem and to subject every socio-political institution to free and unbiased criticism.

CIVIL SOCIETY AND HUMAN AUTONOMY

In the 11th century, the creation of towns and the development of international trade disrupted feudalism by giving rise to a new socio-political system. Moreover, the townspeople made serious attempts in order to codify and standardize customary feudal practices, and they developed a corporate view of society practically organized by the guild system and culturally underpinned by Roman law justifications for self-authenticating autonomous groupings of men. Thus, in the 11th and the 12th centuries, we begin to see the first fully-fledged theories of popular sovereignty[‡]. For instance, John of Salisbury, in his book *The Policraticus* (1156—9), argues that 'aequitas' (equality) is the application by man of his own capacity for reason and right and that the good ruler must be a man of the state and an image of natural equality. According to John of Salisbury, the chief difference between a tyrant and a prince is that the latter obeys the

---

* The term "fork and spoon Masons" refers to those Freemasons who understand and experience Freemasonry merely as a charitable fraternity of men who organize private dinners and socialize with each other, while maintaining some ceremonial traditions in a mechanistic, spiritually sterile manner.

† These attitudes often cause corruption and several scandals, which give Freemasonry a bad reputation. In Italy, the scandal of the notorious Masonic "Propaganda Due" (P2) Lodge is a characteristic case in point. In Greece, in 2009, a major scandal and schism broke out in the Supreme Council of the Ancient and Accepted Scottish Rite that was associated with the Grand Lodge of Greece, which has often attracted negative publicity due to its sectarian ethos and blurred spiritual orientation. In France, in 2011, a major scandal broke out in the National Grand Lodge of France, and members of that Grand Lodge publicly demonstrated against their Grand Master.

‡ Quentin Skinner, *The Foundations of Modern Political Thought*, 2 Vols, Cambridge: Cambridge University Press, 1970; Walter Ullmann, *Principles of Government and Politics in the Middle Ages*, London: Methuen, 1961.

laws and accounts himself as but their servant[*]. Henry de Bracton, in his book *De legibus et consuetudinibus angliae* (ca. 1239), stated that the royal 'voluntas' (will) is primarily concerned with adjudication rather than with legislation[†]. According to Henry de Bracton, laws are promulgated through a co-operative process, and, therefore, the law of the land is not dictated by the royal will but is truly 'common'. Moreover, Marsilius of Padua, in his book *Defensor Pacis* (1324), a landmark in the history of civil political thought, argued that the legislator, or first and proper efficient cause of law, is the people or whole body of citizens, or a prevailing part of it, commanding and deciding by its own free will within a formally instituted context that something among the civil acts of human beings be done or omitted, on pain of penalty or punishment[‡].

According to Georg Wilhelm Friedrich Hegel's *Philosophy of Right*[§], the towns of the 11th century Western Europe were created in order to fight despotism and to establish a system of free and constitutional governance. Hegel argues that the essence of despotism is lawlessness and the essence of free and constitutional government is that it excludes lawlessness and safeguards security. According to Hegel, despotism means any state of affairs where the rule of law has collapsed and where the particular will as such, whether of a monarch or a mob takes the place of law[¶]. Furthermore, Hegel argues that it is precisely the fact that everything in the state is fixed and secure which is the bulwark against arbitrariness and dogmatism[**]. Thus, according to Hegel, civil society is inalienably related to what later German jurisprudence came to call a *Rechtsstaat* (state of law).

In monarchies of increasing administrative and bureaucratic centralization, such as that of Henry II of England, and especially as the king had to levy additional taxes in order to finance increasing

---

[*] See: John Dickinson (ed. and trans.), *The Statesman's Book of John of Salisbury*, New York: Knopf, 1927, Book IV, ch. i.

[†] See: C.J. Nederman, "Bracton on Kingship Revisited", *History of Political Thought*, Vol. 5, 1984, pp. 63-77.

[‡] See: Alan Gewirth (ed. and trans.), *Marsilius of Padua, the Defender of the Peace*, New York: Harper and Row Publishers, 1956, Book I, ch. xii.

[§] G.W.F. Hegel, *Philosophy of Right*, trans. T.M. Knox, Oxford: Oxford University Press, 1942 (originally published in 1821).

[¶] Ibid, section 278.

[**] Ibid, section 270.

defence budgets, incipient representative institutions emerged. In the Middle Ages, the parliaments were bodies that represented socially privileged groups, namely, the Church, the nobles and wealthy citizens of the towns. The first full English Parliament convened in 1265: the House of Lords was representing the Church and the nobility, and the House of Commons was made up of elected representatives from wealthy citizens of the towns. Thus, by the 14th century, the king was seen as ruling more or less in concert with his wealthier noble and non-noble subjects.

Towns helped people to create new institutions: a more egalitarian judicial system, relatively stable policing and military institutions (as opposed to the notoriously unstable feudal armies, which usually were breaking up after their terms of service were up), a new tax system (by the end of the Middle Ages, monarchs were gaining the right to tax their subjects directly, and, in the 13th century, parliaments gained the right to rule on any proposed changes in taxation), etc. Gradually, towns became free republics, and the members of several different professions were organized into guilds. By the late Middle Ages, guild membership and citizenship went hand in hand. For instance, in Florence, membership in a guild was a requirement of citizenship. The guild system created rules that governed taxation, established electoral processes and gave rise to new authorities and offices. The members of the guilds were pledged to assist one another in sickness or distress and to express solidarity to one another in danger. Moreover, some of the guilds maintained schools for the instruction of the children of the members; remnants of such schools exist in England to this very day, e.g. Corpus Christi at Cambridge.

The Concordat of Worms, which was a compromise arranged in 1122 between Pope Callistus II and Holy Roman Emperor Henry V settling the 'investiture dispute', promoted the civil ethos of the townspeople. The king was recognized as having the right to invest bishops with secular authority in the territories they governed (however, not with holy authority), and, therefore, bishops owed allegiance in worldly affairs both to the pope and to the king, since they were obliged to affirm the right of the secular authority (the king) to call upon them for military support. Furthermore, in 1122, in Cologne a revolt against the local archbishop-feudal lord broke out.

Towns were attracting more and more people not so much for the pursuit of financial gain as for the pursuit of freedom. Serfs could earn their living by cultivating the land, but they could not enjoy enough freedom. Henri Pirenne[*] has pointed out that the quest for freedom was the strongest motive of the people who were leaving their agricultural jobs in order to live in a town. For instance, in the Middle Ages, many Germans used to say "Stadtluft macht frei" (i.e. "city air makes you free"). Carlo M. Cipolla[†] argues that, like the first immigrants to America, the liberated serfs were moving to towns in order to live in an 'open society' and to have more opportunities for social and economic success than those supplied by the traditional agricultural societies.

The townspeople, namely, liberated serfs, tradesmen, impoverished aristocrats and various other opportunists and fugitives from the feudal system, built their own walls around their towns, and, thus, they became permanent inhabitants of those towns and were called 'bourgeois' or 'burgenses', which literally means 'of a walled town'. Some of them managed to excel in their professions and participate in the king's council. Additionally, members of the civil class often created secret societies, whose purpose was the protection of the community's interest. As we read in the *Annales Beneventani*, in 1003—1005, after the rebellions of the citizens of Benevento against their local prince, Landulf V, "facta est communitas prima", i.e. "the first commune is made". The first reference to a secret society organized by the bourgeoisie is found in the *History of Milan*, which was written in the 11th century by the historiographer Arnulfus of Milan: Arnulfus of Milan writes that, among the participants to the rebellion that took place in Milan in 980 against the local archbishop was the union of the bourgeois, and he characterizes this union as a "coniuratio" (i.e. "conspiracy") because its members were bound by mutual oaths.

The civil institutional framework abolished the feudal monolithic social pyramid and promoted a higher degree of social homogeneity. Within the framework of the civil system, social stratification is based on social and economic success and is subject to criticism by the citizens. Moreover, it should be stressed that, in the late Middle Ages and the Renaissance, the concept of economic success

---

[*]   Henri Pirenne, *Medieval Cities: Their Origins and the Revival of Trade*, trans. F.D. Halsey, Princeton: Princeton University Press, 1952.

[†]   C.M. Cipolla, *Before the Industrial Revolution: European Society and Economy 1000—1700*, 3rd edition, trans. C. Woodall, New York: W.W. Norton & Company, 1993.

had a broader meaning than that of the accumulation of economic wealth, because the medieval bourgeois understood economic success as a consequence of the civil ethos, i.e. of a spiritual cause. In those eras, the transition from a rural to an urban society was primarily a cultural question, because the transformation of a rural person into a bourgeois presupposed and depended on the adoption of a new system of morality and a new code of social conduct.

The medieval bourgeois saw their civilization as the manifestation of great spiritual principles in the political sphere. Thus, for instance, according to Marsilius of Padua, the city is a "perfect community" or one able to supply all that is needed for a good life. Moreover, Albertus Magnus, the major instructor of Thomas Aquinas, had admitted that a town can supply security (munitio), mental refinement and elegance (urbanitas), unity (unitas) and liberty (libertas), and, through this prism, he had attempted to explain why the Apostle Matthew used the term town in order to refer collectively to the Church Fathers (as we read in *Matthew* 5:14: "A town built on a hill cannot be hidden"). However, the emergence of civil society goes hand in hand with the emergence of a new and pervasive form of domination and stratification.

Civil society pursued its emancipation from the political and spiritual despotism of the Papacy and from feudalism by asserting that civil society itself is the exclusive source of the legitimacy of political authority. Therefore, civil society is intimately related to the democratization of the political system. Nevertheless, civil society's commitment to the logic of capitalism has not allowed civil society to democratize the economic system, too. Thus, in the context of civil society, there is a significant disharmony between the degree of democratization that characterizes the sphere of constitutional law and the degree of democratization that characterizes the sphere of economic/business institutions. Moreover, civil society is prone to totemism, because the intrinsic 'logic' of the civil system imposes itself as an unavoidable nexus of necessities* and the morality of the civil system is identified with the civil system's own logic. Therefore,

---

* Thus, as Karl Marx pointed out in his *Critique of Hegel's Philosophy of Right* (1843), in the context of civil society, the democratic element is admitted only as a formal element, since the state organism is merely a formalism of the state (Karl Marx, *Critique of Hegel's Philosophy of Right*, trans. A. Jolin and J. O'Malley, Cambridge: Cambridge University Press, 1982).

instead of leading to a democratic polity, ultimately, civil society leads to a liberal oligarchy.

The Papacy's and the feudal political elites' authority was based on arguments that are derived from philosophical realism. Using philosophical realism as an instrument of cultural diplomacy, the Pope managed to impose his "plenitudo potestatis". On the basis of philosophical realism, the Pope could behave like his 'archetype', i.e. God. In general, since, from the viewpoint of philosophical realism, the individual has meaning and value only if and to the extent that it serves the universal, the authority that supposedly represents the universal has the right and the duty to suppress the individual in order for the universal to be served according to the judgment of the established authority. The bourgeoisie was the first social force that understood that the Papacy's despotism had to be struck at its core, i.e. at its philosophical underpinnings. But, instead of refuting philosophical realism itself and stressing the 'otherness' of the human person, the 18th century bourgeoisie attempted to substitute its own realist philosophical arguments, which are collectively known as Physiocracy and stress "natural order", for the Papacy's realist philosophical arguments. Therefore, in civil society, too, necessity takes primacy over human autonomy. In other words, instead of fighting totemism itself, the bourgeois substituted their own political and economic totems (and especially the logic of market capitalism) for the feudal elite's totems. In the context of civil society, the labor force is led toward a spiritual state that is characterized by insignificance, because civil society stresses conformity to the established formal system of organization and the substitution of discipline for discretion, and also it produces a 'citizen' who is detached from the life of the 'city' by unemployment, which leads to disintegration, and by precariousness, which leads to submission.

CULTURAL AND POLITICAL CLASHES BEHIND THE CREATION OF MASONIC DEGREES AND ORDERS

There has been a persistent tradition among Continental writers on Freemasonry that the Jacobites had much to do with the development of Masonic degrees beyond the Craft and the Royal Arch during the 18th century. The Scottish adherents of King James II, who followed him into exile after the landing of William the Prince of Orange in

1688, brought to the English Court at Saint Germain (which had been placed at the disposal of the exiled King James II by King Louis XIV of France) the ancient Masonic rites of Heredom and Kilwinning intermingled with Templar traditions. When King James II fled from England, he took refuge at the Jesuit Abbey of Clermont, which had attached to it a so-called College of Clermont, which was founded by Guillaume du Prat, Bishop of Clermont, in 1550.

King James II attempted to use Freemasonry as an institution that could assist him in his endeavor to regain the British throne, but this attempt failed. However, the Jacobite influence on the development of new Masonic degrees is important; for instance, under some Obediences of the Ancient and Accepted Scottish Rite, the 14th Degree is called Grand Scottish Knight of the Sacred Vault of James VI, even though its older name was Grand, Elect, Ancient Perfect Master. Therefore, given that the Grand Lodge of London and Westminister, which was founded in 1717, and the first Grand Master of the United Grand Lodge of England were loyal to the Hanoverian Dynasty, they endorsed a negative attitude toward the Masonic degrees that had been created by the Jacobites, who were supporters of the House of Stuart.

After the year 1740, 'Scots Degrees' sprang up throughout France, and their creation and development can be attributed to the celebrated Oration delivered in 1737 in the Provincial Grand Lodge of England in Paris by Chevalier Andrew M. Ramsay; although the first published reference to a "Scotch Masons' Lodge" occurs as early as 1733 in London[*]. Ramsay, a Scot from Ayrshire, managed to become the Orator to the Grand Lodge of France. He was raised a Presbyterian, but he was converted to Roman Catholicism by François Fénelon, Archbishop of Cambrai, and, after that, he became a tutor to the two sons of King James II in Rome. His first Masonic oration was due on 20 March 1737, but he first submitted his oration to André-Hercule, Cardinal de Fleury, Bishop of Fréjus and Prime Minister of France, asking for André-Hercule's protection for Freemasons and stating that the ideals of Freemasonry were noble, connected with the medieval Crusaders' values and most useful to religion, literature and the State. Ramsay did not know that Freemasonry had already been condemned by a secret conference of his own Church. Thus, André-Hercule rejected Ramsay's Oration,

---

[*]   See: *A.Q.C.*, XVI, 44.

and, on 28 April 1738, Pope Clement XII issued a papal prohibition against Freemasonry. The previous papal prohibition against Freemasonry did not include any theological arguments against Freemasonry, and it is considered by many historians to be the result of the Papacy's authoritarian reaction against the emergence of a new spiritual organization.

Even though Ramsay's Oration failed to build bridges between Freemasonry and the Roman Catholic Church, it exerted decisive influence on the development of new Masonic Orders, particularly the Masonic Knights Templar and other Masonic organizations with a chivalric emphasis. The so-called 'Scots Masters' claimed extraordinary privileges in the French Craft Lodges, and, indeed, their privileges were officially instituted by the Grand Lodge of France in 1755. In particular, the Scots Masters had their own distinctive regalia, they claimed the right to participate as Scots Masters in the ordinary Master Masons' Lodges and to confer the Craft degrees with or without a ceremony. Eventually, in France, Scots Masters' Lodges were appointing the Worshipful Masters of the corresponding Craft Lodges, instead of allowing the Brethren of the latter to elect their Worshipful Masters, as it was the case in England. These Scots Lodges and mainly the Royal Order of Scotland, from which they arose, were the major driving force behind the creation of several 'higher' Masonic degrees during the second half of the 18th century.

The major center for the development and dissemination of new, 'higher' Masonic degrees was the "Chapter of Clermont", which was arguably founded by Chevalier de Bonneville in 1754; this Chapter was based on the three degrees of Symbolic Masonry, the Scottish or Saint Andrew's Degree (4th degree), and, additionally, it worked three higher grades, namely: Knight of the Eagle or Select Master (5th degree), Illustrious Knight or Templar (6th degree), and Sublime Illustrious Knight (7th degree). It is in this Chapter of Clermont and in the "Council of the Emperors of the East and West" into which it was transformed in 1758 that the origins of the Ancient and Accepted Scottish Rite can be found.

The Council of the Emperors of the East and West practiced a ritual that was called the Rite of Perfection, and it consisted of 25 degrees. The 25th Degree of the Rite of Perfection was called Most Illustrious Prince of Masonry, Grand and Sublime Knight Commander of the Royal Secret, and it corresponds to the 32nd Degree of the Ancient and

Accepted Scottish Rite. In 1761, three years only after its foundation, the Council of the Emperors of the East and West granted a patent to one Stephen Morin "to establish perfect and sublime Masonry in all parts of the world," officially pronouncing him a Grand Inspector of the Rite of Perfection. According to Mackey's *Encyclopedia of Freemasonry*, in 1761, Stephen Morin arrived in San Domingo, where he commenced the dissemination of the Rite of Perfection, and he appointed many Inspectors both for the West Indies and the United States. However, many of the Inspectors of the Rite of Perfection that had been appointed by Stephen Morin proved to be persons of low moral and intellectual standards, and, therefore, the Rite of Perfection passed through a period of obscuration, during which the Rite's degrees were being cynically traded for money. In the USA, new degrees were added to the original 25 degrees of the Rite of Perfection, and, thus, the Ancient and Accepted Scottish Rite, which has 33 degrees, was created.

The members of the Council of the Emperors of the East and West were mainly men of noble birth, high culture and deep interests in esotericism and the occult. Thus, the Masonic Rite of the Council of the Emperors of the East and West helps one to understand the cultural differences between the English Freemasonic tradition and the French Freemasonic tradition: English Freemasonry emphasizes its professional roots, i.e. its descent from Operative Masonry, whereas Freemasonry to be acceptable to the French had to be noble (and, therefore, the French aristocracy connected Freemasonry with chivalry); English Freemasonry emphasizes science and the British legacy of empiricism, whereas Freemasonry to be acceptable to the French had to be mystic and often related to the occult (since occultism was very popular among the 18th century French nobility); England sought the civil ethos and the moral chiseling in Freemasonry, whereas France the bizarre and the sensational; English Freemasonry is focused on the trowel, whereas French Freemasonry is focused on the chivalric sword. However, it should be mentioned that the French Revolution exerted significant influence on the ethos of French Freemasonry, and it transformed it, from a fraternity focused on the occult, into a fraternity focused on humanism and on the French political principle of 'état laic'. Moreover, in the 18th century, American Freemasonry, instead of being focused on the occult, became substantially politicized. The Masonic doctrine enunciated by Thomas Jefferson in the Declaration of American Independence, "We hold these truths to be self-evident that all men are created equal, and that they are endowed with certain inalienable rights, among which are life, liberty and the pursuit of happiness", is the keystone of genuine American Freemasonry and of the political ideology of the Founding Fathers of America.

Furthermore, the history of Freemasonry is characterized by intense geopolitical competition among Freemasonic organizations. For instance, after the end of the Cold War, the United Grand Lodge of England, the Ancient and Accepted Scottish Rite of the Southern Jurisdiction of the U.S.A., the United Grand Lodges of Germany and the Grand Orient of France competed against each other to gain control over the new Masonic Jurisdictions of Russia, Poland, the Czech Republic, Croatia, Slovenia, Bulgaria, Romania, Serbia, the Former Yugoslav Republic of Macedonia (FYROM) and Albania.

THE POLITICAL RAMIFICATIONS AND ETHOS OF THE KAIROLOGICAL QABALAH

A polity that is founded on the kairicity of human consciousness does not tell people what to do; it tells them that they have the ability to make decisions about the issues that affect them. Such a polity rejects Physiocracy and admits that the future of history is not given, but it emerges from human action. Thus, the political ramifications of the Kairological Qabalah are about emancipation, empowerment and agency.

In the light of the arguments that I put forward in Chapter 7 about the four-fold dialectic of the kairic action of human consciousness and according to the wisdom of the Kairological Qabalah's Middle Pillar, every system of political-economic institutions must satisfy the following conditions:

(i) The political-economic system must operate in a manner that gives priority to personal and social autonomy (as opposed to technocratic goals* and to bureaucratic programs and structures). Beyond the moral and humanistic significance of the principle of social autonomy, the democratic organization of political

---

* The inefficiencies of technocratic management in the era of advanced modernity and super-industrial societies have been exposed by Alvin Toffler as follows: technocratic planning reflects the values of the fast-vanishing economic model of "industrialism", is short-sighted and "essentially undemocratic", and it gives rise to inefficient bureaucratic structures (Alvin Toffler, *Future Shock*, New York: Bantam Books, 1971, pp. 448-449).

economy is a necessary condition for development. Alvin Toffler[*] has pointed out that the development of modern democracy in the West was intimately related to and dictated by the historical pressure toward social differentiation and toward more efficient systems of social organization, which demanded "sensitive social feedback". In complex differentiated societies, vast amounts of information must flow at ever faster speeds among the members of the social system, and political democracy, by incorporating more and more social agents in decision-making facilitates feedback and of course averts information thrombosis. This is a necessary condition for development, because, as the Nobel Prize-winning economists George Akerlof, Michael Spence and Joseph E. Stiglitz have shown, information asymmetry[†] is a major cause of economic crises.

It is important to keep in mind that, in contrast to bureaucratic and rigidly rationalistic management methods, factories and public services manage to function because employees violate to a large extent the regulations in order to be able to do their jobs. This is proven by the fact that one of the most effective forms of strike is what French call "zeal strike", according to which the employees begin to apply the regulations to the letter, and this can make everything collapse within a short time. Michel Anteby, a professor in the organizational behavior area at Harvard University, has pointed out that so-called "moral grey zones" exist in more or less every sector or enterprise, and they rely on personal trust, at all levels, and of course it is not appropriate in all contexts. However, Anteby maintains, this flexible approach to official rules increases competition within the workplace and the impetus of staff to prove themselves, bringing a greater desire for autonomy and challenge, and cultivates discretion and critical thought.

Furthermore, social cohesion and the exercise of rational control over social change presuppose that people have a deep sense of civic responsibility. The levels of civic responsibility and rationality, in turn, are directly analogous to the extent to which people are actively and constantly engaged in decision-making about socially significant questions. Therefore, democracy is a necessary condition

---

[*] Toffler, *Future Shock*, pp. 475-476

[†] For more details, see: Beth Allen, "The Economics of Information: An Exposition", *Empirica*, Vol. 23, 1996, pp. 119-128.

for social cohesion and for the exercise of rational control over social change.

In the light of the above-mentioned arguments, the democratization of corporate law, along the lines of the democratization of constitutional law, is necessary in order to transform (public and private) corporations into adequately chiselled building stones of a democratic polity. The four defining characteristics of the modern corporation* are:

1. Separate legal personality of the corporation;

2. Shares;

3. Limited liability of the shareholders;

4. Delegated management (i.e. control of the company placed in the hands of a board of directors).

In order to be in harmony with the spirit and the word of democratic constitutional law, corporate law must oblige every corporation to form its board of directors as follows: one portion (e.g. the two thirds) of the members of the board of directors must be elected by the annual general assembly of the company's shareholders (i.e. by the 'capital') and another portion (e.g. the one-third) of the members of the board of directors must be elected by the annual general assembly of the company's employees (i.e. by the 'labor').

(ii) The political-economic system must operate in a manner that allows and encourages social actors to experience and realize the indeterminate dynamics of interpersonal relations in the context of their participation in a common symbolic universe. Therefore, the fundamental significations (i.e. the values) that underpin any society that is founded on the kairicity of human consciousness derive from the four-fold dialectic of the kairic action of human consciousness. For this reason, the fundamental significations that underpin a society that is founded on the kairicity of human consciousness are incompatible with any idea about 'natural necessity' or 'historical determinism'. Hence, the idea of a society founded on the kairicity of human consciousness and hence on the Kairological Middle

---

*   See: Clark, R.C., *Corporate Law*, New York: Aspen Publishers, 1986.

Pillar leads to the rejection of the 'school' of Physiocracy and its offshoots.

(iii) The political-economic system must operate in a manner that manifests an understanding of the material world not as a neutral object but as a structure of logical qualities. The material world is not a neutral object that can be arbitrarily utilized by the human being, but it manifests the mode of the human being's existence. For instance, such material elements as the DNA, the functions of the central nervous system and the human beings' fingerprints are modes through which the existential *otherness* of each and every human being is manifested. Moreover, quantum physics has revealed the logical constitution of matter: matter is not constituted simply by atoms of matter itself, but it is constituted by behavioral qualities, or energies*. The ethos that derives from the Kairological Qabalah transcends every contradiction between spirituality and materialism, and it leads to the creation of a political-economic reality that is founded not on assumed natural necessities but on free relations. Man's freedom and creativity are not consequences of his nature, but they are consequences of the fact that he is an autonomous person (at least potentially).

In the light of the above-mentioned way of understanding the material world, conventional business and national accounting are misguided and inadequate for the implementation of anthropocentric development policies. According to conventional accounting methods, economic growth is measured in terms of economic goods and income categories only, whereas changes that happen in the stock and quality of human and natural resources are ignored. The world of traditional accounting has two dimensions, i.e. the quantity of economic goods and the quantity of income. This two-dimensional picture of economic reality must be replaced by a three-dimensional approach, where the third dimension will represent the values of culture, education, natural resources and biodiversity. For instance, in the previous two-dimensional economic reality (where narrow-minded financial approaches prevail), nation A may be 20% poorer

---

* Paul Dirac, who shared the Nobel Prize in physics for 1933 with Erwin Schrödinger, "for the discovery of new productive forms of atomic theory", has argued that natural scientists must depart from the concepts and the methodology of Newtonian physics when they wish to account for the ultimate structure of matter (P.A.M. Dirac, *The Principles of Quantum Mechanics*, 4th edition, Oxford: Oxford University Press, 1958, p. 3).

than nation B, but, in the previous three-dimensional economic reality (where the values of culture, education, natural resources and biodiversity factor in every economic equation), nation A may be 10% poorer, or even richer, than nation B. Evaluations of GNP and trade potential and generally country analyses should always include variables that represent culture, education, natural resources, biodiversity and people's attitude toward the fauna and the flora.

BIBLIOGRAPHY

Adams, S., *Relativity: An Introduction to Space-Time Physics*, London: Taylor & Francis, 2000

Addis, L., "Aristotle and the Independence of Substances", *Philosophy and Phenomenological Research*, Vol. 54, 1972

Allen, B., "The Economics of Information: An Exposition", *Empirica*, Vol. 23, 1996

Anagnostopoulos, G., *The Blackwell Guide to Aristotle*, Oxford: Blackwell, 2007

Anteby, M., *Moral Gray Zones*, Princeton: Princeton University Press, 2008

Bamford, C., *An Endless Trace: The Passionate Pursuit of Wisdom in the West*, New York: Codhill Press, 2003

Barnes, J., *The Cambridge Companion to Aristotle*, Cambridge: Cambridge University Press, 1995

Barnes, J., *The Presocratic Philosophers*, 2nd edn, London: Routledge & Kegan Paul, 1982

Barry, K., *The Greek Qabalah: Alphabetic Mysticism and Numerology in the Ancient World*, York Beach: Samuel Weiser, Inc., 1999

Bauer, W., *Orthodoxy and Heresy in Earliest Christianity*, trans. and ed. R. Kraft and G. Kroedel, Philadelphia: Fortress Press, 1971

Bengtson, H., *History of Greece: From the Beginnings to the Byzantine Era*, trans. E.F. Bloedow, Ottawa: University of Ottawa Press, 1997

Bennett, J., *Locke, Berkeley, Hume: Central Themes*, Oxford: Oxford University Press, 1971

Bentham, J., *An Introduction to the Principles of Morals and Legislation*, ed. J.H. Burns and H.L.A. Hart, London: Athlone Press, 1970 (originally published in 1789)

Berger, P.L. and Luckmann, T., *The Social Construction of Reality: A Treatise in the Sociology of Knowledge*, Garden City, N.Y.: Doubleday & Co., 1966

Bergson, H., *The Creative Mind: An Introduction to Metaphysics*, trans. M.L. Andison, New York: Carol Publishing Group, 1992 (originally published in 1946)

Bergson, H., *Time and Free Will: An Essay on the Immediate Data of Consciousness*, tr., F.L. Pogson, Montana: Kessinger Publishing Company, 1910

Block, I., "Substance in Aristotle", in G.C. Simmons (ed.), *Paideia: Special Aristotle Issue*, Brockport, NY: State University College at Buffalo and State University College at Brockport, 1978

Block, N. (ed.), *Perspectives on the Philosophy of Wittgenstein*, Oxford: Blackwell, 1981

Braudel, F., "Histoire et sciences socials: la langue durée", *Annales*, Vol. 4, 1958

Britton, K., *John Stuart Mill*, Harmondsworth: Penguin, 1953

Bromiley, G.W. (ed.), *The International Standard Bible Encyclopedia*, Vol. II, fully revised, Michigan: Wm. B. Eerdmans Publishing, 1994

Bronowski, J., *The Ascent of Man*, Boston: Little, 1974

Brzezinski, Z., *Out of Control: Global Turmoil on the Eve of the 21st Century*, New York: Collier Books, 1993

Bullock, A., *Hitler and Stalin: Parallel Lives*, New York: Vintage Books, 1993

Busch, T., *The Power of Consciousness and the Force of Circumstances in Sartre's Philosophy*, Bloomington: Indiana University Press, 1990

Carnap, R., *The Unity of Science*, London: Kegan Paul, Trench, Teubner and Co., 1932/1934

Carr, E.H., *What Is History?*, London: Penguin, 1961

Carré, M.H., *Realists and Nominalists*, London: Oxford University Press, 1946

Cassirer, E., *The Philosophy of Symbolic Forms*, Volume One: Language, Volume Two: Mythical Thought, trans. R. Manheim, New Haven: Yale University Press, 1955

Centrone, S., *Logic and Philosophy of Mathematics in the Early Husserl*, Dordrecht: Springer, 2010

Charles, D., *Aristotle on Meaning and Essence*, Oxford: Clarendon Press, 2002

Churton, T., *The Golden Builders: Alchemists, Rosicrucians, and the First Freemasons*, Boston: Red Weel/Weiser, 2005

Cipolla, C.M., *Before the Industrial Revolution: European Society and Economy 1000-1700*, 3rd edition, trans. C. Woodall, New York: W.W. Norton & Company, 1993

Comte, A., *The Early Essays*, in R. Fletcher (ed.), *The Crisis of Industrial Civilization*, London: Heinemann, 1974

Cooper, J.L., III, "Who Was Hiram Abiff?", *The Alberta Freemason*, Vol. 75, No. 6, June 2010

Cottingham, J. (ed.), *Descartes*, Oxford: Oxford University Press, 1998

Cresswell, M.J., "Essence and Existence in Plato and Aristotle", *Theoria*, Vol. 37, 1971

Crisp, R., *Mill on Utilitarianism*, London: Routledge, 1997

Crowley, A., *The Book of Thoth*, York Beach, Maine: Weiser Books, 2000 (originally published in 1944)

Curd, P.K., *The Legacy of Parmenides: Eleatic Monism and Later Presocratic Thought*, Princeton: Princeton University Press, 1998

Curley, E.M., "Analysis in the Meditations: The Quest for Clear and Distinct Ideas", in A.O. Rorty (ed.), *Essays on Descartes' Meditations*, Berkeley: University of California Press, 1986

Descartes, R., *The Philosophical Writings of Descartes*, trans. J. Cottingham, R. Stoothoff, D. Murdoch and A. Kenny, Cambridge: Cambridge University Press, 1984-1991

Dickinson, J. (ed. and trans.), *The Statesman's Book of John of Salisbury*, New York: Knopf, 1927

Dillon, J.M. and Gerson, L.P. (eds), *Neoplatonic Philosophy*, Indianapolis: Hackett, 2004

Dirac, P.A.M., *The Principles of Quantum Mechanics*, 4th edition, Oxford: Oxford University Press, 1958

Drury, N. and Tillett, G., *The Occult: A Sourcebook of Esoteric Wisdom*, London: Grange Books, 1997

Durand, G., *Les Structures Anthropologiques de l'Imaginaire: Introduction à l'Archétypologie Générale*, Paris: P.U.F., 1963

Earnshaw, S., *Existentialism: A Guide for the Perplexed*, London: Continuum, 2006

Epicurus, *The Essential Epicurus*, trans. and introduction by E. O'Connor, New York: Prometheus Books, 1993

Faivre, A., *Access to Western Esotericism*, New York: State University of New York Press, 1994

Fine, G. (ed.), *Plato 1: Metaphysics and Epistemology*, Oxford: Oxford University Press, 1999

Flynn, T., *Existentialism: A Very Short Introduction*, Oxford: Oxford
    University Press, 2006
Fortune, D., *Mystical Qabalah*, San Francisco: Red Wheel/Weiser,
    2000 (originally published in 1935)
Franklin, W.S., "The Second Law of Thermodynamics: Its Basis in
    Intuition and Common Sense", *The Popular Science Monthly*,
    March 1910
Friligos, K. (trans. and intro.), *Josephus, Against Apion*, Athens:
    Daedalus — I. Zacharopoulos Publications (in Greek)
Gadamer, H.-G., *Truth and Method*, London: Sheed and Ward, 1975
Gane, M., *Auguste Comte*, London: Routledge, 2006
Gaukroger, S., *Cartesian Logic: An Essay on Descartes's Conception of
    Inference*, Oxford: Clarendon Press, 1989
Gerson, L.P. (ed.), *The Cambridge Companion to Plotinus*, Cambridge:
    Cambridge University Press, 1996
Gewirth, A. (ed. and trans.), *Marsilius of Padua, the Defender of the
    Peace*, New York: Harper and Row Publishers, 1956
Gilson, E., *Thomism: The Philosophy of Thomas Aquinas*, trans. L.K.
    Shook and A. Mauer, Toronto: Pontifical Institute of
    Medieval Studies, 2002
Gracia, J.J.E. and Noone, T.B., *A Companion to Philosophy in the
    Middle Ages*, Blackwell Companions to Philosophy, Oxford:
    Blackwell Publications, 2003
Greenwood, S., *The Anthropology of Magic*, Oxford: Berg, 2009
Gregory, J. (ed.), *The Neoplatonists: A Reader*, 2nd edition, London:
    Routledge, 1999
Griswold, C.L. (ed.), *Platonic Writings, Platonic Readings*, London:
    Routledge, 1988
Gruenber, C.D. and Moutsopoulos, E. (eds), *The Idea of Europe — Its
    Common Heritage and Future*, New York: PWPA, 1991
Guthrie, W.K.C., *Orpheus and Greek Religion: A Study of the Orphic
    Movement*, revised edition, Princeton, N.J.: Princeton
    University Press, 1993
Guyer, P. (ed.), *The Cambridge Companion to Kant's Critique of Pure
    Reason*, Cambridge: Cambridge University Press, 2010
Hamill, J., *The Craft: History of English Freemasonry*, London: Aquarian
    Press, 1986
Hawkes, C.F.C., *The Prehistoric Foundations of Europe to the Mycenaean
    Age*, London: Methuen & Co., 1940
Hegel, G.W.F., *Collected Works*

Hilgenfeld, A., *Die Ketzergeschichte des Urchristentums*, Leipzig 1884

Hobsbawm, E., *The Age of Revolution: 1789-1848*, New York: Vintage Books, 1996

Hoyos, A. de and Morris, S.B. (eds), *Freemasonry in Context: History, Ritual, Controversy*, Maryland: Lexington Books — Scottish Rite Research Society, 2004

Huntington, S.P., *The Clash of Civilizations and the Remaking of World Order*, New York: Touchstone, Rockefeller Center, 1996

Inwood, B., *The Cambridge Companion to the Stoics*, Cambridge: Cambridge University Press, 2003

Jaeger, W.W., *Paideia: The Ideals of Greek Culture*, Oxford: Oxford University Press, 1945

James, W., *Pragmatism*, Cambridge, MA: Harvard University Press, 1979 (originally published in 1907)

Jones, B.E., *Freemasons' Guide and Compendium*, New and Revised Edition, Nashville: Cumberland House Publishing, 2006

Jones, B.E., *Freemasons' Book of the Royal Arch*, London: Harrap, 1957

Jung, C.G., "The Relations Between the Ego and the Unconscious", in: J. Campbell (ed.), *The Portable Jung*, New York: Penguin Books, 1971

Kant, I., *Collected Works*

Kelman, H., "Kairos: the Auspicious Moment", *The American Journal of Psychoanalysis*, Vol. XXIX, 1968

Kelman, H., *Helping People*, New York: Science House, 1971

Kleene, S.C., *Mathematical Logic*, London: Dover, 2002

Knight, G., *A History of White Magic*, Cheltenham: Skylight Press, 2011

Kockelmans, J.J. (ed.), *Contemporary European Ethics*, New York: Anchor Books, 1972

Köhler, W., *Gestalt Psychology*, New York: Liveright, 1992

Laos, N., *Foundations of Cultural Diplomacy: Politics Among Cultures and the Moral Autonomy of Man*, New York: Algora Publishing, 2011

Laos, N., *Topics in Mathematical Analysis and Differential Geometry*, London: World Scientific Publishing Co., 1998

Larchet, J.-C., *La Divinisation de l' Homme Selon Saint Maxime le Confesseur*, Paris: Éditions du Cerf, 1996

Larchet, J.-C., *Thérapeutique des Maladies Mentales: L' Expérience de l' Orient Chrétien des Premiers Siècles*, Paris: Les Éditions du Cerf, 1992

Lassen, C., *Indische Alterthumskunde*, Bonn: H.B. König, 1847

Layton, B., "The Hypostasis of the Archons", *Harvard Theological Review*, Vol. 67, 1974

Lévi-Strauss, C., *Structural Anthropology*, trans. C. Jacobson, New York: Basic Books, 1963

Lévi-Strauss, C., *The Raw and the Cooked*, trans. John and Doreen Weightman, Chicago: The University of Chicago Press, 1969

Lévy-Bruhl, L., *Primitive Mentality*, New York: AMS Press, 1978 (originally published in 1922)

Lipsius, R.A., *Der Gnosticismus*, Leipzig, 1860

Lloyd, A.C., *The Anatomy of Neoplatonism*, Oxford: Oxford University Press, Reprint edition, 2005

MacIntyre, A., *A Short History of Ethics*, London: Routledge and Kegan Paul, 1967

Mackey, A.G., *Encyclopedia of Freemasonry*, new and revised edition, New York and London: The Masonic History Company, 1914

Magee, B., *The Philosophy of Schopenhauer*, Oxford: Oxford University Press, 1997

Malherbe, M., "Bacon's Method of Science", in M. Peltonen (ed.), *The Cambridge Companion to Bacon*, Cambridge: Cambridge University Press, 1996

Marcel, G., *Being and Having*, trans. K. Farrer, Westminister: Dacre Press, 1949

Marrou, H.I., *A History of Education in Antiquity*, trans. G. Lamb, Wisconsin: The University of Wisconsin Press, 1982

Martin, C.F.J., *Thomas Aquinas: God and Explanations*, Edinburgh: Edinburgh University Press, 1997

Marx, K., *Critique of Hegel's Philosophy of Right*, trans. A. Jolin and J. O'Malley, Cambridge: Cambridge University Press, 1982

Marx, K., *A Contribution to the Critique of Political Economy*, Moscow: Progress Publishers, 1977

Marx, K., *Theories of Surplus Value*, New York: Prometheus Books, 2000

Matt, D.C., *The Essential Kabbalah: The Heart of Jewish Mysticism*, San Francisco: Harper San Francisco, 1995

McCabe, M.M., *Plato's Individuals*, Princeton: Princeton University Press, 1994

McGrade, A.S. (ed.), *The Cambridge Companion to Medieval Philosophy*, Cambridge: Cambridge University Press, 2003

Merleau-Ponty, M., *Phenomenology of Perception*, London: Routledge Classics, 2002 (originally published in 1945)

Mill, J.S., *Utilitarianism*, London: Parker, Son and Bourn, 1863

Miller, D.W., "Wealth Creation as Integrated with Faith: A Protestant Reflection", *Muslim, Christian, and Jewish Views on the Creation of Wealth*, April 23—24, 2007, Habsburg Center Auditorium

Moore, G.E., *Principia Ethica*, New York: Prometheus Books, 1988 (originally published in 1903)

Moutsopoulos, E., "Kairos ou minimum critique dans les sciences de la nature selon Aristotle", *Revue Philosophique*, Vol. 24, 1999

Moutsopoulos, E., *He Poreia tou Pneumatos: He Axie* (The Itinerary of the Spirit: Values), Athens: 1977, in Greek

Müller, K.H., "Neurath's Theory of Pictorial-Statistical Representation", in T.E. Uebel (ed.), *Rediscovering the Forgotten Vienna Circle*, Dordrecht: Kluwer, 1991

Nederman, C.J., "Bracton on Kingship Revisited", *History of Political Thought*, Vol. 5, 1984

Nicholson, M., *Causes and Consequences in International Relations — A Conceptual Study*, London: Pinter, 1996

Nietzsche, F., *Daybreak: Reflections on Moral Prejudices*, trans. R.J. Hollingdale, Cambridge: Cambridge University Press, 1997 (originally published in 1881)

O'Meara, D., *Plotinus: An Introduction to the Enneads*, Oxford: Oxford University Press, 1993

Orth, J.V., "Jeremy Bentham: The Common Law's Severest Critic", *American Bar Association Journal*, Vol. 68, 1982

Papus (Gérard Encausse), *The Qabalah: Secret Tradition of the West*, York Beach, ME: Samuel Wesier, 2000 (originally published in 1903)

Peters, F.E., *The Harvest of Hellenism: A History of the Near East from Alexander the Great to the Triumph of Christianity*, New York: Simon and Schuster, 1971

Piaget, J., *The Child's Conception of Time*, trans. A.J. Pomerans, London: Routledge and Kegan Paul, 1969

Pieri, P., *Le società segrete e i moti degli anni 1820-1821 e 1830-1831*, Milano, 1931

Pirenne, H., *Medieval Cities: Their Origins and the Revival of Trade*, trans. F.D. Halsey, Princeton: Princeton University Press, 1952

Pirenne, J., *The Tides of History*, Vol. I, trans. L. Edwards, New York: E.P. Dutton & Co., 1962

Popper, K.R., *Conjectures and Refutations: The Growth of Scientific Knowledge*, New York: Harper & Collins, 1968

Potter, J., *Clementis Alexandrini opera quae extant omnia* (Oxford, 1715; Venice, 1757), reproduced in J.P. Migne, Patrologia Gaeca, Vol. VIII, IX

Ramberg, L., "In Dialogue with Daniel Stern: A Review and Discussion of the Present Moment in Psychotherapy and Everyday Life", *International Forum of Psychoanalysis*, Vol. 15, 2006

Reeve, C.D.C., *Substantial Knowledge: Aristotle's Metaphysics*, Indianapolis: Hackett, 2000

Regardie, I., *A Garden of Pomegranates: Skrying on the Tree of Life*, St Paul, Minnesota: Llewellyn Publications, 2002 (originally published in 1932)

Richard, C.J., *Twelve Greeks and Romans Who Changed the World*, Oxford: Rowman & Littlefield Publishers, 2003

Romanides, J.S., *The Ancestral Sin*, trans. G.S. Gabriel, Ridgewood, New Jersey: Zephyr Publications, 2002

Rosa, J.-J., *Euro Exit: Why (and How) to Get Rid of the Monetary Union*, New York: Algora Publishing, 2012

Schaff, P. and Wace, H. (eds), *A Select Library of Nicene and Post-Nicene Fathers of the Christian Church*, Grand Rapids, MI: Wm. B. Eerdmans, 1991, Vol. 7

Schilpp, P.A. (ed.), *The Philosophy of Karl Jaspers*, New York: Tudor Publishing Company, 1957

Schwartz, P., *The New Political Economy of J.S. Mill*, London: Weidenfeld & Nicolson, 1972

Searle, J., *The Rediscovery of the Mind*, Cambridge, Mass.: MIT Press, 1992

Segal, L., *The Dream of Reality*, New York: Norton, 1986

Sheperd, S.H., *The Landmarks of Freemasonry*, Whitefish, MT: Kessinger Publishing, 1997

Shields, C., *The Oxford Handbook on Aristotle*, Oxford: Oxford University Press, 2008

Smith, A., *The Theory of Moral Sentiments*, ed. D.D. Raphael and A.L. Macfie, Oxford: Oxford University Press, 1976 (originally published in 1759)

Smoryński, C., "The Incompleteness Theorems", in J. Barwise (ed.), *Handbook of Mathematical Logic*, Amsterdam: North-Holland, 1982

Solomon, R. (ed.), *Existentialism*, New York: Random House, 1974

Solomon, R. and Higgins, K. (eds), *Routledge History of Philosophy*, vol. VI: The Age of German Idealism, London: Routledge, 1993

Soofi, A., "Economics of Ibn Khaldun Revisited", *History of Political Economy*, Vol. 27, 1995

Spence, L., *An Encyclopaedia of Occultism*, New York: Dover Publications, 2003 (originally published in 1920)

Spiegelberg, H., *The Phenomenological Movement*, 3rd revised and enlarged edition, The Hague: Nijhoff, 1982

Steiner, R., *The Science of Knowing: Outline of an Epistemology, Implicit in the Ghoetean World View*, trans. W. Lindeman, New York: Mercury Press, 1988

Stern, D.N., *The Present Moment in Psychotherapy and Everyday Life*, New York: Norton, 2004

Ströker, E., *Husserl's Transcendental Phenomenology*, Stanford: Stanford University Press, 1993

Tarn, W.W., "Alexander: The Conquest of the Far East", in *Cambridge Ancient History*, Vol. VI, Cambridge: Cambridge University Press, 1933

Tawney, R.H., *The Acquisitive Society*, London: Bell, 1921

Tawney, R.H., *Equality*, London: Allen & Unwin, 1931

Thucydides, *The Peloponnesian War*, trans. B. Jowett, Oxford: Clarendon Press, 1900 ("Funeral Oration of Pericles")

Tiles, M., *Bachelard: Science and Objectivity*, Cambridge: Cambridge University Press, 1984

Toffler, A., *Future Shock*, New York: Bantam Books, 1971

Truman, N.E., *Maine de Biran's Philosophy of Will*, New York: Macmillan, 1904

Veatch, H.B., *Realism and Nominalism Revisited*, Milwaukee: Marquette University Press, 1970

Versluis, A., Fanger, C., Irwin, L. and Phillips M. (eds), *Esotericism, Religion, and Nature*, East Lansing: Association for the Study of Esotericism, 2010

von Balthasar, H.U., *Cosmic Liturgy: The Universe According to Maximus the Confessor*, San Francisco: St Ignatius Press, 2003 von Glasersfeld, E., *The Construction of Knowledge*, Salinas, CA: Intersystems, 1987

Waite, A.E., *Secret Tradition in Freemasonry*, Whitefish, MT: Kessinger Publishing, 1992 (originally published in 1937)

Wallis, R.T. and Bregman, J. (eds), *Neoplatonism and Gnosticism*, New York: State University of New York Press, 1992

Ware, T., *The Orthodox Church*, second edition, London and N.Y.: Penguin Books, 1993

Wavre, R., "Is There a Crisis in Mathematics?", *American Mathematical Monthly*, Vol. 41, October 1934

Weishaupt, A., *Apologie der Illuminaten*, 1786

Weishaupt, A. und von Knigge, A.F., *Illuminatus dirigens, oder schottischer Ritter*, 1794

West, M.L., *Hesiod: Theogony, edited with prolegomena and commentary*, Oxford: Clarendon Press, 1966

Westphal, K.R., "Hegel's Phenomenological Method and Analysis of Consciousness", in K.R. Westphal (ed.), *The Blackwell Guide to Hegel's Phenomenology of Spirit*, Oxford: Blackwell, 2009

Whitehead, A., *Science and the Modern World*, New York: Macmillan, 1944

Wilson, M.D., *Descartes*, London: Routledge & Kegan Paul, 1978

Wolff, R.P., *In Defense of Anarchism*, Berkeley: University of California Press, 1998

Wood, A., *Kant*, Oxford: Blackwell, 2005

Wood, L., "Solipsism", in D.D. Runes (ed.), *Dictionary of Philosophy*, Totowa, NJ: Littlefield, Adams and Company, 1962

Zizioulas, J.D., *Being as Communion*, New York: St Vladimir's Seminary Press, 1985

INDEX

www.ingramcontent.com/pod-product-compliance
Lightning Source LLC
Chambersburg PA
CBHW030728150426
42813CB00051B/331